CUOIAAAAEE

D1759207

WITHDRAWN

Design Management Case

Design Management Case Studies r̲ ̲-ee W̲ ̲̲̲̲̲ and timely contribution to knowledge of the managem̲ ̲̲̲̲̲̲̲̲̲ ̲ service innovation.

The six design management case st̲ ̲t be r̲ ̲̲bed are from large and small companies in the UK and abroa̲d̲. They include architecture, consumer products and services, textiles, clothing and services. All the case studies show an audit procedure, the main research methods used and key findings. Audits have been selected from some 90 detailed studies conducted by design management staff and postgraduate researchers in design management at the University of Central England, Birmingham. Design management policy audits from selected companies with a focus on communication form the core of this book, and also included are descriptions of the overall nature of design management together with review and project questions which will enable the development and teaching of design management and design auditing.

A progressive developmental definition is used where the design facility is normally viewed as a clear and positive attribute to a company even though it may often be integrated with a range of other business functions. A design manager therefore is seen as a specialist team member who utilizes all at his/her disposal towards positive business development.

The research attempts to provide working definitions of design management in action, for those studying, teaching and practising in the area.

Robert Jerrard is Professor of Design Studies at the Institute of Art and Design, University of Central England. He has published widely and his research interests include risk assessment in design, ethnicity and entrepreneurism, and work-based learning.

David Hands is Senior Research Assistant at the Institute of Art and Design, University of Central England. He has worked and published widely in the area of design policy analysis.

Jack Ingram is Chair of the Programme of Postgraduate Design courses at the Institute of Art and Design, University of Central England. He has published widely and is co-founder and executive editor of *The Design Journal*.

Design Management
Case Studies

**Robert Jerrard, David Hands and
Jack Ingram**

London and New York

CUMBRIA INSTITUTE
OF
THE ARTS

745
2
JER

First published 2002 by Routledge
11 New Fetter Lane, London EC4P 4EE

Simultaneously published in the USA and Canada
by Routledge
29 West 35th Street, New York, NY 10001

Routledge is an imprint of the Taylor & Francis Group

© 2002 editorial matter and selection, the editors; individual
chapters, the contributors

Typeset in Times by Wearset Ltd, Boldon, Tyne and Wear
Printed and bound in Great Britain by Biddles Ltd, Guildford
and King's Lynn

All rights reserved. No part of this book may be reprinted or
reproduced or utilized in any form or by any electronic, mechanical,
or other means, now known or hereafter invented, including
photocopying and recording, or in any information storage or
retrieval system, without permission in writing from the publishers.

British Library Cataloguing in Publication Data
A catalogue record for this book is available from the British Library

Library of Congress Cataloging in Publication Data
Jerrard, Bob.
　Design management case studies / Robert Jerrard, David Hands,
　and Jack Ingram.
　　p. cm.
　Includes bibliographical references and index.
　1. Design, Industrial–Management. I. Hands, David. II. Ingram,
　Jack, 1959– III. Title.
TS171.4 .J47 2002
658.5'75–dc21   2001058966

ISBN 0-415-23378-X (hbk)
ISBN 0-415-23379-8 (pbk)

Contents

Figures

Tables

Notes on contributors

Bob Jerrard, David Hands and Jack Ingram are members of the Birmingham Centre for Design Research at Birmingham Institute of Art and Design in the University of Central England. This book is their first collaborative project and has been prompted by a shared commitment to postgraduate design education and the development of design research methodologies within taught Master's courses.

David Hands is a Senior Research Assistant who has worked broadly within the area of design policy analysis, recent publications include *Design In-House: Twelve Case Studies Describing how the TCS has Improved In-House Design Capability*, with T. Inns Design Research Centre Publications (Brunel University, 1998) and *Applying Quality through Interactive Design Tools*, with John D. Law. He is the editor of *Quality Reliability Maintenance, 3rd International Conference*, University of Oxford, 2000.

Jack Ingram is Chair of the Programme of Postgraduate Design Courses and manages collaborative product development projects with local manufacturers. He is co-founder and executive editor of the *Design Journal*, an international refereed journal for all aspects of design, a Council member of the Design Research Society and a founder member of the European Academy of Design. He has published both in academic journals and through commissioned articles and reviews for publications such as *Design* and *Design Week*. His published case studies of university–industry collaboration in new product development include *Product Values and Brand Values in Small and Medium-sized Enterprises: A Case Study* (with S. Andrews and D. Muston) (2001), and *The Design Information Needs of Small and Medium-sized Enterprises* (with K. Burns and R. Newport).

Bob Jerrard, the principal author and editor, is Professor of Design Studies with particular research interests in technology diffusion and work. His current research interests include risk assessment in design (funded by the Design Council), ethnicity and entrepreneurism, and work-based learning. Recent publications include *Managing New Product Innovation*, (ed. with M. Trueman and R. Newport) (Taylor & Francis, 1999). He has published research widely in journals including *Design Issues, The Design Journal, Fashion Theory, Digital Creativity* and *Ethnic and Migration Studies*. Recent publications include contributions to Haptic Interface Theory, Migration Studies, and Doctoral Education in Design. He is a Council member of the Design Research Society and a member of the Reference Group of the Art, Design and Communication – Learning and Teaching Support Network and an Editorial Board Member of Art, Design and Communication in Higher Education.

The Birmingham Centre for Design Research (BCDR) seeks to deepen and focus research in design and design management. In addition to supervising research degrees, this has involved a wide variety of funded work and collaboration with commercial organizations. Its projects include the Centre for Product Design Information, a European Regional Development Fund-supported £1.4 million project to establish a web portal (www.cpdi.co.uk) meeting the needs of both design professionals and the manufacturing companies who might seek to engage in design activity. BCDR has a number of approaches to its work including design analysis, design history, design management, social and cultural aspects of design and electronic learning. Key collaborators include the Higher Education Funding Council (England), the Design Council, the Design Research Society and several publishers.

The case studies in Part II of the book were researched by students undertaking the Master of Arts course in Design Management at the University of Central England. All students on the course undertake a design policy audit in a company. The contributors all came to the course from a design background.

Andrea Lee gained her MA in 1998, having graduated with a BA(Hons) in Visual Communication at the University of Central England.

Maria Morse joined the course with a BA(Hons) degree in Design Management from de Montford University, and also graduated in 1998.

Sarah Parker, who joined the course with BA(Hons) in Design Studies from Nottingham Trent University, graduated in 1998.

Alexandra Smith graduated in 1997, having entered the course with a degree in Design.

David Williamson graduated in 1997, having entered the Master of Arts course in Design Management at the University of Central England with a degree in Interior Architecture.

Preface

The case studies presented in this book are the product of postgraduate studies in Design Management at the University of Central England. The five design management policy audits which comprise Part II of the book have been selected from some ninety detailed studies conducted by postgraduate student researchers enrolled on the Master of Arts course in Design Management between 1994 and the present. The study of Electrolux has been developed by the authors through interviews with senior Electrolux personnel, with reference to secondary sources which include the results of postgraduate student research.

The large body of data that has been accumulated over this period provides insights into the practices and attitudes that shape design management policy in a wide range of companies, both large and small, in manufacturing and service sectors. Researchers typically spend a minimum of ten weeks tracking the day-to-day activities of the company, before presenting the findings in the form of a report that includes recommendations for feedback to the company. The adoption of novel, taught research methodologies facilitates the accumulation of data from many studies: this approach of shared research methodologies over such a large number of researchers has been possible within the structure of a taught Master's degree programme. Development of a sustained programme of policy audits within a Master's course led to the invitation by Routledge to publish selected examples as a contribution to the diffusion of the findings of research into contemporary design management practice. The selection of company cases is intended to provide a range of examples in manufacturing and service organizations: a constant theme is the nature of communication, both within design teams and between such teams and other individuals and groups in the organization.

The opening case study, which has been written expressly for this book describes New Product Development processes in Electrolux, and identifies issues that are critical in large, mature manufacturing organizations operating internationally. The development of a maturity in design management, and the learning process within organizations contributing to that maturity, is explored in the introduction, setting the scene for the Electrolux study – an excellent example of a company whose design management maturity has kept pace with its commercial success.

Acknowledgements

The authors wish to thank all those who have contributed to the production of this volume. In particular, the collaborating companies that opened their procedures to the scrutiny of the researchers for extended periods. Electrolux, for their generosity in making available senior managers Jim Hanson, Director Product Management, Electrolux Home Products Corporation NV (Product Category Management, Refrigerators), and Sean Carney, Design Director, Electrolux Home Products, Industrial Design Centre, UK.

Thanks also to Angela Summers (MA Industrial Design, 2000) whose student design policy audit of Electrolux identified the company as a potential contributor, and provided vital references. We are grateful to Jill Harthill, for her secretarial assistance.

We acknowledge the assistance of the Birmingham Centre for Design Research and the Birmingham Institute of Art and Design for their encouragement and support, and in particular Kathryn Burns, Manager of the Centre for Product Design information.

We would also like to thank Routledge, for their patience and encouragement in the development of the original manuscript.

Introduction

How to use the book

It is intended that the book may be used either as a text from which appropriate sections are chosen by the tutor for detailed analysis, or for independent learning. The Summary, Review Questions and Project Questions provided with each audit are intended to aid comparison of management practices. Direct comparison of policies in large companies with the equivalent in small enterprises is not always appropriate, although valuable benchmarks may be found. There is a variety of common strategies used within the case studies which elicit very different types of information.

Whether studying individually or in groups, students are invited to seek similarities and differences in the policy issues and their management across the companies, and debate the company characteristics that generate them. The study examples at the end of each audit are intended to be indicative of how the case studies may be used. For example, within a seminar, common formats for analysis may be chosen in the study of either problem detection or solution recommendation. Students should be encouraged to find their own alternative solutions and their own examples of similar issues within other companies.

All the studies from postgraduate student researchers follow a similar format, showing the purpose, methodology and outcomes of the audit. The audits, although very different, are derived from very similar initial intentions: they all deal with issues elicited from an 'insider' focus and are published in the manner in which the individual authors reported. They share a common methodology and approach but are appropriately respectful of the individual nature of design policies in each of the selected companies. Summaries and suggested topics for discussion have been added in this compilation, identifying issues that encourage comparisons between the reported case studies.

It is recommended that a combination of private study and seminars be used when exploring each chapter. Additionally, these audits may be used as examples for students' own policy audits, the results of which may then be compared with those within the book. Readers are encouraged to take a critical view of both the research methods employed and company practices and strategies they identify.

Part I
Notes on the nature of Design Management

Introduction to the case studies

This book adopts an empirical approach to Design Management: the researchers who provided the case studies generated them experientially, spending extended reflective periods working with the designers and design managers they reported upon. The research attempts to define design management by describing examples of it in action. An underlying assumption is that design has a clear and positive contribution to make to a company when effectively integrated with a range of other business functions. A design manager therefore is seen as a specialist team member who utilizes everything at their disposal in positive business development.

Experience of this audit programme suggests that, among both academics and commercial managers, any coherent and consistent view of the complex set of disciplines that comprises Design Management is constantly evolving. This book attempts to contribute to the continuously developing design management curriculum by presenting both research results and novel associated methodologies. An acknowledgement of the importance of academics working collaboratively with partners in the commercial world is seen as central to the development of the full potential in studies in design management.

There is an increasing body of published work in the area of design management, which reflects an increase in design management activity, as promoted and encouraged by organizations such as the UK's Design Council and recognized in the curriculum of business schools. To reflect this increased activity, there has been a corresponding development of academic publishing in this area, stimulated in part by the Research Assessment Exercise within UK universities.

The case studies in this book identify a sample of design management issues common in a range of commercial and industrial organizations. Readers will be able to gain insights of both research methods and management processes – they are intended to provide a stimulus for thought rather than simply recording fresh data. It is the authors' intention to demonstrate some of the variety of issues which engage design management practice rather than promote any particular model of design management process.

However, in offering these examples, we recognize that there are some underlying influences which play a part in determining the design management issues of concern to companies, and how they deal with them. The audits provide a timely insight into both policy and process at a specific period when all the companies displayed a particular commitment to design. Previous experience always has a profound effect on design management performance: all organizations evolve, and with evolution there develops a corporate knowledge evidenced in changing management expertise and mechanisms that reflect shifts in priorities at key stages in that evolution.

Such evolution is not directly related to the size and age of the organization: just because a company is large, and has management systems for dealing with complexity does not mean that it necessarily is mature in design management terms. Equally, some small companies that have not yet evolved sophisticated management systems may well have a highly evolved view of design management and practise it successfully. Indeed, small companies are sometimes focused on their products and services simply because they are young, having come into being to derive commercial benefit from some new product. Equally, it is not uncommon for a company that has been created to market a new product to find that its energies are concentrated on the business of becoming established, a development phase in which quality, price and delivery performance tend to dominate product development. For many companies, the achievement of targets in these three areas makes such demands on management that further new product development may be perceived as relatively unimportant, and may slip off the management agenda completely. Within many long-established industries, this phenomenon is easily recognized; the reluctance to see design as a source of commercial benefit has taxed successive generations of the Design Council whose efforts have been directed towards encouraging companies to take a first step towards integrating design within commercial management. However, the emphasis on encouraging businesses to recognize the commercial benefit of design deflects attention away from the complexity of design management. In this book, it is assumed that design has a part to play in most organizations. The case studies reported here illustrate a range of design issues, reflecting the variation in design maturity attained by the companies as they progress from the first realization of the benefits design can bestow on their operations, through the gaining of experience in the use of design at successively more strategic levels. The companies reported here all subscribe to the idea that design is beneficial: the case studies show how design is managed, how its contribution to the business is perceived, and the extent to which design understanding is shared by key personnel.

The case studies demonstrate some of the variety of design management issues that companies face and that the issues are not necessarily related to company size or age. Experience of working with a large number of organizations suggests that it is useful to differentiate between stages of evolution of design 'knowledge' within organizations. A general evolutionary direction has been suggested in Andrews *et al.* (2001). While it does not suggest that the stages are discrete or occur in a precise order, the model attempts to describe a broadly hierarchical path from the first recognition of the potential commercial benefits of design through to a level of mastery of management techniques and the inclusion of design perspectives into company policy and vision.

The case study of Electrolux demonstrates that the company focuses both on mechanisms for handling the day-to-day complexity of a very large multinational company and on the strategic issues of design policy. In particular, it shows how policy issues at the highest level of abstraction (the definition and maintenance of the values that differentiate the products of its component brands) ensure the maintenance of the company vision and other policies. The company models for new product development include both business strategy and the policy issues that shape it.

Reference

Andrews, S., Ingram, J. and Muston, D. (2001) *Product Values and Brand Values in Small and Medium-sized Enterprises: A Cast Study*, proceedings of the 4th European Academy of Design Conference, Aveiro, Portugal, March 2001.

Electrolux

The management of complexity in a large organization

Bob Jerrard, David Hands and Jack Ingram

This introductory policy audit features design management processes of
The Electrolux Group and is presented to complement the other studies.
Electrolux is as mature in matters of design management as it is as a business entity. The design management issues in Electrolux reflect the
company's size and complexity: design management policies are explicit,
and are integrated with the company business strategy. Company policies
and management procedures such as the *Integrated Product Development
Process* (IPDP) reported in this study are published internally, contributing to the coherence of corporate effort through a shared understanding of
strategic issues.

The Electrolux Group, with sales of 124 billion SEK in 2000, is the
world's largest producer of appliances for kitchen, cleaning and outdoor
use, such as refrigerators, cookers, washing machines, chainsaws, lawn-
mowers and garden tractors. Each year, the Group sells more than 55
million products to consumers in more than 150 countries. Products are
sold under famous brand names such as AEG, Zanussi, Frigidaire,
Eureka, and Husqvarna. A brief history of the company's development
shows how the size and complexity of the company today have developed
over a one hundred-year period from being a manufacturer of a single
product.

The early years: realizing opportunities in the electrification of the home

AB Lux, Stockholm, was established in 1901, launching the Lux kerosene
lamp for outdoor use, which proved to be a huge success; it was also used
in lighthouses around the world. In 1910, having felt the competition from
electric lighting, the company moved to new premises and looked for new
products. The company Elektromekaniska was formed, producing the first
vacuum cleaner, Lux 1 at Lilla Essingen in 1912. Sales were established in
Germany, the United Kingdom, France and Sweden, and in 1917, all the

shares of Elektromekaniska were purchased by the sales company Svenska Elektron. In 1919, the company name AB Elektrolux was adopted by Elektromekaniska – a combination of Elektromekaniska and Lux. A ten-year agreement was reached, under which Elektron had sole sale rights to AB Lux vacuum cleaners, with Lux as its sole suppliers. Four years later, in 1923, a newly formed company, AB Arctic, started producing refrigerators based on a newly patented application of the absorption process. In 1925, Elektrolux purchased Arctic and launched the first absorption refrigerator, the 'D-fridge' for the domestic market.

Company expansion: developing international markets

From 1926 until 1940, the company expanded its operations worldwide. In 1928, share capital increased tenfold from 6 million SEK to 60 million SEK. Turnover of five plants, some 20 subsidiaries and 250 offices throughout the world was 70 million SEK. The Group was consolidated and introduced on the London Stock Exchange (1930 on the Stockholm Stock Exchange). Throughout the 1930s, there was continued expansion of business based on vacuum cleaners and refrigerators.

In 1940, production was reorganized when many plants and subsidiaries were closed due to World War II. New products included air filters for Swedish defence forces and a domestic food processor.

Diversification, new product development and further expansion in the post-war years

In 1944, Elektrolux purchased Bohus Mekaniska Verstads in Goteborg, giving a new product area – industrial washing machines. Penta, manufacturer of outboard engines, also was purchased; and 1951 saw the introduction of the first Elektrolux domestic washing machine. Production of steel shelving moved from Motala to Säffle, the foundations of what would later become Elektrolux Constructor. Five years later, the first chest freezer was launched, and in the same year, 1956, group sales passed the half billion kroner mark.

Within the next ten years, in which turnover doubled, there were changes which established many new products for which the company has become known in its second half-century. In 1957, the spelling of the Group's name was changed throughout the world from Elektrolux to Electrolux. New products included its first dishwasher, a benchtop model, and the first combined fridge/freezer in 1959. In 1962 came the acquisition of Elektrohelios, providing new production facilities and a new product group – cookers. Sterilization equipment was added to the product portfolio in 1964 through the acquisition of Getinge Mekanista Verkstands AB.

International expansion through acquisition of established brands

Group turnover passed the 1 billion kroner mark in 1965, and in just over 25 years would increase to one hundred times that figure, due in no small part to a sustained programme of acquisitions on an international scale. The company purchased Norwegian Elektra (cookers), Danish Atlas (refrigerators), and Finnish Slev (cookers, sauna units) in 1967, then lawn-mower manufacturer Flymo and 50 per cent of cleaning company ASAB in 1968, when the Group head office was moved from Stockholm to the factory premises at Lilla Essingen.

The year 1969 brought the establishment of subsidiaries in the USA (Domestic Sales Corp), and Hong Kong. A large-scale face lift for the Electrolux range took place, and the environment began to take a central position in public debates. Then, 1973 saw the acquisition of office machinery, the production of kitchen and bathroom cabinets, and manu-facturing facilities in Luxembourg and Germany to meet demand in Euro-pean markets.

In moves to gain a strong foothold in the US household appliance market, the acquisition, in 1974, of what is now the Eureka Company made Electrolux the world's number one producer of vacuum cleaners, and boosted the Group's air conditioning technology research and know-ledge resources. White goods were marketed under new brand names, and commitment to nature conservation products continued.

In the five years from 1975 to 1979, acquisition of many new companies, in sectors such as laundry service, materials handling, agricultural machinery, in addition to French, Belgian, Dutch, US and Swiss manufac-turers of white goods and vacuum cleaners, strengthened the Group's position in household appliances. The acquisition of Husqvarna also brought the addition of chainsaws to the product range, which in turn initi-ated new purchases in the same industry.

The year 1980 saw the important acquisition of metals conglomerate Gränges (mines, steel works, aluminium and copper, vehicle safety belts). The Group's turnover was almost 23 billion SEK, an increase of 51 per cent over the preceding year.

In 1984, the Italian company Zanussi was acquired, including its sub-sidiaries in Spain, making Electrolux the unquestioned leader in Europe for household appliances, and number one in food service equipment. In the following five years, acquisitions included white goods manufacturers Zanker in Germany and Duo-Therm in the USA. White Consolidated Inc. (USA) brought brands such as Frigidaire, Gibson, Kelvinator and White-Westinghouse, while the outdoor products business area expanded with new acquisitions which included Poulan/Weed Eater (USA). The white goods division of Thorn-EMI (Britain) brought brands Tricity, Scott Benham and Parkinson Cowan, and white goods were further strengthened by the purchase of Corbéro and Domar, Spain's leading companies in this sector. American Yard Products (USA), Unidad Hermética (Spain) and Buderas Group's manufacturing operations (Germany) were added, and an agreement was reached with Sharp Corporation for the sale of white goods in Japan. Group sales first exceeded the 100 billion SEK milestone in 1993, in which year Electrolux exercised its option to buy a second 10 per cent of AEG, having purchased 10 per cent in the previous year, and began negotiations to take over the remaining shares.

Consolidation and restructuring: the reduction of complexity

In 1997, the Group began a two-year restructuring programme with the aim of improving profitability. Streamlining led to the divestment of the industrial products sector and the production of sewing machines, agricultural implements and interior decoration equipment, followed in 1998 by operations in recycling, kitchen and bathroom cabinets, professional cleaning equipment and heavy-duty laundry equipment. A new brand policy was adopted to focus resources on a smaller number of large and well-defined brands. The core business now comprised household appliances, professional appliances and outdoor products.

Design management at Electrolux

In 2000, the three core business areas were further redefined as just two areas: consumer durables (indoor and outdoor) and professional products (indoor and outdoor). Consumer durables account for approximately 75 per cent of Group turnover, and include white goods, floor-care products, garden equipment and light-duty chainsaws. Professional products include food-service and laundry equipment, leisure appliances, chainsaws, trimmers, etc., landscape maintenance equipment and power cutters. The size and complexity of the business affect the design management processes. In this study we shall concentrate on just one aspect of the consumer durables product area – refrigeration – illustrating some key features of Electrolux's project management mechanisms. Consumer durable products are mainly white goods such as refrigerators, freezers, cookers, washing machines and room air conditioners. In 2000, they accounted for 79.1 per cent of Group sales. Electrolux Group is the world's largest producer of appliances, the market leader in Europe, the third largest producer in the USA, and second largest in Brazil (AB Electrolux, 2000).

Of the white goods produced, refrigeration products provide a good example of design management practice. Refrigeration products are designed, engineered and manufactured in several European countries for world market; brands include AEG, Electrolux, Frigidaire, Kelvinator, White-Westinghouse and Zanussi. New product development builds on excellence in product design and engineering to bring the benefits of standardization of technological features across the range of brands, while maintaining brand differentiation.

Research for this case study centred on detailed discussion with key company employees within the Electrolux Home Products Division: the Director for Product Management and the Design Director. Semi-structured interviews, questionnaires and reviews of company literature and publications were conducted over a twelve-month period. The study of refrigeration products came at the end of a six-year development period and at the start of a new product launch. Research centred on key themes in the overlap between industrial design and product category management in the UK, Belgium and Spain. In order to provide a clear perspective of the research process, Table 1.1 shows the central themes, together with the key company procedures for addressing them.

At the centre of the discussions at Electrolux was the 'Integrated Product Development Process' (IPDP), which provides the link between the long-term perspectives of company strategy and the immediacy of project management for the launch of new products. Figure 1.1 gives an overview of its role, and shows how company business strategy is influenced by three key areas: Electrolux Group stated policies, customer needs, and the business environment. The Group has published policies on the environment and on quality, together with statements about its vision and values.

In assessing customer needs, customers include both trade customers and end users. Evaluation of the business environment takes in consideration of trends, legislation, suppliers and competitors. Business strategy comprises strategies for products, markets and technology, and the IPDP includes the development of both complete products and technology applications for future use in products.

In order to establish and update the portfolio of projects being undertaken at any given time, plans for generations of both technological features and whole products are devised with reference to the relevant influences. For example, the evolution of product technology can be seen as the successive adoption of features made possible by technological trends, whereas the evolution of products may be described in terms of product families in particular market segments. To be included in the project portfolio, proposals for the development of new technological features and product families are subjected to a financial evaluation and are dependent on resource availability (see Figure 1.2).

Once included in the portfolio, a project may proceed as either 'primary development' or 'product development'. In each case the project is structured with checkpoints, of which 'Checkpoint Zero' (CP0) marks the point of decision whether or not to commit to investment in hardware or industrialization. At this point, all product specifications are frozen, and a project timescale is set. The importance of CP0 as a critical decision point extends beyond the financial commitment: Electrolux have estimated that

Table 1.1 Key aspects in refrigeration new product development and design at Electrolux

	Industrial design	*Product category management*
New product development	Baseline procedures involving designers, practical use of products and retailers within design centre	Team approaches across the division 'Ideas' internal market
	Product generation plan Technology generation plan	Product generation plan Technology generation plan
International management communication	Role of software	Role of software, staged electronic signing off
Product development communication	Project meetings	International policy-resource allocation and relocation
	Sign-off procedures	Internal market
Strategic policy	Brand derived Integrated product development process	Internal market-based policies centring on brands and competitors Financial evaluation Competition cost manufacturing Integrated product development process
Manufacturing technology	Balance between life style based experimental design and timed release of technologies	Longer-term technology development and 'shelving' policy
Project management	Role of software	International sourcing team Large-scale divisional conference
Competitor and market awareness	Internally derived, trends, features, tech. and features	Regular detailed analysis Uncertainty reduction

management ability to influence the outcome of projects is greatly reduced once CP0 has been passed and the industrialization phase is underway, which can be contrasted with an increase in management time spent on the project. Management time expended before CP0 is limited to approximately 5 per cent of total management input into the project from specification through to market launch (see Figure 1.3). What has been described

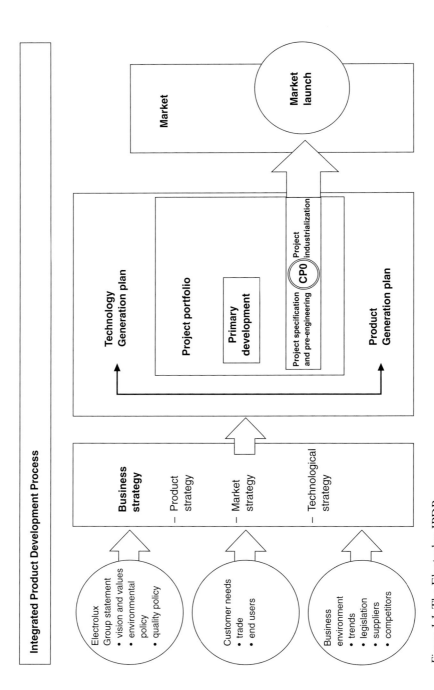

Figure 1.1 The Electrolux IPDP

Source: Adapted from Electrolux *IPDP Manual* (1994 and 1997)

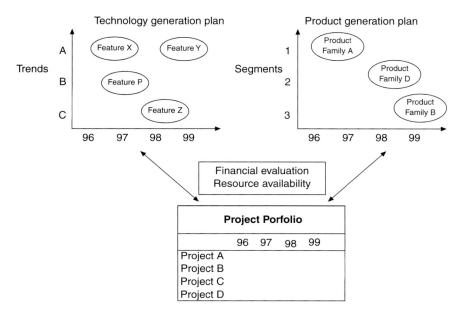

Figure 1.2 Electrolux IPDP: continuous development of the project portfolio
Source: Adapted from Electrolux *IPDP Manual* (1994)

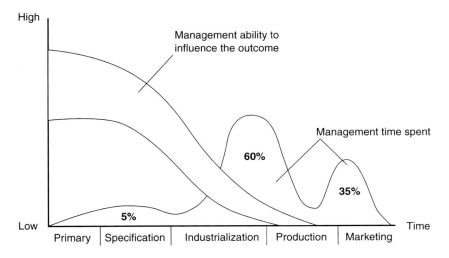

Figure 1.3 Electrolux IPDP: management focus
Source: Adapted from Electrolux *IPDP Manual* (1994)

so far follows conventional new product development practice, linked to broader business strategy perspectives. However, contained within the IPDP model there is also the concept of primary development, which is employed for more than just products.

To quote the *IPDP Manual*:

> Primary development is the systematic testing of new technologies, marketing concepts or production methods for the eventual creation of new or next generation products, production processes and marketing. The purpose of primary development is to reduce uncertainties concerning technology, customer demands, feasibility, time and cost before product development projects are started.

Primary development projects are extremely varied: they may be large or small, theoretical or concrete, technical or market-oriented, but they all share the characteristic of a *high degree of uncertainty* (see Figure 1.4). Because of this uncertainty, they cannot be a sequential part of product developments that work towards a fixed launch date. The results of primary development projects are classified as either 'verified ideas' or as

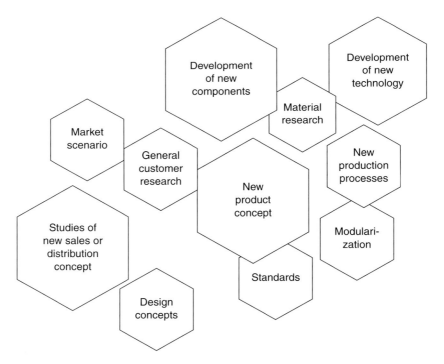

Figure 1.4 Electrolux IPDP: examples of primary development projects

Source: Adapted from Electrolux *IPDP Manual* (1997)

'hardware solutions'. Verified ideas are solutions to core problems that have been evaluated and tested. Hardware solutions have been realized as functional prototypes. All outcomes of the primary development process are stored for later use in a 'primary development bank' (see Figure 1.5). The policy of investing effort in the accumulation of tested ideas allows Electrolux to be prepared for both changes in legislation and market expectations.

While the project portfolio at any one time will contain both primary and product development projects being pursued in parallel, this practice is not to be confused with conventional concurrent engineering. The concurrency described in Figure 1.1 is that of separate projects run in parallel: they appear in the same diagram to show how Electrolux manage what in some companies might be separately described as 'Research & Development', 'market research' and 'new product concepts' as part of the same process as new product development. A major advantage of this approach is that so many interdependent processes can be placed in a context which includes strategic business issues. By taking primary development projects out of the time constraints of product development projects, they are able to concentrate on addressing core issues. The *IPDP Manual* states that:

Primary development projects should:

- *support business strategy.* The idea must be an appropriate and logical extension of the Electrolux business strategy. It must complement the Electrolux statement of vision and values.
- *be innovative.* Innovation is any characteristic, feature, or function of a product that surprises the target customer in a positive way.
- *add value.* Added value need not be a product feature. It may also be a new marketing strategy, a method for reducing production costs, or anything else that makes people choose to actively do business with Electrolux.

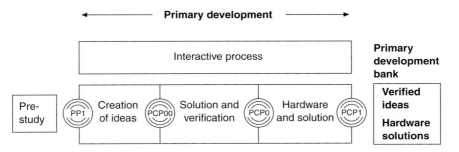

Figure 1.5 Electrolux IPDP: primary development of features, structures and systems

Source: Adapted from Electrolux *IPDP Manual* (1997)

- *have a market message.* If a message about a new product or feature cannot be communicated, the result will not be noticed, and energy invested in the project will be wasted.

Product development projects are also responsive to the core, strategic company concerns, partly because of explicit stages in the IPDP, and partly because they incorporate ideas and hardware solutions from the primary development bank. The process has checkpoints that require 'signing off' by the owner/steering team of the project. The checkpoints are shown in Figure 1.6, grouped into three phases: project specification, project industrialization, and production. An outline of the contents of each phase shows how a typical project might progress.

The project specification and pre-engineering phase has two stages, project initiation and concept analysis. In the run-up to the initial checkpoint at the start of the project, project initiation (PI), the product development pre-study considers the desired market message, and includes target formulation, a proposal for project organization, and an outline time plan and budget. Following checkpoint PI, the development of a business plan and initial concept definition leads to CP '00'. In this stage, the market message is refined and the target formulated is updated. Analysis of market data and competitor analysis leads to a product concept definition. In addition to generating a test plan and a project plan, project organization is firmed up, together with design verification. A patent search is made at this stage.

The second stage of the project specification phase, concept analysis, concentrates on concept solutions and verification. The market message and target formulation are finalized, in line with results of an analysis of market data. A final product concept is generated, providing the basis for an industrialization plan. A number of design factors are taken into account at this stage, including an environmental analysis, manufacturability issues, design for variation, FMEA (failure mode effect analysis) and safety analysis. A functional prototype is made, and key suppliers are selected; internally, a project plan is finalized and an investment request made. These efforts lead to CP '0', Checkpoint Zero, the critical point at which investment approval is either given or withheld.

The project industrialization phase comprises three stages: product and process engineering (CP '1'), process verification and investment release (CP '2'), and process set-up and market launch (CP '3'). The first of these three stages, product and process engineering, in addition to planning the industrial system in detail and testing and design verification, including the production of a fully representative functional prototype, also sees a first preliminary market launch plan, an instruction book draft, an authority approval plan and agreement with key suppliers.

Key components of the process verification stage are a market launch plan and sales material, the installation of production equipment, initial

Project Specification and Industrialization

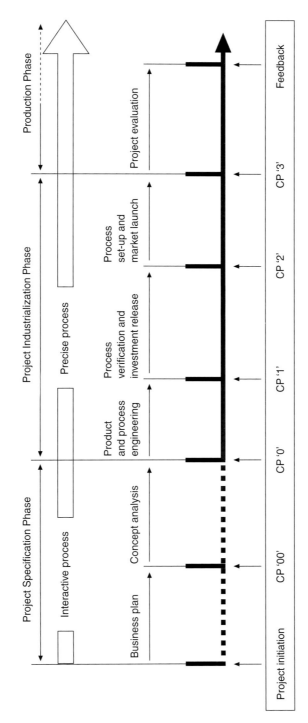

Figure 1.6 Electrolux IPDP: project specification and industrialization

Source: Adapted from Electrolux *IPDP Manual* (1994 and 1997)

training of the production team, development of the instruction book, status and test results from prototypes tested, and the preparation and initiation of field testing.

Process set-up and market launch (CP '3') is the final pre-production stage. In addition to finalizing preparations for production, and the market launch details, the instruction book is printed, together with service instructions. A spare parts plan is devised, and authority approvals are obtained.

The IPDP extends beyond market launch into the production phase, in the form of project evaluation, informed by feedback from the market, follow-up of organization and production targets. The information gathered in this evaluation phase aids preparation for the ramp-up to full production rates.

Conclusion

Electrolux, like any successful, large manufacturer, has a well-defined new product development process. However, some features of the Electrolux process are less common, and mark out the company as one of considerable maturity and sophistication in matters of design management. Within a single model of design process, the company explicitly links company vision and values to business strategies and thence into products that embody them. The same model shows how generations of technologies and products are created, and how many of these developments are outside the time constraints of normal NPD process, being held in a primary development bank to await incorporation into products when the market is deemed to be ready for them. Such sophisticated practices are more typical of the motor car industry than domestic consumer products, and their publication and use for developing aspects of the company culture are as worthy of note as the processes themselves.

Further reading

AB Electrolux (1994 and 1997), *Electrolux IPDP Manual*, Stockholm.
AB Electrolux (2000), *Annual Report 2000*, Stockholm.
Andrews, S., Ingram, J. and Muston, D. (2001) *Product Values and Brand Values in Small and Medium-sized Enterprises: A Case Study*, proceedings of the 4th European Academy of Design conference, Aveiro, Portugal, March 2001.
Birmingham Institute of Art and Design (1996), *Research Training Initiative*, Birmingham: Birmingham Institute of Art and Design.
www.electrolux.co.uk (2000)

Part II

Research methodologies for postgraduate studies in Design Management

Design Management audits

The researchers were all students on the Master of Arts course in Design Management, which has attempted to define Design Management in relationship to other management topics. It is clear that there is a paucity of usable research for the purpose of teaching Design Management in the context of related management subjects: the approach taken attempted to redress such imbalances by identifying and then utilizing a broad curriculum.

The teaching of research methods with specific audit techniques is central to this philosophy; students are developed as potential insiders within their chosen companies, able to research and subsequently inform at a professional and specialist level. The practice of working in collaboration with the company team tends to highlight issues dependent on design leadership as much as design management. In particular, training of the researchers has benefited from Birmingham Institute of Art and Design's Research Training Initiative (1996), which has been developed to include elements of policy.

The companies and audit arrangements

Companies are selected on the basis of matching student interest to in-house requirement. Almost all of the researchers are graduate designers, usually with commercial experience; companies vary from large communication or manufacturing multinationals to small designer-based enterprises. For the studies selected here, the researchers all had specific design management interests which were matched to company aspirations to find out more about how their design function was being managed and integrated into their wider business practices. Within the conclusions at the end of each audit, the researcher makes recommendations for development of the company design management function and these have been included here, as appropriate. The recommendations are generally perceived by the companies as extremely valuable, and have in many cases radically changed the company outlook and practices, resulting in major policy change in some cases. The audits are central to a programme established in 1994, and are still ongoing: as the body of data has steadily accumulated, the value of the audits has emerged through post-research analysis.

Managing and marketing creativity

Perspectives on design consultancy and architectural practice

Company:	Associated Architects
	19 Newhall Street
	Birmingham
	West Midlands
	B3 3PJ
Business:	Architectural services, feasibility studies, landscape design, project management
Auditor:	*Sarah Parker*

Introduction

Consultant design agencies, in order to generate effective design solutions, must first win their clients. For the client, the process of selecting an architect is undertaken with care – architectural projects are always a major financial commitment, and once completed, the outcome must be lived with. For the architects, the winning of contracts requires the wooing of potential clients, and the establishment of the conditions which attract clients often consumes a significant proportion of staff time. Architects can rely on their track record: it is in the nature of architecture that the outcomes are visible to a greater or lesser degree, and attract attention and comment in the public domain. Reaction to individual examples of work accumulates into more general reputations, within the world of architecture and in the world at large.

A central problem for Associated Architects (AA) is how to build on these largely unmanaged and uncontrolled processes, to communicate to potential clients the benefits of choosing them over their competitors. In order to reap the maximum benefit from the marketing effort, client retention is important. Qualitative aspects of architect–client relations during the design phase need management with regard both to achieving design outcomes and establishing respect and rapport with the client.

This case study looks at opportunities for developing control of the factors which combine to influence the generation of business, and makes suggestions for the development of a marketing plan. Marketing planning is a concept which is relatively new in many design professions: practitioners tend to think in terms of acceptance directly through their design work, relying on publicity generated through the trade press, and, to a lesser extent, awards from peer organizations.

The approach here builds on McDonald's (1992) definition of a marketing plan, in which an organization articulates a perception of its own position in its market relative to its competitors; its objectives; its strategies for achieving them; its resource requirements; and expected results. Associated Architects operate in several construction sectors: arts, education, housing and industry. It is suggested that each sector has to be analysed separately, and that these separate analyses be combined into a composite plan.

A Boston matrix is applied as a first step towards articulating the practice's perceptions of sectors in which they operate, followed by a SWOT analysis, and leading to a repositioning strategy. A previously completed competitor analysis is criticized for failing to categorize competitor strengths by sector, and a set of objectives to remedy the deficiencies is identified.

The study looks in some detail at a wide range of factors which can influence the marketing success of practices such as Associated Architects, and over which, in turn, the practice has control. Identified 'marketing mix decisions' include:

- *Product* (detailed definition of design services offered)
- *Price* (fee levels indicate the practice's positioning in the markets in which they are competing)
- *People* (staff qualities to support the practice's objectives)
- *Process* (project management, financial control and attention to detail)
- *Response to enquiries/opportunities* (systems to increase speed of response)
- *Quality assurance* (procedures to ensure implementation of stated policy)
- *Project review and control* (internal and external communication).

Strategies for implementation take into account press releases, promotional materials, presentations, and the use of the practice premises. It is suggested that each partner should be responsible for prospecting for new work, adopting common principles and sharing a common contacts database. Marketing roles and responsibilities are defined, with suggestions for establishing and managing future marketing activities.

The architectural dimension

Architectural design is a creative service, often requiring a one-off solution to solve unique problems. Therefore, unlike consumer products, creative services cannot be tried and tested before use. Clients have to take an added risk appointing architects on the basis of reputation, track record and expertise, which makes the process more intangible than most, as the results and nature of the end product are not known until after completion, well after the purchasing decision has been made. The situation is further complicated by the fact that some design companies tend to concentrate on the quality of the end product rather than the quality of the service and communication process that procured it. As the two fundamental principles of marketing are to retain and to attract new customers, the quality of service is essential and should be comparable with the quality of the end result in order to understand the needs of the clients and to champion better design and an increased quality of built environment. Indeed, effective communication of a good quality design service (as many clients do not understand its true importance or nature), and its intelligent application to clients needs, are now more important than ever to remain competitive.

Creative products require creative marketing, marketing 'design practice' should not be viewed as a separate function, but as an integral part of the same process. Marketing should occupy a core role within both business and design, looked upon as an investment rather than an expensive 'add-on'. Furthermore, its function should be collectively understood throughout every facet of organizational activity.

As a consequence of deregulation, the abandonment of mandatory fee scales and the introduction of alternative building procurement methods have significantly contributed to structural changes in the way architects work. Notably, the last ten years has precipitated a transition, which has resulted in a shift in values towards a more commercial awareness in practice management. Fierce competition on fees has resulted in numerous architectural practices 'down-sizing' or going into liquidation, all affecting the quality of built solution in preference to the clients' commercially orientated objectives.

National Lottery monies have been beneficial in improving the quality of the built environment, particularly in the public sector while also educating the wider general public and potential clients about the value and benefits that design can offer.

However, in order to maximize future business growth in today's volatile marketplace, Associated Architects must not become too complacent as many design and architectural practices did throughout the 1980s. To remain competitive, architects need to embrace business and organizational issues, once considered peripheral and alien to the designer, and to have the most effective marketing strategy in place.

Market planning

The initial process of conducting the AA audit was to consider how the practice related to principles involved in planning. It is widely considered that marketing planning is a continual process. A marketing plan should be an integral part of the business plan, setting out an agenda to achieve business objectives. The first phase is to define 'strategic aims' and 'objectives' in both the long and short term – where are we now? And where do we want to be? Or alternatively:

> a plan for 3 or more years ... is the intellectualism of how managers perceive their own position in their markets relative to their competitors (with competitive advantage accurately defined), what objectives do they want to achieve, how they intend to achieve them (strategies), what resources are required and what results are expected (budgets).
>
> (McDonald, 1992)

The second phase is to formulate 'operational' objectives and requirements – how do we get there? And what will we do? Once all the strategic issues have been reviewed, the marketing plan should detail, schedule and cost the actions required to meet strategic objectives over a twelve-month period and be up-dated annually. It should outline the responsibility delegated to individuals against a planned timetable and budget. Milestones should be set as targets with each area of the plan reflected upon until a workable solution is established. Therefore the marketing planning process can be split into four areas, see Figure 2.1:

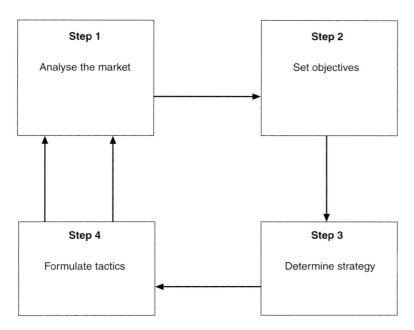

Figure 2.1 The marketing planning process

1   Analyse the market.
2   Set objectives.
3   Determine strategy.
4   Formulate tactics.

Implementation and control

It is very important that the implementation of a marketing plan is taken seriously and planned systematically. An irresolute attempt will only provide unrealistic expectations and minimal results, which not only will be counter-productive but also probably will later be abandoned. Common problems of implementation can be identified as:

- Lack of clearly defined business objectives.
- Lack of control and feedback by not allocating responsibility effectively, and setting unrealistic deadlines.
- Resources allocated unevenly and in the wrong areas, i.e. spending an excessive amount on an open competition which the practice has a small chance of winning.
- Marketing seen as an expensive resource rather than an investment.
- Reluctance by partners to adhere to marketing objectives in favour of fee-earning work.
- Difficulty in obtaining up-to-date information. Marketing may be seen as threatening because it challenges the status quo and does not fit in with the culture of the practice.
- Lack of communication and personality clashes between partners, teams and administration staff does not facilitate strategic decisions and can result in antagonism and breakdown in the marketing planning system.
- Not involving the staff can result in an unrealistic perception of the practice service offer.
- Lack of knowledge and understanding of marketing concepts generally due to different education and training. According to Schneider (1993), 'most firms' marketing tended to mean promotion rather than the total process of satisfying client and societal needs profitability'.

To overcome these problems, marketing strategy must be implemented holistically throughout the practice with every employee understanding marketing initiatives and being committed to the implementation of the plan. Marketing strategy should be consistent with the culture of the practice, with each partner responsible for identifying prospects in their own area of expertise under the umbrella of a unified set of procedures. All employees are ambassadors of the practice and should be encouraged to identify opportunities and to communicate them to their team leader. At present 50 per cent of staff interviewed in the author's survey considered that they were not encouraged to do this.

In Schneider's (1993) report it was noted that at AA 'there is a lack of energy to implement change', therefore it should be the responsibility of one partner to champion the change. He or she should be responsible for developing the plan, co-ordinating the marketing tools and systems, and opening up channels of communication between partners and staff, to make sure that effort is made to achieve objectives. A control system should be designed to monitor and review the results of the marketing plan so that corrective action can be taken if the strategic objectives are not being met.

Budget and expenditure

Both direct and indirect marketing expenditure should be closely monitored against a fixed budget. Marketing should be given a job number and all staff should record time spent on marketing. Direct marketing costs, such as the production of promotional and presentation material, reprographics, and advertising, etc. will be more obvious than indirect labour expenses which account for a much larger percentage of overall expenditure. A core brochure, for example, may cost £20,000 to produce but the amount of labour hours devoted to researching, planning and developing its contents will greatly exceed this amount. The time spent working on speculative and or feasibility work which the practice does not win, and hours spent by partners on indirect marketing should be recorded against the marketing job number and monitored closely. Without these systems in place, a realistic marketing budget cannot be implemented.

Once AA has decided which areas of the marketing plan are the highest priority, budgets can be set accordingly. It is important that analysis is undertaken to establish the marketing return rate by dividing the total fee volume by the marketing expenditure to give the plan accountability. By doing this the practice can establish whether they are getting adequate returns for their marketing efforts and, if need be, can reduce or increase different percentages of the marketing budget.

Strategic aims and objectives of the marketing plan

These provide the foundation on which a marketing plan can be based. They need to be reviewed and analysed before operational requirements can be suggested and actioned. The marketing plan must include different analyses to help it progress in the right direction.

Market segmentation

The potential of each of AA's core sectors: arts, education, housing and industry should be assessed on their growth rate, fee-earning capability, degree of competition and the practice's core capabilities of meeting client needs. Key points to consider are:

- Do AA have the relevant track record and experience which potential clients require?
- What is the profit ratio of both the top and the bottom line?
- Are the sectors both large and stable enough to give AA adequate returns for their profits?
- Do the clients in each sector have a high level of similarities?
- How easily can the sectors be subdivided, i.e. private, public, commercial?
- Are the sectors economically stable, growing or shrinking?

The marketing plan needs to identify a system of establishing a profile of each of AA's core sectors and focusing on them. One suggested way of doing this, according to Schneider (1993), is to telephone clients' marketing departments to obtain sources for up-to-date market intelligence information. Also it is important to attend industry conferences and seminars. Additionally, the practice can get information from the following sources:

- National media, i.e. *Financial Times* industrial surveys;
- the trade, both technical and professional press;
- government departments and official publications;
- local and national Chambers of Commerce;
- professional and trade organizations – yearbooks and directories;
- subscription services, to provide periodic sector reports on market intelligence and financial analysis;
- Mintel and Keynote Market Intelligence Reports. FAME and Company House CD ROMS can provide financial information.

In addition to AA's core sectors, look at other secondary sectors and identify key opportunities. Which other developers are offering partnering packages?

Portfolio analysis and strategic thrust

The marketing plan needs to identify strategic objectives of the services AA offers in each of the sectors in which it operates. By monitoring the potential growth rate in each of these core sectors, AA will be able to make strategic decisions on which sectors are likely to do the following:

- provide the practice with adequate returns for its efforts;
- provide the practice with a high probability of repeat work;
- raise the practice's national profile through prestigious design-led projects, which are likely to generate favourable publicity.

Focusing on sectors in which AA has extensive experience makes commercial sense; however, putting all its efforts into offering a narrow range of services to a small number of sectors is potentially dangerous. Markets are unpredictable, therefore it is important not to become complacent. The economic forecast may be optimistic at the moment but as the construction industry is cyclical, it is important to have an open view and a contingency plan to avoid being pigeonholed. Dividing services and sectors into strategic categories, i.e. premium, standard/steady, and discount is important in establishing strategic objectives (build, hold, harvest, divest).

Portfolio analysis is a marketing method used to monitor, plan and balance high risk, attractive and innovative work (such as National Lottery competitions) against the more mundane and predictable work such as design and build projects and professional management consultancy services.

By way of illustration, the 'Boston matrix and strategic objectives' (Jobber, 1995) is a commonly used tool to analyse the position of consumer products throughout their lifecycle. The same principle can be applied to services (see Figure 2.2). Ideally a 'Star' would be a National Lottery Project – an opportunity to raise AA's National profile by doing prestigious high profile architecture. However, certain projects which due to the resources required to enter competitions and probability of winning against some 'signature' architectural practices, may be 'Problem Children' depending on which sector they are in and how much experience the practice has with the particular type of work.

Therefore, resources acquired from 'Cash Cows' (could be an area of work in which the practice has extensive experience/high profitability ratio and/or little competition) can be used to build a 'Problem Child' into a 'Star'. This could be achieved by investing in and building up a portfolio of 'arts' projects.

While the Boston matrix has been criticized for being too simplistic, it is nevertheless useful for assessing which areas of AA's service sectors are: (1) profitable; (2) prestigious but high risk; (3) steady cash generators; and (4) not profitable and/or likely to tarnish the practice's reputation – 'signature' architects, for example, would never consider doing design and build projects. Hence it may be better to focus on getting more professional management consultancy work, rather than get involved in designing buildings which are likely to compromise quality.

The marketing plan needs to define the allocation of resources to meet strategic objectives by dividing the practice's product-service offer and sectors into strategic categories. A review system must be set up to monitor progress and assess the success rate.

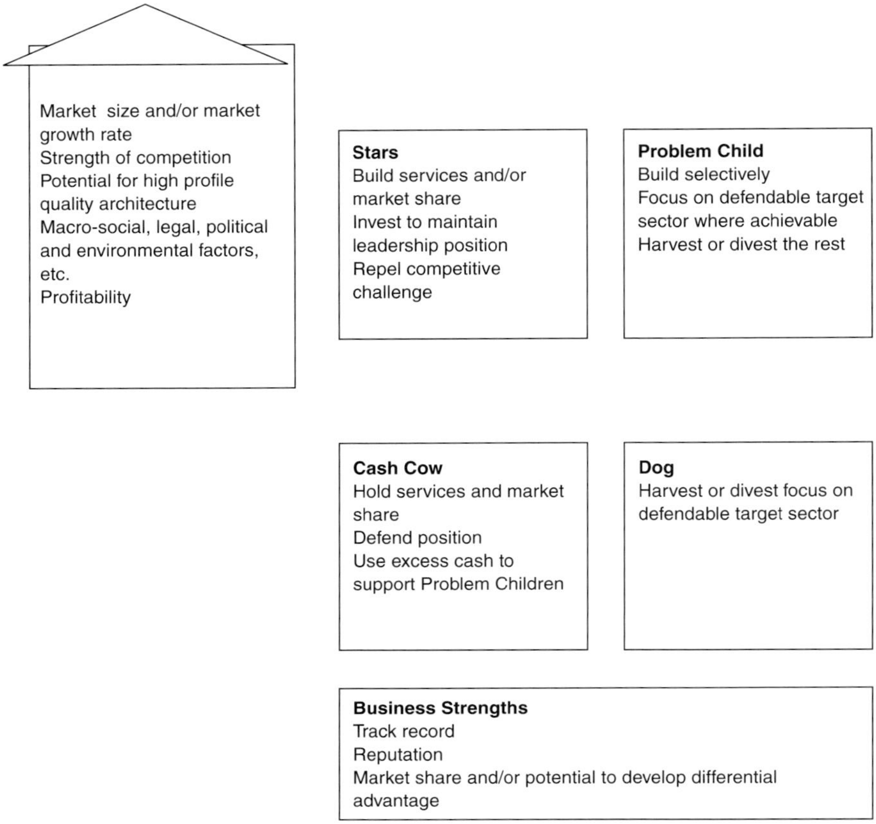

Market size and/or market growth rate Strength of competition Potential for high profile quality architecture Macro-social, legal, political and environmental factors, etc. Profitability	**Stars** Build services and/or market share Invest to maintain leadership position Repel competitive challenge	**Problem Child** Build selectively Focus on defendable target sector where achievable Harvest or divest the rest
	Cash Cow Hold services and market share Defend position Use excess cash to support Problem Children	**Dog** Harvest or divest focus on defendable target sector
	Business Strengths Track record Reputation Market share and/or potential to develop differential advantage	

Figure 2.2 Services marketing

Source: Jobber (1995)

SWOT analysis

This analysis is the synthesis of the marketing audit (an examination of the internal and external marketing environment). Therefore the SWOT analysis carried out by Eric Schneider in 1996 should not be considered as complete. It needs to be reviewed to take account of any new developments in the external environment including:

- review and analysis of the macro environment 'SLEPT' (Social, Legal, Ecological, Political, Technical factors)
- market trends in AA's chosen sectors
- competition analysis
- the internal environment as: 'what might appear at first sight to be an

opportunity may not be an opportunity when examined against an organisation's resources and feasibility of implementing strategies' (McDonald, 1992).

Therefore, in order to exploit AA's opportunities, there have to be the internal organization and resources to do so. If not, these features, some of which are identified by Schneider as 'key weaknesses', need to be addressed in the marketing mix.

Positioning

Establishing AA's actual market position is a key element of the strategic marketing plan. By reviewing the SWOT analysis undertaken by Eric Schneider, a more up-to-date view can be established to form the basis of the practice's positioning strategy or repositioning strategy.

To be competitive, AA must differentiate themselves by offering key attributes which their target clients value more than the competition. Therefore the services AA offer should be customized to specific sector/client needs demonstrated through the practice's marketing mix. The main principle of this is illustrated in Figure 2.3.

Although AA are design-led, the level of design quality and 'orientation' is entirely dependent on the client's culture and commercial objectives. Figure 2.4 illustrates the opinions of staff interviewed in the survey,

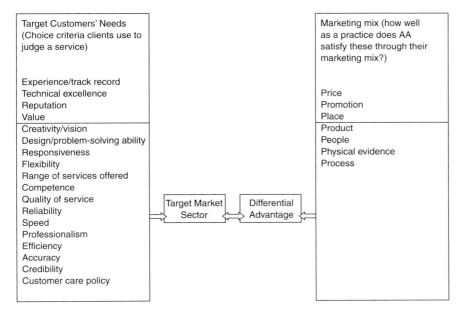

Figure 2.3 Marketing principles for AA

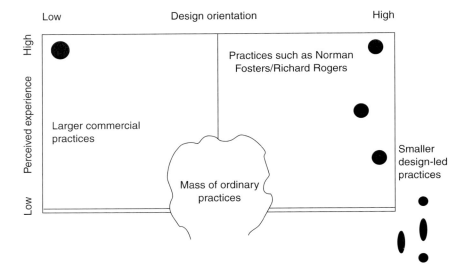

Figure 2.4 Perceived experience and design orientation at AA

who stated that AA moved between the top and bottom right-hand quarters, depending on the sector the client occupied and design service commissioned.

Competitive analysis

To create differential advantage AA needs to understand its clients better than their competitors. In Schneider's 1996 survey, AA clients list who they thought the practice's main competitors were. However, there was no mention of which sectors they were active in and to what extent they proved a threat. Although AA's staff were aware of local and national competitors, some were unaware of specifics and only knew the competitors in their chosen area of work.

Rather than relying on received wisdom, the marketing plan needs to consider methods of monitoring and building up profiles of key competitors. AA need to answer such questions as:

*   What is their market share in your chosen sectors?
*   What is their market size?
*   What are their strengths/weaknesses, opportunities/threats?
*   Are they winning or losing/expanding/downsizing?
*   What is their reputation/track record?
*   What is their national location/area of operation?
*   What awards have they won recently?

This should apply to both AA's regional competitors in their main area of operation, and particularly national competitors, against whom the practice is more frequently competing in National Lottery competitions.

The first step is to monitor and record who AA is competing against in their chosen sectors, establishing whether the practice is winning or losing, to whom and why. This could be for a number of reasons, for example, due to a lower fee bid or a better scheme. From this analysis the next step is to formulate a system to collect information and intelligence on key competitors who are a threat.

Each partner should systematically review relevant data from media analyses and document results. Findings could be recorded in the form of monthly marketing reviews or reports that should be open to discussion at marketing meetings and then circulated to staff. Competitor profiles will only be achieved through perseverance and time and, if successful, new opportunities and threats could be identified. This is not easy to achieve immediately and some data such as financial information (for partnerships) will not be easily accessible.

Marketing mix decisions

All elements of the marketing mix are interdependent. As illustrated in Figure 2.3, marketing mix decisions should relate to the culture of the target sector and the choice criteria of clients to which they are applied.

Product

The product denotes the design services AA offers to a client. What exactly is the practice offering? A client does not just want a building; they want a design solution to satisfy their specific needs. Carrying out market research on the practice's chosen sectors not only establishes growth potential but also facilitates a closer relationship with the client. Although AA is design-led and has designed some high quality and innovative buildings, this physical evidence alone is not enough to win new work. The quality of the end-result is entirely dependent on the sector/building type (as some clients do not value design and just want the cheapest solution). Quality of service is therefore very important, and the client starts consuming this quality as soon as AA answers the telephone.

Therefore, the quality of people the practice employs, the quality of promotional material, the quality and appearance of the practice's premises, the quality of the design process and the practice's fee levels are all essential in influencing the clients' purchasing decision and should be matched with each client's key choice criteria.

Price

Competing on price has become a commercial reality; however, price is also an indication of perceived quality. Therefore discounting too heavily on price could be counter-productive and undermine AA's reputation. The emphasis on fee levels should not be cost-focused but 'value added'. The marketing plan needs to address the services AA are going to offer for the practice's fee. By emphasizing a larger skills base such as quality innovative architecture, expertise in QA, CDM, energy conservation, whole life pricing, CAD, etc.; 'the client may not be comparing like with like, therefore discounts can be made should the client not need all the services the practice has offered' (RIBA). Therefore the statement: 'You get what you pay for' must be highly valued.

In the survey undertaken by Eric Schneider (1996), AA's clients gave mixed reviews on fee levels. Some commented that they thought the practice was high to medium-priced while others stated that the practice was low-priced. This is because the price cannot be isolated from the marketing mix. The product-service offer to each sector has a different cost implication, which determines the overall level of fees. The marketing plan should determine which sectors are premium 'first class' and which are discount 'economy' and a system should be set up to monitor fee levels in each of AA's chosen sectors.

The marketing plan also needs to address how the practice can improve profitability, for example, by doing the following:

- Reducing overheads (what is the progress on 'divesting of unwanted properties?').
- Improving productivity by more integrated use of CAD and IT, with introduction of internal networking and email/ISDN links to consultants/contractors/reprographics, etc.; the purchase of cross-platform software, such as MS Office (Word, Excel, PowerPoint, Access).
- Increased efficiency by enhanced internal and external communication, quicker response to enquiries and problems.
- Improved project management skills/resourcing.
- Monitoring spend on spec and feasibility work and fixing budget.
- Charging for extra work/not doing work for free.
- Improving office management and delegation of responsibilities.
- Asking if it is economical to have partners typing their own submission brochures. Again, cross-platform software will help.

People

Without training, control and a sense of being 'valued' staff performance levels can vary. Every member of staff is an ambassador of the practice. Therefore recruiting the right people to match the practice ethos and reputation is obviously a fundamental element of the marketing plan. There should be a good balance between experienced staff with excellent project management skills, technical staff and young inexperienced staff with high levels of creativity, flair and lack of inhibition.

The practice needs to be in a position where its national profile is so good that high quality staff will come and work for the practice irrespective of location. Most students and high calibre staff want to go and work for high profile 'signature practices' in London, where they are unlikely to be provided with opportunities to express themselves. AA needs to stress its core values of being 'design-led', 'nice people to work with', 'fun and exciting', and perhaps 'the practice that encourages and motivates creativity and innovation'.

AA could also consider giving lectures at key universities around the UK, and building contacts with university placement officers. The Bartlett in London, for example, have built up a large contact base with architectural practices to place students wanting to complete their Part III qualification. They place students into jobs according to their skills and type of work the practice offers.

One way of assessing the development potential of staff is to carry out a SWOT analysis, as shown in Figure 2.5. In addition, consider the following:

- Are there enough staff in the office with the skill base to provide new services such as finance/procurement consultancy, strategic briefing, whole life costing, planning, energy, conservation and Quality Assurance (QA)? If not, then appointing staff or training in-house needs to be considered.

STRENGTHS	WEAKNESSES
• Good creative ideas • Enthusiastic • Willing to learn • Hard-working • Gets on well within the company	• Inexperienced • Poor attention to detail • Low technical ability • Poor time manager • Poor presenter
OPPORTUNITIES	THREATS
• Time management training • Presentation skills training	• May get bored • May leave once trained • May be unable to cope with computer training due to low technical ability

Figure 2.5 SWOT analysis of junior designers at AA

- Are staff aware of their job description and expected levels of performance – are there standards in place?
- Does the practice value its staff and take note of appraisals and action items accordingly? At present, staff commented that appraisals are carried out in an *ad hoc* fashion.
- Are staff skills appropriate to the project and relevant to the relevant RIBA stage? For example, some architects who are highly creative would be best suited to working on the concept, outline scheme and detail design of arts projects, while other more technically minded may make better job runners when the job is at the production stage, or job architect for an industrial shed.
- Are staff being rewarded for their efforts? Through recognition in media or through promotion? An 'internal staff care policy' must be realistic and adhered to. Is there the right synergy between team members and partners?

The marketing plan needs to outline the practice's 'internal staff care policy' and training policy (including continuing professional development). It also needs to outline recruitment policy to identify the practice's recruitment plans for the next twelve months allowing four to six months to find the right people.

Process

The process is the mechanisms and systems which deliver quality of service to the client. Providing an excellent service is critical to maintaining a good reputation, word of mouth recommendation and the securing of repeat work. In the staff survey, partners stated that between 80–85 per cent of projects were delivered on time and within the agreed budget. However, staff interviewed stated that this was between 40–60 per cent. Although the performance of other members of the design team is sometimes out of the architect's control, excellent project management, financial control and attention to detail are very important in reducing expensive overruns. The quality of the process is also critical in eliminating legal claims.

Place

'Place' is the area of operation in which the practice operates. Joint ventures outside AA's area of operation need to be discussed with all partners. At present there are differing views on this topic.

Response to enquiries/opportunities

All potential new work, which comes into the office, must be prioritized and discussed among all partners, in alignment with strategic objectives.

Improved communication and centralized control of opportunities would help break down partner fiefdoms and facilitate better sharing of human resources. At present some partners and staff have commented that in some cases not enough time has been allocated for submission bids, despite the bid being in the office for weeks. Consequently the bid has been left until the last minute.

Strategic discussions of opportunities could take place (as they do at present at Monday partner's meetings) and additionally by the introduction of QMI's (quick marketing information – 15-minute meeting to discuss new opportunities attended by the partners and associates). All meetings should be minuted and any new opportunities documented in a circular distributed to all staff.

The marketing plan needs to define how better resourcing and planning can facilitate quicker response to enquiries and preparation of bids. It also needs to define systems of monitoring and forecasting team migration and man-hours spent on jobs, if this is already not in place. This is also useful for measuring forecasts against actual spend. Migration by team members also facilitates better 'incubation' which is a fundamental element of creative process.

Quality assurance

The marketing plan should clearly define the practice's quality assurance commitment. All the staff interviewed stressed that they were aware of quality assurance procedures but not all of them were following the guidelines. One example is the signing-off of drawings. The QA system need not be bureaucratic, it should be a procedure in which the critical stages in the plan of work are documented and carried out. There is no point in having a policy 'or quoting a policy' in a submission brochure if it is not going to be used.

Project review and control

Does the practice carry out project appraisals on completion? If not, consider doing this and keeping records in the office for reference. These would be useful for gauging a project's success and for setting targets to overcome any recurring problems.

Communication

Internal communication

Both Eric Schneider and AA's staff commented that one of the biggest problems at the practice was internal communication. Some staff commented that they did not always know what was going on. Moving to an open plan office could ameliorate this. However, AA also needs to consider the following:

- regular partners/associate meetings – across teams – to discuss new opportunities, resourcing and project progress;
- regular partner/design team meetings;
- quarterly staff meetings – most staff interviewed in the author's survey stressed that they did not always know what was going on in the practice;
- quick market intelligence meetings (QMIs) – 15-minute meeting to evaluate new opportunities. Programme of office socials – visits to buildings (all should be minuted);
- design crits/reviews – all staff interviewed stated that they thought design crits would be useful as long as a structured approach was implemented. They would improve internal communication, shed light on design problems, facilitate a breakdown in partner fiefdoms, and enable designers and non-designers to gain fresh insight into key projects in the office;
- operating a 'non-judgemental and informal approach' (similar to brainstorming techniques) as creative personalities are very fragile. This is particularly relevant for junior designers, as they may feel intimidated by senior designers with strong views on design;
- doing a 'spring clean' of key projects, at different stages of their lifecycle, which either celebrate the practice's ambitions, or have complex problems, etc.;
- having a member of staff taking minutes and distribute them to all those present.

The marketing plan needs to outline how often meetings are to be held (with the exception of QMIs, which should be spontaneous), and a programme for design crits and projects to be reviewed.

External communication

The marketing plan needs to define the 'customer care policy' (if published, it must be adhered to, otherwise the practice could face similar problems to failing QA accreditation). External communication would also be improved by establishing a programme for publicity, public relations and the development of promotional materials; improving administration and organization of information technology; and operating a focused development strategy.

Better use of IT

- Better implementation of IT in the office will improve productivity and efficiency.

- The practice needs to co-ordinate its hard/software to suit both Mac and PC platforms. At present PC and MAC software is not compatible.
- Consider a PC on reception to monitor phone calls and facilitate internal email to PA/team secretaries. Also consider a good way of monitoring incoming telephone calls. This could also be the source of a contacts database.

Promotion of the company

There are many opportunities to promote and sell the philosophy and ethos of Associated Architects, from public relations and networking activities; seminars, lectures, exhibitions and socials (each augmented with relevant materials), to presentations and the appearance of the practice premises and attitude of the staff. Combined, each element is important in raising the practice's profile and should be presented in a holistic way to communicate the practice's corporate identity and vision. There are only three key words to remember: 'Attention to detail'.

Public relations

All client–consultant and intermediaries social functions should be in keeping with the practice's ethos. Visits to completed projects and invitations to lectures, exhibitions and seminars which directly promote the practice's design efforts are essential, rather than ostentatious invites to the opera.

Social functions should be timed to coincide with any new practice work, completion of a building, or the winning of awards, etc. They should provide an opportunity to encourage existing and potential clients to communicate, and inform others of their satisfaction. Consider having a client reception when the practice moves offices.

The marketing plan needs to develop a framework and budget for public relation activities (which need not be expensive or flamboyant), complete with a list of possible clients, consultants and intermediaries the practice wants to target.

Publicity – press releases

Cultivating contacts with journalists and editors is an ongoing activity. It is important that AA sends press releases to individual contacts rather than to just a journal or newspaper. To raise the national profile of the practice it is important to inform the press on a regular basis as to new work; winning competitions; new awards; an activity or project which is particularly topical or when the company breaks new ground, etc.

Whether AA writes its own articles or has a journalist write them is entirely dependent on the level of experience and personal preference of each partner. Listed below are some quick tips regarding press releases:

- Obtain the contact names of editors and journalists and nurture relationships.
- Decide which projects to promote, when to promote them and who is going to be the single point of contact.
- Gauge the 'personality' of the journal and its audience (ask clients which journals they read? There may be an opportunity to write a topical feature for one of their industry journals.
- Always ensure that 'Press Release' is at the top of AA's letterhead. Always provide a contact name and a single telephone number for point of contact.

The marketing plan needs to define which projects to promote, and to establish a timetable for cultivating contacts. It should also list recommendations for a 'publicity policy'. All contacts made should be put on the contacts database.

Promotional materials

All promotional materials should be 'design-led' to reflect the architectural philosophy of the company. Therefore, the same attention to detail, vision and innovation applied to architectural design should be applied to the design of all visual material from brochures to presentation boards, computerized slides, drawings, reports, recruitment ads, etc.

There are many opportunities to send out promotional literature, from mailshots, letterheads, company brochures, presentation boards, Christmas cards etc. The promotional material employed by Associated Architects should be presented in a holistic way to match the practice's corporate identity. Currently all presentation materials, especially brochures, are sent out in varying formats depending on which partner is responding to an opportunity. Therefore, the design of a comprehensive new brochure is now an urgent requirement. This must be co-ordinated in a unified way, balancing the impact of a quality brochure and materials against bespoke in-house system, as 'core brochures' are not very flexible, are expensive and have a very short shelf life. All materials should show buildings in their best light. It is pointless hiring a professional photographer and then having a low quality output.

One way to achieve this would be to appoint a graphic designer to design a high quality cover into which bespoke contents could be inserted. These could be the combination of project sheets and texts arranged in a unified format, taking advantage of in-house binding facilities, DTP systems and RS's IBM contact (perhaps through modem link). It would be beneficial to design the contents at the same time as the brochure programme cover so that the entire brochure programme could run parallel with both in-house and out-house elements completing at the same time. The amount of money to be spent on the brochure is entirely dependent on the practice's overall marketing budget, and importance of the brochure within it.

The marketing plan needs to formulate a timetable and programme for the design of a new promotional cover and design of in-house layouts and contents; plus, the design of any other promotional material the practice wants to employ. A broad overview of the design process and possible budget requirements for doing this can be split into the following stages:

Practice time – indirect labour costs
- Interview and select designer
- Prepare design brief – decide on in-house/external split
- Brief designer
- Collect information (i.e. written contents, history, philosophy, core capabilities, experience, awards, résumés, etc. This information needs to be compiled in-house and stored on the computer under different headings so that it can be modified to suit different opportunities.
- Source illustrative material – appoint photographer as necessary
- Discussions
- Working meetings
- Presentations
- Content discussions/draft preparation
- Writing of text
- Checking and proofing.

Consultants' fees and expenses
- Design fee (lump sum or hourly)
- Artwork production fee
- Out of pocket expenses
- Presentation costs
- Travelling expenses.

Services and subcontractors' fees and costs
- Photography
- Illustration
- Technical drawing
- Printing
- Finishing.

It is important to be realistic about the practice's capabilities and core values in the text of the brochure rather than supply philosophical hyperbole.

The marketing plan should include a design policy for the presentation of all visuals so that they are consistent with the practice brochure and corporate identity. Also include any plans for training on DTP systems.

Presentations

The most important person at a presentation is obviously the client. All presentations should be designed to match the client's key choice criteria. Therefore appropriateness and sensitivity to client's aims and self-image are essential. This can only be achieved by thorough researching and questioning the client's needs in relation to the culture of their organization, and design service they are commissioning. Then and only then can an accurate 'diagnosis' be made.

The quality of the presentation and way in which this is visually communicated should again be design-led to reflect the philosophy of the practice. Hence the same amount of creativity and attention to detail should be applied, with a consistent and holistic approach to fit in with all other promotional material and corporate identity. The presentation should also be personalized to embrace the culture of the client organization.

Other points to consider are:

- The presentation visuals should not be too esoteric; the majority of clients do not understand architectural drawings. Therefore, using a 'mixed media' approach should be beneficial.
- This approach could be facilitated by the use of basic card models, perspectives, 3D CAD Models and QTVR (Quick Time Virtual Reality). Using these techniques would give the client better spatial awareness.
- All visuals should be appropriate to the type and size of project. This is especially important when using IT. The use of 3D CAD (especially if communicated digitally – through PowerPoint) does impress the client, however, it must be used in context because some buildings such as 'high-tech' take better to CAD rendering than others. Traditional brick, for example, tends to look 'pseudo-real' if heavily rendered and better suited to 'hand-held' techniques and traditional rendering such as crayon.
- Using computer technology for a large 'arts' project over a certain value may be appropriate, but may be too flash and 'cutting edge' for a one-off house or church. Used out of context, it may also suggest that the practice is not as responsible with costs as the client would like.
- Make sure, as noted by Schneider, that the practice puts forward the appropriate team and also make sure that this team is going to undertake the project throughout the lifetime of the project.

Premises

AA's premises are a gallery of the practice's work. If AA goes 'open-plan', it needs to consider the following:

- There are models, photographs of work and architectural reading material in the reception area.
- Need to identify a suitable location, which has the right support facilities nearby, and the right ambience.
- Consider also ease of access and adequate car parking for clients.
- What better publicity tool than occupying a building designed by the practice? Michael Hopkins and Partners house in Hampstead was a model for future work.

New business development

Prospecting for new work

Each partner at AA should be responsible for prospecting for new work within their own area of expertise. At present, the practice covers a broad spectrum in which to identify new opportunities with each partner sitting on professional/civic bodies. AA has done an extensive amount to nurture contacts within urban regeneration at English Partnerships, Housing Associates and the Urban Village Forum, etc. However, it was noted in Schneider's survey that the practice does not do enough to keep their clients motivated. Therefore, through effective PR and market research, AA should concentrate on a focused and pro-active approach to targeting possible new opportunities. Personal contact is far better than cold calling/direct marketing attacks that are time-consuming, have a limited success rate and are foreign to the culture of the practice. Therefore AA should embrace Eric Schneider's suggestion of 'hot-housing' and targeting a 'general' sector specific group where AA has a high probability of winning new work. It is important that the practice sets up a formal system of monitoring and following up any new leads with relevant promotional material. (In the author's opinion, tri-annual mini-brochures would be more appropriate than monthly newsletters.) Additionally, these should follow the culture of the client organization. Partners should be encouraged to share information and prioritize any new opportunity in alignment with strategic objectives. Figure 2.6 illustrates the principle of prospecting for 'new' clients.

As well as prospecting for new clients, the practice should also focus on targeting and nurturing existing clients, past clients, jobs lost and intermediaries. AA should ask, which clients are going to be targeted for future work/new services? AA could also consider targeting past clients with whom they have not had contact for some time in sectors which typify the

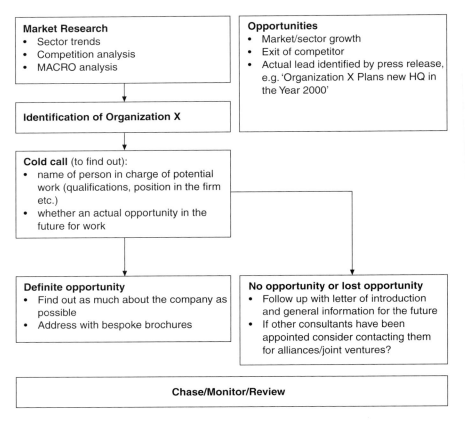

Figure 2.6 A proposal process for finding new clients at AA

practice's ambitions. AA could consider following up any key shortlisted job opportunities they did not win, to keep the lost client in touch with the practice's activities.

Intermediaries should also be kept informed of any new practice work. Relationships should be nurtured with teams structured appropriately so that AA can assemble the 'A Team'.

Contacts

As already noted, all joint ventures and alliances with other architects should be discussed among all partners in alignment with strategic object-ives. These contacts should be nurtured and kept up-to-date with the prac-tice's work. All contacts should be put on the contacts database, including brief profiles of key players and their relationship with the practice.

The marketing plan needs to determine which prospects to target, and fix a budget and timescale for doing so. Every opportunity should be discussed between partners in line with strategic objectives.

Marketing structure and systems

Market research – methodology

Each partner should be responsible for initiating their own research. However, who is responsible for the actual collection of information could be delegated by partners to PAs or a marketing PA with relevant experience but this person must be properly briefed. The practice must decide how much of the research to be carried out is to be field research and desk research. Field research consists of market research carried out externally on behalf of the practice, usually by a market research agency. This could include quarterly sector reports and market intelligence on AA's core sectors.

Desk research consists of market research carried out internally by partners and staff, i.e. reviewing national, local and professional press for analysis. This entails analysing the macro-environment, market trends, competitions and identification of new opportunities; calling clients' marketing departments for list of sources for client press, industry trade journals and details of forthcoming seminars, etc.

Marketing tools – databases

Without constant up-dating any computerized system of storing data and information is going to become obsolete and a waste of time and resources. The prospect of setting up such systems initially appears daunting, but like other systems already in place in the company, if systematically planned and clearly matched to AA's objectives, these could become valuable resources.

In order to set up databases to store marketing information, the practice must first establish how these systems are going to be used, implemented and managed, and their potential benefit must be analysed in alignment with meeting strategic objectives. The practice may want to ask the following questions:

- In which areas of the marketing environment will the database be most useful?
- What are the practice's main enquiries/what information does it want to glean?
- How will this information be used? For what purpose? To what end?
- How will this information be analysed, in what form and by whom?
- How will the databases be integrated within the practice?
- Who is going to be setting up the databases?

- Who is going to be inputting the data?
- What is the learning curve of using the database?
- How confidential is the stored information?
- How much is it going to cost to purchase the software?
- How many licensed copies will the practice need?

The database must be simple to use, and although it may require a person with detailed knowledge to set up, its lifecycle must not be dependent on skilled personnel. Microsoft Access is a simple database package to use, allowing the user to build databases by using set wizards, and clearly defined icons. It also contains hyperlinks to other MS Office software, such as Word or Excel. Databases can also be published on the Internet by use of HTML (Hypertext Mark Up Language). Once the database has been set up, the user can sort and filter information by a number of means. The database can be sorted into marketing/projects, clients, fees, design services, field headings, or contacts.

Marketing/project database

As already outlined in the market/project database, it can be used for analysis of strategic objectives – Build, Hold, Harvest, Divert and Portfolio analysis, thus which projects are Stars, Problem Children, Cash Cows, and Dogs (see Figure 2.2).

It can also be used for the analysis of strategic risks, which jobs are the practice winning and which are they losing? How much is the practice spending on entering competitions and what is the return rate on marketing spend? For example, possible filter criteria, and field headings respectively.

Client

How many times has the practice worked for a particular client? What is the percentage of repeat work? If high, then this particular client could be targeted for new work.

Fee

Which sectors or design services are more profitable than others (cross-sector fee analysis)?

Design

Which sector/design services are more design-led than others, dependent (on procurement process, design service, client, etc.)? A coding system could be used to grade the design innovation potential on each project.

For strategic risks – field headings

- Job title
- Client
- Selection process
- Intermediaries (if team bid)
- Competitors/teams on the shortlist
- If lost, why did the practice lose?
- Name of practice/team that won.

To have one very large database containing all information on projects, fees, sectors, selection processes, etc., would be problematic and very difficult to update. Therefore the marketing/project database should be a series of databases broken down into manageable parts, coherently structured and interrelated. Each part can then be up-dated by the appropriate personnel. Sensitive fee information, for example, can be stored on separate spreadsheets and accessed through hidden field by appropriate senior members of staff. Figure 2.7 illustrates the key principles of this system. The database would be divided into core information, sections/facets and specific details.

Contacts database

The contacts database should be the practice's live 'old boy' network and must be constantly up-dated. Therefore it would ideally be located at Reception and networked to team secretaries and PAs. All staff at AA stated that this would be very useful. All relevant contacts, such as appropriate past clients, existing clients, intermediaries, journalists, personal

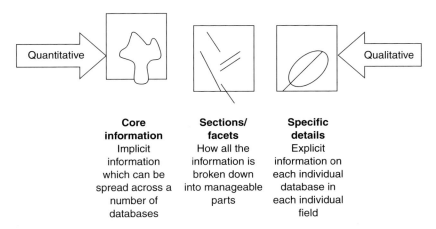

Core information	**Sections/ facets**	**Specific details**
Implicit information which can be spread across a number of databases	How all the information is broken down into manageable parts	Explicit information on each individual database in each individual field

Figure 2.7 A proposed marketing/project database for AA

contacts, etc. should be stored and profiles built of key players. The field headings could include:

- Name of contact, title and qualifications
- Company, address, telephone, etc.
- Discipline
- AA contact name
- Length of relationship with the practice
- Projects worked on if appropriate
- No. of times worked with
- Key profiles.

Marketing organization

Marketing communication

Figure 2.8 illustrates the communication process in the marketing planning system with every member of staff understanding marketing initiatives. Marketing is a team activity within AA, and Figure 2.9 illustrates the network of roles and responsibilities.

Marketing documentation and procedures

All documentation of marketing information should be kept simple. Ideally the practice could start with minuting all marketing-related meetings. When a market research programme is in place the practice can begin to think about producing quarterly marketing reports to be circulated to staff preceding quarterly staff meetings and starting to build profiles on key competitors.

AA should implement a centralized filing system for all marketing information and publicity files, contacts, etc. At present partners keep their own files.

Marketing 'hub'

The marketing 'hub' should be a central area containing all marketing information, including:

- marketing/project databases;
- marketing intelligence information;
- key presentation boards, CAD visuals, perspectives, etc., filed in referenced portfolios;
- slides and photographs;
- centralized filing system;
- Power Mac/server with all in-house promotional material scans;
- résumés, project sheets, texts, etc.

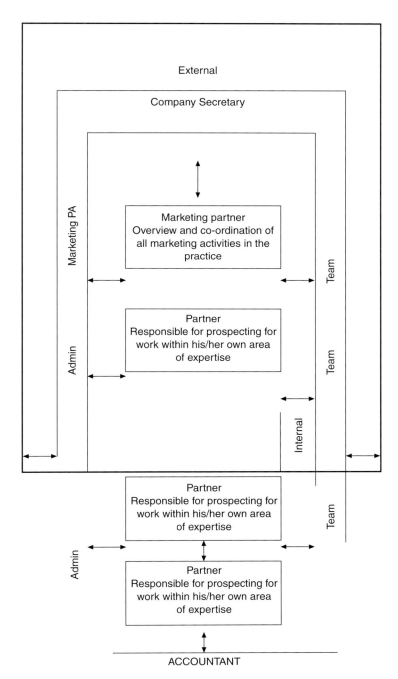

Figure 2.8 Proposed marketing communication at AA

Marketing partner	Partners	Marketing PA
Responsible for implementation of management and control of marketing planning systems	Responsible for prospecting for work in own area of expertise and initiating market research and publicity	Responsible for maintenance of publicity and marketing files. Monitoring of practice publicity. Marketing systems administration. Organizing marketing 'hub' and maintaining marketing materials. Up-dating marketing database

Company	Administration	Teams
Responsible for setting up financial systems/ spreadsheets, i.e. resources; marketing job numbers	General Marketing Administration for each partner	Responsible for identifying new opportunities and contributing to practice marketing initiatives

DTP/Graphics	Receptionist
Responsible for co-ordinating in-house promotional material on Mac	Responsible for up-dating contacts. Highlighting AA publicity, both local and national press; professional journals and putting on file

Figure 2.9 Proposed network of marketing activity at AA

It would also be beneficial to put the library next to the marketing 'hub' for reference to architectural journals and books for precedents etc.

Marketing programme

Over the next twelve months Associated Architects need to systematically programme the actions required for the implementation of a marketing plan. Each element needs to be prioritized against strategic objectives with every cost implication clearly defined.

To formulate an accurate budget all marketing expenditure must be predicted and measured both directly and indirectly, i.e. forecasting the time in man-hours of completing a given task, and the direct cost of purchasing new software, etc.

In the first year the initial investment of setting up formal systems will obviously be far greater than in later years. However, if properly implemented, monitored and controlled, these initiatives will give the practice considerable returns for their efforts and secure a healthy future.

A summary of the activities required is listed and these need to be programmed against start and finish dates and noted against human and financial resources:

Define strategic objectives

- goals and objectives over a three-year period;
- positioning, review of strategic issues analysis (SWOT);
- definition of primary and secondary market sectors;
- definition of product service offer;
- definition of financial objectives and fee strategy.

Market research

- define scope of market research activities, systems and sources of information;
- competitor analysis, sector/market trends, external environment.

Human resources

- define recruitment programme and policy;
- define training programme for professional practice/new services;
- develop internal staff care policy;
- develop resources spreadsheet;
- identify and target placement officers at key blue chip universities;
- develop schedule for partners/team meetings.

Internal communication

- programme office socials;
- programme visits to buildings.

External communication

- publicity;
- development of brochure brief;
- design of brochure cover;
- collation of texts, résumés and visuals for in-house element of brochure;

- training on DTP systems;
- development of presentation standards policy.

Conclusion

The author would agree with Eric Schneider that AA would survive with little or no change. However, there is a significant difference between surviving and capitalizing on new opportunities and 'riding on the crest of a wave'. Post-UCE College of Art and the Jewellery School, both sensitive and deservedly acclaimed projects, the new generation of partners have an excellent opportunity to take the practice forward into its next phase. A future which could celebrate and build upon past triumphs and wisdom, to provide a new pedigree in architectural direction.

In order to embrace this philosophy and maximize AA's true potential, the practice needs to have the appropriate commercial perception to foresee market changes, and act accordingly, using a pro-active and diagnostic approach to identifying new opportunities in line with strategic objectives and experience.

Current and future projects will provide the opportunity to promote the practice's architectural narrative, outside regional boundaries. National recognition is an important catalyst on which to build AA's portfolio outside the practice's main area of operation. This requires persistence, consistency and creative foresight, which must be reflected in quality of service; quality of staff; and the quality of the design process.

To motivate and nurture creativity, improve management and administrative procedures, the practice must recognize the need to reconcile communication shortcomings and hierarchical fiefdoms.

References

Jobber, D. (1995) *Principles and Practice of Marketing*. New York: McGraw-Hill.
McDonald, M. (1992) *The Marketing Planner*, Oxford: Butterworth-Heinemann.
Schneider, E. (1993) Management Audit, Associated Architects internal report.

Review questions

1   Discuss the differing issues that an architectural practice would need to consider when formulating an effective marketing plan.
2   What are the main four areas of the marketing planning process and why is it important to integrate this with the strategic business plan?
3   Why is it important for the organization to clearly identify its core sectors of business activity?
4   Discuss the different ways it can achieve this.
5   Why was it important for AA to undertake a 'competitor analysis'?

6 Discuss the benefits of a formal quality assurance commitment to both AA and their clients.

7 Referring to the text, could you suggest other suitable ways for the practice to attract and maintain new and existing clients?

8 Explain how the marketing information database could be employed in developing new business opportunities for the practice.

9 Why is it important to maintain and update the marketing database?

10 Referring to the chapter, what other recommendations would you offer regarding the use of information in relation to marketing object-ives and business objectives?

Project questions

1 Consider the particular nature of the marketing planning process at Associated Architects. Use this description and Figure 2.1 in a com-parison with the same process in an interdisciplinary design consul-tancy. List key similarities and differences found between these examples of architectural design and other design consultancies.

2 Is the Boston matrix an appropriate or accurate way to consider Asso-ciated Architects' market position? Consider also the SWOT analysis. Which method provides the best results? Describe your comparison in terms of value to Associated Architects.

3 Develop a questionnaire that would elicit the nature of communica-tion at Associated Architects. This may be applied to your university or work environment but particularly apply to developing the commu-nication section of this chapter. In particular, attempt to elicit the rela-tive amounts of formal and informal communication.

4 Consider the principles of prospecting for new clients. Which of these would apply to a design consultancy? Devise a tabulated comparison of each for such a business.

5 Consider the chapter as a whole. If Associated Architects are to act on the result of the audit, briefly describe the critical process points that will have to be achieved, their time frame and the change manage-ment process involved.

Further reading

Allison, K. (1993) *The Wild Card of Design: A Perspective in Architecture in a Project Management Environment*. London: Butterworth Architecture.

Churchill, S. (1995) 'How to attract the press', *Architects Journal*, 16 November.

Daniels, C.N. (1994) *Information Technology: The Management Challenge*. London: Addison-Wesley.

Eley, J., Seidel, A.D. and Symes, M. (1995) *Architects and their Practices: A Changing Profession*. London: Butterworth Architecture.

Lucas, J. (1997) 'Time to make a profit', *Architects Journal*, 17 July.

Lydiate, L. (ed.) (1992) *Professional Practice in Design Consultancy*. London: Design Council.

Oakley, M. (ed.) *Design Management: A Handbook of Issues and Methods*. Oxford: Blackwell.

RIBA (1992) *Strategic Study of the Profession: Phase One – Strategic Overview*. London: RIBA Publications.

RIBA (1993) *Strategic Study of the Profession: Phase Two – Clients and Architects*. London: RIBA Publications.

Ryness, L.C. (1992) *Marketing and Communication Techniques for Architects*. London: Longman Group.

Slavid, R. (1997) 'On the crest of a wave', *Architects Journal*, 3 July.

Strong, J. (1996) *Winning by Design: Architectural Competitions*. London: Butterworth Architecture.

Whitson, B.A. (1992) *Presentations: A Client's Viewpoint*. California: Arts and Architecture Press.

Wilson, D.A. (1993) *Managing Information*. London: Butterworth-Heinemann.

CASE STUDY 3

The effectiveness of Design Management communication in British Telecom

Company:	BT (British Telecommunications plc)
	81 Newgate Street
	London
	EC1A 7AJ
Business:	UK's largest telecommunications company
Auditor:	*Alexandra Smith*

Introduction

Since becoming a privatized company in 1984, BT has been a vocal champion of design, initially with an in-house design team, but since 1991 choosing to use external design agencies under the direction of a design management team. Its Corporate Design Unit (CDU) is responsible for product, multimedia and interior design, corporate identity and corporate graphics. As a high profile company, constantly in the press, its design decisions in managing the company's corporate identity, and in particular the change of symbol which is the major component of its public presence, have been widely reported, and the subject of much debate in both the general and specialist design press.

The CDU reports to the Design Strategy Group of the Corporate Relations Department, the senior management group responsible for the overall management and control of design in BT. The CDU is the main source of guidance and help for all BT managers on design matters, and has the aim of developing, implementing and managing the visual image of BT to reflect BT's main mission and brand values. Its remit includes the benchmarking of BT design against competitors and leaders in other industries.

In addition to its given remit, the CDU has set itself the mission to demonstrate BT as the worldwide role model telecommunications group through the application of the highest quality of design. Its self-set objectives include being 'the best design management team'.

This case study examines the methods and effectiveness of communications both within the CDU, and between the CDU, its internal clients and external agencies. A sample of thirteen completed and ongoing projects was analysed to establish design management methodologies, in terms of briefings, conduct of meetings, relationships, and communication during the project, and room for improvement. The results of interviews, which used a standard series of questions, are discussed in detail. They offer insights into the feelings of participants about the effectiveness of communications between each of the three pairings of the three groups – CDU–BT internal clients, CDU–external agencies, and external agencies–BT clients. Results of the survey suggest that patterns of communication are uneven across projects, with seven projects using CDU as the sole point of contact between BT and the external agencies, and with six projects using some level of three-way communication.

The study concludes that a three-way relationship offers the greatest opportunity for achieving the satisfaction of all parties. At a more detailed level, guidelines are given for improving aspects of the three-way communication. These include a clearer definition of the CDU role. It is recommended that the CDU should develop its role as a team of design management consultants with a brief extended to include educating BT clients about the benefits of design, and promoting themselves as facilitators: listeners, consultants and communicators. Suggestions are made for achieving this extension of the role.

Another recommendation is for a more formal statement at the start of each project, to specify the project leader, the funding source within BT, members of the project team at each stage, timescales including sign-off stages, and authority for sign-off at each stage.

Overall, it was noted that, whereas in the initial interviews with CDU the impression was gained that CDU's management and communication skills were exemplary, further investigation revealed areas for improvement. Following an expansion of the recommendations made in the study, some of them were immediately adopted by BT.

As a postscript to the study, there is included a summary of the importance of communication policies generally, with reference to the case of the CDU in BT.

A brief history of BT

At the time of the study BT was the UK's largest telecommunications company, and is continuing to grow rapidly in the hope that it will be the largest worldwide telecommunications company.

Telecommunications used to be part of the General Post Office, a department of the British Civil Service. In the 1970s it was then called Post Office Telecommunications, a division of a public corporation, still subject to government control, and still closely linked with postal business. In 1981 BT split from the Post Office as a public corporation, but then in 1984, became a privatized company. BT was then known as 'British Telecom' and identified by the 'T' symbol. This symbol was unique in the UK but not globally, many other communications groups used similar logos. As BT's vision was, and still is, to become 'the most successful worldwide telecommunications group', they had to adopt a new and unique identity. The identity changed in 1991, after much thought and research, to the Blue and Red Piper symbol. This identity change was criticized fiercely by the press at first, but has now been accepted by the UK as one of the most distinguishable identities of the 1990s.

The need for this new identity was brought about by the increase in competition both nationally and internationally, since the privatization of BT. Oftel, the Government's Office of Telecommunications was created to ensure that competition within the telecom industry would increase, which would in turn ensure that customers were treated fairly by providing competitive prices. Although BT is still the market leader in this ever-changing industry, the need to maintain their competitive edge is of paramount importance for its success.

Telecommunications today is not just about the provision of telephones and telephone lines. The increasing use of technology has enabled BT to develop more and more products and services for quicker, easier and more comprehensive communication. However, technological advancement has not yet come to an end, it is the continuous evolution of technology that makes BT one of the most exciting and dynamic industries in the world today, and will continue to do so for many years to come.

BT is very much a high profile company, constantly in the press, purely because telecommunications is now a part of everyday life, rather than a luxury. BT has a great influence on people's lives. However, with other companies offering the same services as BT, customers today are faced with a choice. It is through increased competition that the need for design has increased. The effective use of design as a business resource can affect how the customer perceives a company.

Organizational guide to British Telecom

Personal, Business and Global Communications are at the forefront of the company, as these departments deal with all external customers – residential, business and customers requiring a global service. The structure of British Telecom is shown in Figure 3.1.

Group Business Management provides a framework which helps the divisions to achieve BT's Corporate Objectives, again enabling customer units to deliver what the customer wants. Group Business Management's responsibilities include planning, pricing, assessing and co-ordinating all requests for internal systems development. Group Finance ensures the effective management of finance throughout the Group.

Office of the Chairman and Chief Executive is split into 4 areas: BT Security; Corporate Relations; Strategic Relations; and Corporate

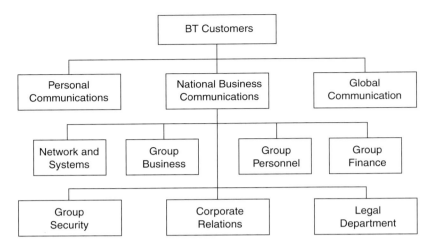

Figure 3.1 Structure of British Telecom

Strategy. These are all services within and for BT working to achieve BT's mission.

Group Personnel ensures that BT has the appropriate resources to support all the other divisions. Group Legal Services delivers quality legal services as an integral contributor to BT's success.

Structure of Corporate Relations Department and Corporate Design Unit

The Corporate Design Unit (CDU) is part of the department (CRD). This is the Unit in which the audit was conducted during the placement (Figure 3.2). The Design Strategy Group is the senior management group responsible for the overall management and control of design in BT. This group oversees the activities of the design management groups in CDU.

Corporate Design Unit consists of the Head, who is part of the Design Strategy Group, five Design Managers and three part-time Contractors. Their aim is to develop, implement and manage the visual image of BT to reflect BT's main mission and brand values. Such aims require BT's design to be of the highest quality, fit for purpose and often setting new standards and strategic direction for the future. The Design Unit is the main source of guidance and help for all BT managers on design matters. CDU's remit is as follows:

- To direct company policy on corporate identity and in all areas of design.
- To create corporate identity and design standards for use by BT people and external suppliers.

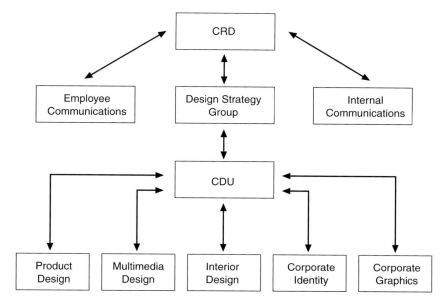

Figure 3.2 Structure of CRD and CDU

- To monitor and maintain the quality of design and use of the corporate identity throughout the company and wherever the BT brand is used around the world.
- To benchmark BT design against their competitors and leaders in other industries.
- To manage design projects for CRD, Group Headquarters and for other divisions where required.
- To provide helpline advice on all matters relating to corporate identity and design in BT.

CDU have developed their own mission and specific objectives in addition to their remit. CDU's mission is to demonstrate BT as the worldwide role model telecommunications group through the application of the highest quality of design, according to the BT corporate brand. CDU's objectives are:

- To establish BT as the leading telecommunications brand in the world.
- To develop and maintain a corporate identity architecture according to the changing needs of the BT group.
- To establish brand, identity and design as an effective strategic business resource.
- To provide BT products and services with a competitive positioning through design and usability.

- To provide leadership and direction on identity and design across the BT group.
- To support BT's image and reputation through the highest quality standards of design.
- To be the best design management team.

The Design Management Team was put in place after the launch of the new BT logo in 1991. Before then, BT had an in-house design team, who were responsible for the design work. However, since the organizational downsizing of the early 1990s all the design work is done externally by large design agencies and consultancies; these projects are still managed internally by CDU's design managers.

Each design manager is responsible for the management of design within the various disciplines. These disciplines are shown in Figure 3.2. Each of the design managers takes a brief given by another BT manager i.e. their internal client and briefs a design agency on the project and then CDU manage the project while the agency actually does the design work.

Purpose of the audit

The purpose of the audit was to analyse and evaluate the methods and effectiveness of communication of the CDU, both 'internally' and 'externally'. Internally refers not only to CDU itself, but also to the internal clients for whom CDU manage design projects. These clients are managers of different departments within BT e.g. Product Managers, Shareholder Managers, Group Property Managers, etc. 'Externally' refers to BT's external suppliers who are commissioned by BT to do specific work. The suppliers can be design agencies and consultants, manufacturers of various products, builders, architects, etc.

A communication audit within this three-way relationship was examined (see Figure 3.3). Within each of these groupings is a complex struc-

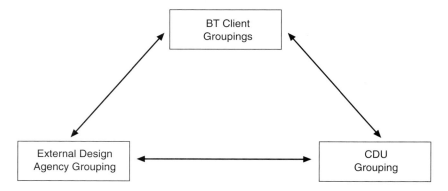

Figure 3.3 Three-way relationship and communication model in BT

ture. In some cases more than one person from each grouping is involved in a project, and in most cases the communication lines linking each grouping are not equal in strength. Each link varies, depending on the kind of project. Sometimes the link between CDU and the external supplier could be much more frequent than others, but there is still a line linking the other groupings.

Project plan

A ten-week project plan and initial brief was set up to provide a route to follow so as to maximize the time spent in CDU. Then once the project began the plan evolved as certain ideas and proposals became irrelevant, and other ideas were more appropriate. A more focused plan was developed once the project was finalized and discussed with CDU.

The time spent in CDU was used to gather as much information and research as possible. A final but informal presentation was given to the Corporate Design Unit managers at the end of the project. An executive summary of the findings and conclusions was sent to David Mercer, Head of CDU, two days before the presentation, to enable David Mercer to have an insight into the issues that were to be addressed during the presentation.

Methodology

During the first two weeks as much background information as possible was gathered about CDU and its role within BT. This was done by briefly interviewing each design manager about their job, what they do, how they do it, and asking general questions about relationships.

Once this information had been gathered, more focused information about specific projects needed to be obtained. In order to get an accurate insight into the way CDU works with clients and suppliers, examples of projects were provided by each design manager and contractors; some of these projects were currently running and some were completed projects. These were chosen randomly, so as to avoid bias. Each design manager provided a brief outline of each project, its background, and the current state of play. They also provided contact names and addresses of other people involved, i.e. a client and a supplier, all of which were design agencies. Letters were sent to each client and design agency explaining the circumstances and providing notice that a phone call would be made to arrange an interview. Altogether a sample of thirteen projects was used, divided up as follows: 1 interior/refurbishment project; 2 product design projects; 2 corporate identity projects; 6 graphics/communications projects; and 2 multimedia projects.

Once the sample had been compiled, access to project files was made available to gather further detailed information. These project files were kindly provided by the design manager responsible for each project. Even though the uncompleted projects cannot be described, they do not affect the way the research was conducted.

Appointments were made with each design agency and client separately for an interview. Four weeks were spent visiting and interviewing clients and agencies. For the interviews a set of questions was drawn up for the clients and another for the agencies. All clients and all design agencies were asked the same questions. This was done so that the data from each project could be compared and conclusions drawn from the findings. The questions, although generic, were very focused on communication, project procedures and relationships. The subjects covered in the questions were:

- briefings;
- conduct of meetings;
- relationships;
- communication during the project;
- room for improvement.

The interviews were recorded and the questions were very open, encouraging the interviewees to raise issues that they felt strongly about. Although thirteen projects were examined in detail, CDU have, on average, twenty projects each current at any one time. Therefore the research is representative of CDU's work.

Interviews were conducted together with a range of observations made from a variety of meetings during the ten weeks, and interview comments were noted down and used to back up any issues raised on that particular situation. Four important meetings were attended to add to the observations made:

- a major presentation meeting with CDU, the design agency and the client committee; eleven attended;
- a minor, *ad hoc* meeting between the client and CDU; four attended;
- an informal meeting with David Mercer (Head of CDU) and two design managers from BAA (British Airports Association);
- a major CDU team meeting; all the design managers and David Mercer attended.

Notes were made at all these meetings and they provided a useful insight into the way CDU is managed.

Once all the interviews have been conducted, the relationship within each project was then analysed. A chart for each 'relationship' was developed. In order to judge whether or not each relationship worked well, a set of compliance criteria was devised for each relationship. If any one of the criteria was not fulfilled, the relationship was considered to have failed. The set of criteria was as follows:

- The client is satisfied with the end product.
- The end product conforms to BT design standards and guidelines and reflects BT brand values.
- The client felt in control and well informed during the project.
- The relationship promotes awareness, internally, of the design management and communication processes.
- The end product is on time and within budget.
- In future, clients buy into the design management process.

Communication within these relationships was analysed and conclusions were drawn from these results.

The interview results were analysed and compared, and consensus opinions were noted as the most important issues to be addressed, as these issues were of great concern to many clients and design agencies. From these findings, recommendations were then developed.

Interview results and evaluation

The following is a detailed evaluation of the results of the interviews, and this represents correlations across respondents within the CDU. All opinions have been included, even if it is the opinion of only one interviewee, as CDU feel that every opinion counts and is equally as important as any issue raised by a majority of interviewees.

Once each question has been evaluated, the main findings will be concluded by providing recommendations as to how these issues can be improved and/or solved.

Results and evaluation of design agency interviews

Q1 How did you come to be working for BT?
Q2 If there was a pitch for the job, did you know who you were competing against?

Results

Q1	Q2
Long term = 6/12	Pitch = 4/7
	No pitch = 2/7
Medium term = 4/12	Pitch = 3/4
	No pitch = 1/4
Short term = 2/12	Pitch = 2/2

There seems to be no correlation between the length of time the agency has worked for BT and whether they had to pitch for the job or not. The theory would be that long-term agencies should not have to pitch and newer, or shorter-term agencies should have to pitch.

Agencies that have had a long-term relationship with BT would like to be asked to do a project on the basis that BT already know the agency and what they are capable of; thus, a certain amount of trust will build up and would boost the morale of the agency and as a result, produce better results.

For these results to be evaluated accurately, size must be considered. However, the size of a project can be assessed in two ways: (1) the size of the budget for the project (e.g. £25K = large, under £5K = small); and (2) the amount of actual design work that was required for the job. Unfortunately, there was no access to information on the size of the budget allocated for each project, therefore point (2) is the only other way to assess each project size.

Of the projects followed during the ten-week period, six were large; two were medium; and four were small. By comparing questions 1 and 2 with the size of each project, a correlation can now be found. The large project for which there was no pitch procedure was the largest project researched. Many different design elements were involved, it was not only a large project in terms of design, but it was also a long-term one.

With such a major project, it seems strange that there was no pitch. The reason for this may be that the design agency was asked to complete one aspect and was then given the other small individual projects to follow on, so that there would be a coherent style throughout the whole project.

However, this was not just a graphic design project, there was also product, interior and fashion design involved. Surely a product design agency should have been given the chance to put their ideas forward. Staying with the same design agency seems to be an easy option and saves time, but it is not necessarily the most professional way to manage a project.

Q3   Did you know who you were competing against before or after the pitch?

Result

Most design agencies did not know who they were competing against, despite operating within a relatively incestuous professional environment. Six agencies said that they would find it very useful to know why they had won a pitch or not and they would also like to know which agencies they are competing against in a pitch situation. This would be useful for agencies that do not mind knowing who is perceived to be in their competitive set.

The only way this would benefit CDU would be via the fact that they would get to know which agencies are prepared to be open about their approach to design business and competition. However, some agencies may consider this to be an unprofessional approach.

Agencies should be so focused on winning the pitch, that they are not concerned about their competitors, although all agencies should be entitled to some confidentiality, and should be asked if they would like their identity to be revealed to their competitors. CDU must keep professionalism in mind and keep competitors anonymous in a pitch situation.

Q4   Before the pitch, were you sent a written brief before being formally briefed by BT? If so, how was it sent to you? Post, Fax, email, etc.?

Q5   Who from BT briefed you?

Q6   How did they brief you? Face-to-face, in writing, over telephone, etc.?

These questions must be compared with each other and with the size of each project.

Results

Size of project	Q4 Written brief?	Sent	Q5 Who?	Q6 Formal briefing
1 Large	Written	Fax	CDU	No
2 Large	Written	Verbal	Client	Yes
3 Large	No	Tel	CDU	No
4 Large	Written	Verbal	CDU	Yes
5 Large	Written	$3\frac{1}{2}$ Disc	CDU	No
6 Large	Written	Fax	Client	Yes
7 Medium	Verbal	Fax	CDU	No
8 Medium	Written	Verbal	CDU	Yes
9 Small	No	Verbal	CDU	Yes
10 Small	Written	Fax	CDU	Yes
11 Small	Verbal	Verbal	CDU	Yes
12 Small	No	Verbal	CDU	Yes

As shown in result number 3, one large project was briefed over the telephone. This is the same project that did not have a pitch. Of the five that did receive a written brief, only three were given a formal face-to-face briefing afterwards. Only one of the medium projects had a formal face-to-face briefing (result 8). This again is not a good result for CDU. Two small projects did not have a written brief, but they had a formal face-to-face briefing. This is not necessary for small projects.

Only one of these small projects did not have a formal face-to-face briefing. Formal briefings are less necessary for small projects, but are essential for large and medium-sized projects. Formal briefings do depend on how well the agency knows CDU. If the agency has a good working relationship with CDU and knows about their design standards and guidelines, then the need for a formal face-to-face briefing may not be necessary. However, there is always a chance that the subtle nuances of a project can be lost in the written brief, and the agency may not fully understand the essence of the brief.

When these questions were asked, the majority of agencies said that the briefings are the most important part of a project. It could be argued that it should be up to the agency to make sure that the briefing is satisfactory for them to create a good result. However, this should only be the case if their client (i.e. CDU) has no knowledge of design. As in BT's case, CDU should be responsible for getting the correct message across to the agency, after all, that is one of their most fundamental roles.

Q7   How does CDU compare to your other clients' methods of briefing?

Results

Size of project	Length	Comparison with other clients
1 Large	Long	Less professional and informal
2 Large	Long	Good
3 Large	Long	Less formal
4 Large	Long	Very good
5 Large	Medium	Same as others
6 Large	Long	Quite good
7 Medium	Medium	Same
8 Medium	Medium	Not detailed enough
9 Small	Medium	Good
10 Small	Short	Good
11 Small	Short	Same

Two agencies working on large projects felt that CDU are less formal and one said it was less professional. These did not have a formal briefing from CDU. It can be assumed that methods of briefing reflect the sense of professionalism of the agencies' clients. CDU should take briefings more seriously and must be aware that their professionalism is reflected during the briefing process. The same two agencies who do not see CDU as very professional have had a long-term relationship with CDU. Therefore, this is not a first impression but one that has built up over time. In that sense CDU are not conveying a good impression.

Q8   Who did BT brief from your company? You or another?
Q9   Was the brief self-explanatory and easy to interpret?
Q10 If not, why?

Results

Q8 Who was briefed?	Q9 Self-explanatory?	Q10 Why?
1 Project leader and designers	Yes	–
2 Design Team	Yes	–
3 Director	Yes	–
4 Design Team	Yes	–
5 N/A	Yes	–
6 Design Manager	Yes	–
7 Director	Yes	–
8 Design Team	No	Too complicated
9 Project Leader and Design Manager	Yes	–
10 Account Handler	Yes	–
11 Design Manager and Designers	Yes	–
12 Director	Just OK	–

From these results there seems to be more senior people being briefed on the project. This is not a problem as it is up to the managers to make sure that the right people are working on the right project. Many directors prefer to be briefed by BT themselves so that they can then put together the resources suitable for that job. A design team is the most appropriate team of people to brief from an agency. This gives everyone a chance to ask questions and enables CDU to ensure that the correct message has been conveyed.

Q11 Was the way in which BT briefed you satisfactory?

Only one agency said 'No'. But when asked if there was anything they would like to see improved about CDU's briefings (Q12), eight agencies made suggestions. Only four said that there was nothing to be improved. This proves that the majority of agencies are not fully satisfied with CDU's methods of briefing. The agencies' suggestions were as follows:

- More face-to-face briefings should be provided after an initial written brief has been sent.
- More marketing and consumer-based issues/information should be included in the brief – after the pitch stage.
- Guidelines should be provided earlier.
- Briefs should not be too long, and not include too much jargon. The brief should take the form of a short statement of requirements and then the more subtle nuances should be conveyed at a face-to-face meeting.
- More background information should be provided e.g. who is funding the project, who is the project leader, etc.

- Brief should be sent out earlier.
- More written briefs, but not too detailed at the early pitching stages.
- More written briefs, but also more people should be at the face-to-face briefings, i.e. marketing people, clients, etc.
- More thought from the heart should form the written brief. CDU tend to write out a standard document for the brief, and there is not much feeling put into them.

Q13 Once BT briefed you, did you then brief the rest of your design team, or did BT do this also?

As shown in the results of Q8, BT briefed the whole design team for only three projects, one of which was briefed by the BT client and not CDU. The other projects were briefed to more senior people, then they briefed their team, as explained above.

Q14 Describe your relationship with BT. Formal, informal, etc.
Q15 Do you prefer formal or informal relationships with your clients?
Q16 Why?

Results

No.	*Q14* *Relationship*	*Q15* *Preference*	*Q16* *Why?*
1	Professional	Professional	Work better
2	None with CDU	N/A	N/A
3	Professional	Professional	Work better
4	Informal/Formal	Informal/Formal	Better results
5	Professional	Professional	Work better
6	Infrequent	N/A	N/A
7	Informal	Professional	More respect
8	Informal	Informal	Work better
9	Informal	Informal	Work better
10	Informal	Professional	No comment
11	Informal	Professional	More respect
12	Informal	Professional	Work better

It seems that agencies prefer to have professional relationships. A professional relationship does not mean a formal one. The more informal the relationship, the less professional CDU seem. Professionalism is the key to gaining more and more respect from people both internally as well as externally.

When the agencies were asked about the frequency of their liaison with CDU (Q17 and Q18), all results varied, and this issue was not one of concern to the agencies. All said that the amount of liaison was enough and appropriate for each project. Therefore it can be assumed that this is not an issue that needs to be improved on.

Q19 Who initiates most of the meetings, you or CDU?

Q20 Do you have to go to BT for most meetings or does CDU come to you?

Results

No.	*Q19* *Initiator*	*Q20* *Where?*
1	Agency	CDU
2	Agency	Client
3	CDU	CDU
4	Agency	Both places
5	Agency and CDU	Both places
6	Agency and CDU	Client
7	Agency and CDU	CDU
8	Agency and CDU	Agency
9	Agency and CDU	Both places
10	Agency and CDU	CDU
11	Agency	Agency
12	Agency	Client

As shown, it is apparent that the initiation of meetings and liaisons is fairly equal between CDU and the agency. It is also equal when it comes to the venues for these meetings. This shows that there is mutual agreement and negotiation when it comes to arranging liaisons and meetings. This is fair as it mainly depends on the nature of the liaison. If there is a presentation of work, the best place to have it is at the agency, so that they do not have to worry about transporting the work across London. This is a general issue that is managed in the most appropriate way by both agency and CDU.

Q21 asked which do the agencies prefer, CDU coming to them or them going to CDU. No agency minded at all where they go for a meeting. This proved to be a minor issue in the management and running of a design project.

Q22 If you go to CDU do you feel that you can conduct a meeting successfully, without any distractions? Is this the same when CDU comes to you?

Of the seven agencies that have attended a meeting in CDU, three have meetings that are mainly conducted in David Mercer's office, not CDU's office. All three agencies said that meetings in David Mercer's office were fine. Two other agencies said that meetings in CDU's office are not good.

The CDU office is open plan and when a meeting is conducted there, there are many distractions, e.g. telephones ringing, people interrupting, desks full of paperwork, etc. To conduct a meeting or a presentation is difficult in this environment.

Q23 Are you comfortable with the way CDU conduct their meetings?

Seven agencies said 'yes'. No one said 'No'. This is a good result.

However, when asked Q24, 'Do you think there is room for improvement in the way CDU conduct meetings?' Five agencies had suggestions: 'Establish a date and stick to it, and set agendas'; 'Have meeting rooms available'; 'Agendas and minutes must be done'; 'Get out more'; and 'Make sure the relevant people are present'.

In correlating the results from Q23 and Q12, it is apparent that agencies will put up with certain issues, but, when prompted, will express their true feelings about the issues that irritate them. A lot of agencies simply take the way CDU work for granted and do not question it.

Q25 Is the majority of your liaison with CDU done by telephone and fax?
Q26 Is this an efficient way of communicating with CDU?
Q27 When you leave a telephone message or send a fax, does CDU respond quickly or do you have to chase them up?

Results

No.	Q25 Liaison	Q26 Efficiency	Q27 Response
1	Phone	OK	Not good
2	Phone (not much)	Not good	No
3	Phone	OK	Yes
4	Phone and meeting	Not good	Not good
5	Phone	OK	Yes
6	Not much	–	Not good
7	Phone and meetings	OK	Yes
8	Face-to-face	OK	Usually good
9	Voice mail	OK	Yes
10	Phone/fax	OK	Yes
11	Face-to-face	OK	Awkward
12	Phone	OK	Not good

Six agencies said that the response to telephone messages by CDU is not good.

Q28 How does CDU compare to your other clients in the way that they work with you – good or bad?

Seven said 'Good'. One said 'Good' but they only liaised with the BT Client. Two said 'OK'. Two said 'Not good'. These statistics are quite favourable.

Q29 Do you see CDU as a 'big bad client' or do you feel part of their team?

No-one said that CDU are a 'Big Bad Client'. However, not all agencies felt part of a team.

Results

Q29	
Team or client?	
1 Neither	7 Not Team
2 N/A only liaise with client	8 Not Team
3 Team	9 Team
4 Team	10 Not Team
5 Team	11 Team
6 Not Team	12 Not Team

Q30 asked why they felt part of a team or not, some of those that said they feel part of a team gave the following reasons:

We have a comfortable and informal relationship with CDU.
A good relationship creates a good team spirit.
Our relationship is brilliant and this has built up trust.

Some of those that said they do not feel part of a team gave the following reasons:

When more people are involved it becomes more formal.
There is more formality than a team spirit.
There is not much direct liaison to build up a team spirit.
CDU is not involved enough for a team spirit.
Not much involvement with CDU.
Not enough contact.

From these results it can be assumed that where CDU have a lot of involvement in the project, there seems to be more of a team spirit. But when CDU are not as involved the relationship is much more formal. This shows that CDU are good at creating a good team spirit during a project. This is one of the secrets to good design management. If the agency feels part of the team, they will take more interest in the project and aim to produce the best possible results. The more formal the relationship, the less interest the agency takes in the project and therefore they do not aim to produce the best results.

Q31 Do you feel that you can get on with a project, without having to check everything with CDU first?

Eight said 'Yes', they can manage a BT project in their own way. Two said 'No'. Two said 'Yes and No'. When asked which they prefer: All interviewees said that they prefer to manage a project in their own way. The reasons why were all very similar: They feel that they can work better and produce better results, knowing that CDU trust them to get on with the project themselves.

This is a difficult issue for CDU, because they have to be careful not to give the agencies too much responsibility, as the BT clients will begin to wonder what CDU are there for. But having too much hands-on influence over projects can be just as bad. This would threaten the agency, as confusion would arise over CDU's role, and this could jeopardize the working relationship.

Q32 What do you think of the design standards that CDU use?

Five said they are 'essential'. Two said they are 'important'. One said they are 'necessary'. One said they are 'OK'. One said they are 'useless'. This shows that design agencies understand the need for standards, especially for such a large organization.

Q33 Do you find them easy to follow and interpret?
Q34 If not, why not?

Four said that they are easy to interpret. Four suggested improvements. Four had not used the guidelines. Their comments were as follows: 'They are not detailed enough'; 'They are out of date'; 'They are a bit obscure'; and 'They need to be revised regularly'. It is apparent that not all agencies are happy with the standards. CDU must keep this in mind and aim to improve their guidelines in the hope of maintaining the respect that has already built up.

Q35 Do these standards limit the creativity you can offer CDU?

Four said 'Yes'. Three said 'No'. Five had no comment. This is not a major issue as there is no consensus response.

Q36 Do you genuinely like the work you do for CDU?

All answered 'Yes'. Most said that if they did not like the work they would not have BT as their client. This shows that agencies do have some choice over who they work for, because no agency is working for BT purely to pay the bills. Some actually choose clients who they enjoy working for, especially those who feel part of a team.

Q37 Do you find BT projects challenging or boring?

Eight said 'Challenging'. One said 'They can be boring'. Two said 'Neither'. This is a good result for CDU. However, if the agency found the work boring, they should not work for BT, as lack of interest will resu t in an uninteresting solution. The interest in a project of the agency is reflected through their work. When asked Why? (Q38) No-one gave a reason.

Q39 If you make a recommendation about a project, is it noted down by CDU, or is it ignored?

All interviewees said that any recommendation is noted down and discussed. However, they are not necessarily used. CDU must appear to be interested in everyone's opinion, whether it is useful or not. However, when they have decided whether to use it or not they must maintain their authority and give reasons why.

Q40 Do you have much contact with the BT client?

Four agencies have much more contact with the client than with CDU. These projects do not have much input from CDU, but whether this is CDU's choice or not is another matter. Eight agencies have some contact with the client. All agencies agreed that this liaison with the client was necessary (Q41).

Q42 With whom do you prefer liaising? CDU or the client or both?
Q43 Why do you prefer liaising with CDU or the client?

Results

	Q42	*Q43*
1	CDU	CDU now about design
2	Client	CDU do not respond
3	Client, especially near a deadline	–
4	N/A	–
5	Both	Need info from both
6	Client	CDU are not involved
7	CDU	CDU know more
8	Both	Need both info
9	N/A	–
10	N/A	–
11	N/A	–
12	Both	They each have different roles

The ideal result here should be all agencies preferring to liaise with both CDU and the client as this would show that there is a good three-way relationship. The three agencies that prefer liaising with the client are those who have much more contact with the client than CDU. Maybe if they had more contact with CDU their answer to this question would be 'Both'. These results show that the communication within the three-way relationship is not as effective or as efficient as it could be. Those agencies who prefer liaising with the client gave the reason that CDU is not as involved, or CDU do not respond. The reason why agencies prefer liaising with CDU is because they already know about design.

Q44 Is the relationship between you and the BT client formal or informal?

Results

Q44			
1	Informal	7	Formal
2	Informal	8	Informal/Formal
3	Formal	9	No relationship
4	N/A	10	Informal
5	Professional	11	Informal
6	Informal/Professional	12	Informal

By correlating results for Q44 and Q14, it is apparent that clients tend to be more formal than CDU. This might have a correlation with either clients' authority or the 'language barrier', so to speak. Formality may be enforced due to the lack of design jargon knowledge on the part of the client. The more the client understands about design, the more relaxed the relationship can be. This, however, is not an issue of concern for CDU. This question was used to assess the kind of relationship between the agency and the client, to get a clearer picture of the three-way relationship, if any.

Q45 Are there any problems with the communication between you, CDU and the client that you feel could be improved?

Results

Q45			
1	No	7	No
2	Yes, CDU are not involved enough	8	No
3	No	9	No
4	N/A	10	N/A
5	No	11	N/A
6	Yes, CDU not involved	12	No

Q46 Are you comfortable with the way you work for BT?

All agencies said 'Yes'. This result is what perhaps should be expected. Any other result would not be encouraging for CDU. In cases where the agency has a good and mutually respectful relationship with CDU, then the agency should be in a position to give CDU constructive criticism about certain issues and offer recommendations on how they can improve the way they work.

Q47 Does CDU ask for your feedback on their performance?

These results were as expected. All agencies said 'No' and none said that they would expect that from a client of theirs.

Q48 Does CDU provide you with any feedback on any completed projects?

All agencies said that they do not receive any formal feedback from CDU. This is an issue that they would like to see CDU addressing. Feedback is useful for CDU as well as the design agency and this ideally should be implemented into the final stage of each project.

Q49 If so, do you have to request this or does CDU provide it anyway?

All agencies said that an informal, verbal feedback is sometimes given, but is only through general conversation after the project is completed. No agency said that they have to ask for it. Some agencies feel that the most honest form of feedback is repeat business, however, it is not necessarily the best.

Q50 If not, do you feel that this should be a standard procedure to end each project?

All agencies agreed that this would be useful to them as well as CDU. From these results, it is clear that there are some issues that CDU must act upon in order to improve their ways of working. It is important that CDU take the criticism from the design agencies and use it to create a much more professional image. The more professional CDU appear, the more respect agencies will have for them.

Results and evaluation of BT client interviews

This section evaluates in detail the results from the interviews with CDU's internal clients that were available.

Q1 How long have you used CDU for design management work?

Results

Q1

1	This is the first time	7	Three years
2	Five years	8	This is the first time
3	Ten years	9	Client unable to interview
4	Client unable to interview	10	Client unable to interview
5	Six years	11	–
6	One year	12	Ten years
		13	This is the first time

This great variety of timescales shows that more and more BT managers are becoming aware of the need for design, because some of these projects are a first for the clients.

Q2   Who initiated this project? Did you seek advice before deciding on what exactly was wanted from the project in terms of design?

Q3   If so, from whom did you seek advice?

Results

No.	Q2 Initiator	Advice	Q3 From whom?
1	Marketing	Yes	CDU
2	Client	Yes	Marketing and CDU
3	Client	Yes	CDU
4	Unavailable	–	–
5	Yes	Yes	CDU
6	Client/CDU	Yes	Design Agency
7	CRD	Yes	CRD
8	Client	Yes	CDU and Marketing
9	Unavailable	–	–
10	Unavailable	–	–
11	CDU	N/A	N/A
12	Client	Yes	CDU
13	Client	Yes	CDU

It is mainly the client who initiates the project in the first place, as they are usually the main funding body for the project. However, in the other cases it is either marketing or CRD who have initiated a project. They have the idea and have to submit a business case to the end client. It is surprising that more projects are not initiated by marketing, as they should know what BT can be doing to keep their marketshare and also to explore new markets. CRD and CDU should be looking for areas of BT that need more design input to improve BT's environment, and make sure that design improves the public's perception of BT.

Possible reasons why more projects are not being initiated by marketing and CRD or CDU are perhaps related to who is funding the project, and which department has the most resources to take on new projects. If this is the case, it can be assumed that CDU, CRD and marketing have insufficient budgets.

It is interesting to see that all clients seek advice about design before a project begins. Only one client asked advice from the design agency directly. This is a result that CDU should be trying to eradicate, as this not only jeopardizes their jobs or undermines their authority, the end result may not conform to BT's design standards.

One client said that to get advice he had to go through various channels before he got to CDU. This was apparently purely through lack of knowledge about CDU. He did not know that BT had a Design Unit at all.

Q4   Did you approach CDU for the design work to be done, did they approach you, or did you go straight to the design agency?

Results

Q4	
1	Client approached CDU
2	Client approached CDU
3	Client approached CDU
5	Client approached CDU
6	Client approached design agency
7	CRD approached client
8	Client approached CDU
11	CDU approached client
12	Client approached CDU
13	Client approached CDU

Maybe CDU should approach more clients for design projects, as this would be beneficial to all parties involved. The only reason why CDU do not approach clients could be a lack of resources to cope with the increase in work load.

Q5   For whom did you write the brief? CDU or the design agency?

Results

Q5	
1	CDU wrote the brief
2	For design agency
3	–
5	–
6	For design agency
7	For both
8	–
11	CDU wrote the brief
12	CDU wrote the brief
13	CDU wrote the brief

Where there are no answers in these results means that the client could not remember who wrote the brief.

The assumption here is that CDU should always write the brief for the design agency as they already know design jargon. Many clients do not know how to write a brief for a design project. However, the reality is that clients do write briefs, but what has not been found is how detailed and clearly written the briefs were. Therefore there is no evidence to decide whether clients with no design knowledge can write a good brief or not. It would be best to assume that CDU should write better briefs than their clients.

Q6   If you wrote the brief, did you write it alone or with others? Who?

There were only four answers:

1 Joint between CDU and marketing.
2 The design team.
6 and 11 Client alone.
7 CDU and client.

Q7   When writing the brief, did you consult any guidelines to do so?

All clients said 'No' as they feel this is CDU's role to consult the guidelines and make sure they are being followed. Perhaps CDU should make sure that clients are consulting a guideline that shows them how to write a brief, and general advice on how to deal with a design agency. A glossary of terms could be included so that all relevant design jargon is understood. A guideline on how to write a brief does exist. However, it is quite vague and only describes the kind of headings that should be included in the brief.

Q8   Were you aware of the kind of work CDU does before contacting them for work?

Results

Q8			
1	No	7	Yes
2	Yes	8	No
3	Yes	11	Yes but don't use them
5	Yes	12	Yes
6	Yes but don't use them	13	No

This suggests that CDU is not known by all departments in BT. This is understandable as BT is such a large organization, with large departments situated all over the UK. Even so, one client (project 13) did not know CDU existed even though they are in the same building only two floors apart. This is a result of lack of self-promotion by CDU. For design in BT to be consistent and keep up with fierce competition, CDU must champion themselves, to increase awareness of their role within the BT Group. Yet, this may be due to BT's own culture.

Q9   Did you decide which design agency to use, was this left to CDU or was it a joint decision?

Results

Q9			
1	Joint decision	7	Joint decision
2	Client decided	8	Joint decision
3	CDU decided	11	CDU decided
5	Joint decision	12	CDU decided
6	Client decided	13	CDU decided

Those three projects for which CDU decided on the agency are the same three projects for which CDU wrote the brief. It seems that those three projects were left very much in CDU's control.

Q10   Which would you prefer? To decide on the agency alone, leave the decision to CDU, or to let everyone involved have a say in the matter?

Results

Q10			
1	Let everyone decide	7	Let everyone decide
2	Decide alone	8	Let everyone decide
3	Let CDU decide	11	Let everyone decide
5	Let everyone decide	12	Let everyone decide
6	Let everyone decide	13	Let CDU decide

Those clients who prefer to leave it to CDU feel that this is one of CDU's roles and they are the most appropriate people to decide which agency is the best for that particular job. Also CDU know which design agencies are good at specific design work, and therefore who would be the most suitable design agency for each individual job.

Joint decisions should not only be made at the very beginning of a project, but during the project and right through until the end. Thus, all those involved will be informed about every aspect of the project. Some may even prefer not to be involved in the decision-making, but at least they have the choice.

Q11 How did you decide on the agency (if not chosen by others) e.g.
      pitching, recommendation, etc.?

Results

Q11		
1 Pitch	6	Track record
2 Pitch	7	Pitch
5 Credentials	11	Track record

The majority of agencies were chosen through a pitch situation. The
design agencies were also asked this question, to see if all parties knew
whether or not there was a pitch. This gives a good idea of how well clients
and design agencies were informed of the project; this seems to be accurate. Clients answered in a similar way to the agencies.

Q12 Did you seek advice before deciding on the agency? (If you decided
      alone) from whom?

Advice was asked of CDU and CRD when a client was choosing the
agency themselves. This issue is not one of great concern, as clients did
seek advice.

Q13 Did you brief the design agency as well as CDU, or was this left to
      CDU only?

Results

Q13		
1 Agency only	7	CDU and agency
2 Agency only	8	Marketing only
3 CDU only	11	N/A
5 CDU and agency	12	CDU only
6 Agency only	13	CDU only

In three of the projects, CDU were not briefed by the client. The design
agency was briefed only in two and marketing was briefed in one and then
CDU got involved at a later stage. This shows that CDU are not always
involved at the right stage in the project. Some clients appear unsure as to
when CDU should be brought in on a project. This may be due to lack of
education about CDU and its role. Educating clients is the only way CDU
will be able to get involved at the beginning stages, as CDU cannot
monitor every design project because they do not have enough resources
to keep a check on all design activity within BT.

Q14 How were all the briefings carried out?

Results

Q14			
1	Written	7	Face-to-face/Written
2	Face-to-face	8	–
3	Telephone	11	Face-to-face
5	Face-to-face	12	Face-to-face
6	Face-to-face	13	–

It is good that the majority of briefings are done face-to-face. Project 3 that was briefed over the telephone was discussed earlier.

Q15 Please describe your relationship with CDU.

Results

Q15			
1	Informal	7	Informal
2	Informal/limited contact	8	Informal
3	Informal/formal	11	No relationship
5	Informal	12	Informal
6	No relationship	13	Informal

It is good to find that most relationships are informal. This should create a good team spirit, and the project should run smoothly.

Q16 Is this how you would prefer it to be?

All clients said 'Yes', even the client that has no relationship with CDU said that is how it is preferred. This should be rectified for future projects. Correlating these answers to those of the design agencies, it seems that formal relationships are no longer the norm in business. Informal but professional relationships seem to be favoured much more. Informal relationships break the ice and allow feelings to be shared. It is human nature to enjoy working with people who get on well together. This kind of relationship also tends to break down hierarchical status. Only when it is necessary is that status used, for example, when major decisions have to be made.

Q17 Once a project has begun, how often do you actually meet with CDU face-to-face?

Results

Q17			
1	Monthly	7	Weekly
2	Not often	8	Not much
3	Depends on stage	11	Never
5	Monthly at first	12	Not much
6	Never	13	Not much

Looking at these results, it seems that CDU do not have very much contact with their clients. Too much liaison may not be necessary in some cases. Nevertheless, clients must be kept informed of the project's developments. In some projects CDU tend to share project control with their clients. CDU should strike a balance between controlling a project and also letting the client feel they are in control.

Q18 Is this too often or not often enough?

Results

Q18			
1	Not often enough towards the end	7	Fine
2	Not enough	8	OK
3	OK	11	Not often but OK
5	Fine	12	Fine
6	Not often but OK	13	Fine

Only one client (project 2) found that liaison was not enough. The other clients that do not have much liaison with CDU felt that this was enough. Those clients apparently do not need to be kept informed very frequently about their project. The client involved with projects 6 and 11 seems not to need CDU to be involved in those two projects.

Q19 Who initiates the majority of meetings? You, CDU or the design agency?

Results

Q19			
1	Equal	7	Equal
2	Client	8	–
3	Equal	11	Agency
5	Equal	12	Agency
6	Agency	13	–

There is not a lot that can be concluded from these answers, only that where there is a good working relationship between all three parties, the initiation of meetings tends to be equal. There is no one person initiating projects. In project 2 where the client initiates the meetings, this may be because CDU are not very involved and therefore the client is taking full control over the project. This seems to be how this client prefers it.

Q20 Do you like to know exactly where the project is up to, or do you leave it completely to CDU until the deadline?

Results

Q20			
1	Know	7	Know
2	Know	8	Deadline
3	Deadline	11	Know
5	Know	12	Know
6	Know	13	Deadline

Most clients prefer to know where a project is up to, after all, it is their project, so to speak. Those clients who leave it to CDU must obviously have trust in CDU to manage the project and deliver what is required. Again, CDU must strike a balance between informing the client of the project's development and managing it themselves. Asking the client at the beginning of the project would make sure that a good balance is achieved.

Q21 Does CDU fill out status forms during a project, to let you know which stage in the brief they are up to?

All answered 'No'. Maybe CDU should think about status forms as a routine way of informing all the relevant people about the project's development. Having all transactions and developments written down makes accessing project information much easier and efficient. If anyone involved has been away or absent they can get up to date on a project's progress immediately, by simply referring to the status forms. This way, anyone who needs to know about a project can do so very easily.

Q22 If you do like to know, do you contact CDU mostly, or do they contact you regularly?

Of those clients who do like to know, only one is informed through weekly meetings. The design agency is the informant for other clients. Only one client said that both the design agency and CDU report back regularly.

Q23 When you meet with CDU, do you approach them or do they come to you?

Results

Q23			
1	Meet at agency	7	Specific meeting room at BT
2	Meet on site	8	Meet at agency
3	Meet at CDU or agency	11	–
5	Compromise	12	Meet at agency
6	–	13	Mixed

These answers are varied and therefore do not seem to be a problem.

Q24 Which would you prefer?

All clients said that they do not mind where they go for a meeting. This confirms that there is no problem with varying venues for meetings. The phrase 'horses for courses' seemed to be an appropriate way of emphasizing their answer. A meeting is usually held where it is most appropriate. If these results showed that everyone always has to go to CDU for meetings and that this was not what clients preferred, then there would be cause for concern.

Q25 If you go to CDU, do you feel you can conduct a meeting successfully, without any distractions?

Results

Q25			
1	N/A	7	Fine
2	N/A	8	David Mercer's office
3	Prefers David Mercer's office	11	N/A
5	N/A	12	N/A
6	N/A	13	Better if in a room

Only one client said that a meeting in the CDU office is 'fine'. However, for this project (7) the meetings are held weekly in a specific room with all the appropriate people present. Only *ad hoc* meetings are conducted in the CDU office and these are generally to iron out small problems or to answer simple queries. These *ad hoc* meetings do not usually last longer than 5–10 minutes from what was observed frequently. The private meeting room for CDU is the Design Director's office, which is used frequently while he is out. Clients and design agencies prefer this office to CDU's office. This is understandable as there is no privacy in the CDU office. However, David Mercer's office is not always available. When interviews with clients are compared to interviews with design agencies, the design agencies all had an available meeting room in which the interviews were conducted without distraction. Only two clients were able to use a meeting room for their interviews. One client had a separate office, and the rest were conducted in open-plan offices with many distractions, no privacy and were generally uncomfortable. One client said that it is not BT's culture to have private meeting rooms and cellular offices. Open plan is the norm at BT in order to create an open, team-like spirit in each department. Open-plan offices are a good idea, but the need for private meeting rooms is also essential for professional business practice. A private meeting room does not mean that the working relationship or the meeting has to be formal.

Q26 Is the majority of your liaison with CDU done by telephone or fax, email?

Q27 Do you feel this is an efficient way of communicating?

Results

Q26		Q27
1	Phone	Yes
2	Phone and fax	Yes
3	Phone and fax	Yes if there is a response
5	Phone and fax	Yes
6	–	–
7	Face-to-face	Yes
8	Phone and fax	Yes
11	–	–
12	Phone, fax and face-to-face	Yes
13	Face-to-face	Yes

This does not seem to be a major problem. Only one client has a problem with getting a response.

Q28 When you leave a message at CDU, do they return your call promptly or do you have to chase them up?

Results

Q28			
1	Response is quite good	7	CDU respond
2	Response is quite good	8	Response is good
3	No, have to chase up	11	–
5	Response is good	12	Response is good
6	–	13	N/A (face-to-face)

The same client has a problem with CDU's response. Through observation it was found that CDU are not always in their office. Many messages are left by phone and it takes CDU a while to return those messages. This perhaps is not a good system, especially for a telecommunications company. CDU have pagers, but not everyone is comfortable paging someone, as they do not know how important the matter has to be before paging CDU.

This does not seem to be a problem, but using the general observations made during the placement, this matter needs to be addressed not only to keep up a professional image of BT, but also to make life easier for CDU and anyone who calls.

Q29 How does CDU compare to other people who work for you? Good or bad?

Results

Q29

1	Useful	7	Good
2	When it's good it's very good, when it's bad it's dreadful	8	Good only because they provided some budget
3	Not good	11	Not used
5	Good	12	Good
6	Not used	13	Good

There are mixed feelings here. CDU should be striving to make these results a unanimous 'Good'. Otherwise clients will avoid using CDU and will go straight to the design agency.

Q30 Is there anything you would like to improve about the way in which CDU work? If so, in what way?

Results

Q30

1	Promote CDU	7	Clarify their role
2	Improve timescales	8	Get more budget
3	CDU should clarify its role more	11	Make roles clearer
5	Roles need clarifying	12	–
6	Make roles clearer	13	Promote themselves

Here there are two consensus issues. CDU should perhaps clarify its role, and they should promote themselves to the rest of BT. An awareness campaign is needed to tackle these two issues. This is one of the most important issues that has arisen from this research.

Q31 Do you see CDU as part of your team/colleagues, or is CDU simply people who work for you?

Results

Q31			
1	Team member	7	Team member
2	Team member	8	Supplier
3	Supplier	12	Team member
5	Team member	13	Supplier/Service

Most see CDU as a team member. What is interesting to find is that project 2, who does not have much liaison with CDU still sees them as a team member.

Q32 Does CDU ask for your feedback on their performance?

All except one client (project 12) said 'No'. This should be a standard procedure to end a project. That way CDU will learn from any mistakes and continue to carry out those procedures that the client preferred. A feedback session can be beneficial to all parties concerned, as it will improve procedures every time.

Q33 Please describe your relationship with the design agency.

Results

Q33			
1	Informal	7	Informal
2	Informal	8	Formal
3	Formal	11	Informal
5	Informal	12	Informal
6	Informal	13	None

Again, the majority of relationships are informal, with the exception of two. Where there is a formal relationship this tends to be when the client does not have very much contact with the design agency. This is covered in question 34.

Q34 How much contact do you have with the design agency?

Results

Q34			
1	A lot	7	Weekly
2	Most	8	Not much
3	Frequent	11	Most
5	Most	12	More than with CDU
6	Most	13	None

Four clients have more contact with the design agency than with CDU. This can be good and bad: good in the sense that the client is learning about the design process, but bad in the sense that the guidelines may not be used.

Q35 Is this degree of liaison necessary or not?

All said 'Yes', it is necessary, including the client who has no contact with the agency. This client does not feel the need to be involved. This is again good and bad. Good that CDU can make sure that standards are being conformed to, but bad in that this client has not been educated in the design process for future situations.

Q36 Do you prefer to liaise with CDU or the design agency or both?
Q37 Why?

Results

No.	Q36	Q37
1	CDU	CDU have more design knowledge
2	Agency	Get more response from agency than CDU
3	Agency	CDU do not add any value to the project and it saves time and money to go straight to the design agency
5	Both	No reason
6	Agency	There is no need for CDU
7	Both	Easier
8	Marketing	Marketing is my main interface
11	Agency	There is no need for CDU
12	Agency	Much quicker
13	CDU	CDU know more

More clients prefer to liaise with the design agency. This is not a good result for CDU, as they should make their clients feel comfortable liaising with both CDU and the design agency for different reasons. This result could be damaging to CDU's value to BT. There are mixed feelings about CDU and its worth, however, the reasons why clients prefer liaising with the design agency are usually detrimental to CDU.

Q38 Are most of your liaisons with the agency done over the telephone or by fax, or are most done face-to-face?

Results

Q38

1	Phone	7	Phone and face-to-face
2	Face-to-face	8	Not much
3	Phone and fax	11	Phone
5	Phone	12	Fax
6	Phone	13	None

Q39 Is this efficient enough?

All said 'Yes'. This does not seem to be a problem for either clients or design agencies.

Q40 Do you tend to let CDU deal with the design agency, or do you prefer to have a hands-on approach?

Results

Q40

1	CDU handle agency	7	CDU handle agency
2	Hands-on	8	CDU handle agency
3	Hands-on	11	Hands-on (totally)
5	Hands-on	12	Hands-on
6	Hands-on (totally)	13	CDU handle agency

Many clients do prefer to have a hands-on approach, which is a good thing. However, leaving it to CDU shows that the client trusts CDU to deliver the work. It is important for CDU to find out early on in the project whether or not the client prefers a hands-on approach. This will let everyone involved know where they stand.

Q41 When you leave a telephone message, or send a fax to the design agency, do they respond quickly, or do you have to chase them up frequently?

Results

Q41

1	Chase	7	Respond
2	Respond	8	Respond
3	Chase	11	Respond
5	Respond	12	Respond
6	Respond	13	Respond

This does not seem to be a major problem. However, the client in project 3 seems to be very uncomfortable with both CDU and the design agency as this client has to chase both parties up. This may be due to clashes in personality, rather than through bad conduct. However, project 3 seems to be the one project that has not followed the normal procedure at all, compared to the others. Therefore it is more likely because of bad conduct by both CDU and the design agency that the client is unsatisfied.

Conclusion

After examining the results of the twenty-one interviews conducted, it is possible to find which issues are the most important and should be taken into consideration by CDU. These issues are as follows:

- Briefings at the beginning of projects. Formal briefings are not being taken seriously.
- Comparing CDU to other clients, some design agencies feel that CDU is less professional and very informal.
- Agencies feel that there is room for improvement in the way CDU conducts their briefings.
- Meetings should be conducted in a more professional manner.
- Response to messages and general communication should be improved.
- The design guidelines should be improved to suit the needs of the BT Group and also be easy to interpret.
- CDU should be more involved in the design process.
- Feedback should be provided at the end of each project.
- CDU is not very well known by other departments in BT. CDU should be promoted to increase design awareness.
- CDU is not involved at the right stage in design projects.
- More liaison with clients is necessary in some cases. CDU should find out whether the client wants to be involved or not, and to what extent.
- All transactions should be put in writing and status forms should be completed.
- CDU must keep all communication channels open.
- CDU should clarify its role.
- Feedback should be asked by CDU of the client.

These issues can be put into four main categories:

1   Promotion of CDU and definition of its role.
2   General communication.
3   Basic managerial procedures
    (i) Meetings
    (ii) Briefings

    (iii) Status forms
    (iv) Feedback sessions.
4   Guidelines.

Review questions

1 Referring to the text, would you consider the method of project briefing by CDU to be satisfactory? How would you increase the quality of briefing?
2 Discuss the problematic areas so often associated with verbal briefing.
3 Discuss the benefits to both the client and design team that result from having a close working relationship.
4 Do you think that design standards inhibit creativity? Provide examples to underpin your argument.
5 How important do you think the role of feedback is to increasing project performance and as a means of increasing the quality of design solution?
6 What mechanisms would you suggest to increase the effective free flow of information between client and design team?
7 How would you raise the profile of CDU within BT?
8 How closely involved should the client be with the design team over the duration of the design project? At particular stages or occasionally?
9 What important stages of the design project do you feel require client input and feedback?
10 CDU are often perceived as too informal by their clients, what suggestions would you offer for them to overcome this image?

Project questions

1   Consider the question on the briefing process in the Review questions. Produce a proforma brief for BT'S various designs that would attempt to meet all criteria.
2   The BT case is complex and presented in such a way as to show the question and answers involved in the audit. Consider three questions and their results and provide research correlations between them, which do not appear fully in the Conclusion.
3   Devise a short questionnaire designed to elicit the relative values of formal and informal communication within BT's strategic design management. This may then be used with research within other companies.
4   Devise a relationship model (see 'Relationship 4') that would operate via the web, based internationally. Given language and cultural differences in Europe, how much would BT have to change its communication processes as described?

5   Describe how BT may 'choreograph' points of contact. How should BT prepare for this and use the resultant information?

Further reading

James, D. (1996) 'The web-wise lack the will to communicate', *Management Today*, September, p. 23.

Japan Business Consultants Ltd. (http://www-personal.engin.umich.edu/~gmazur/jbc/).

Morgans, J.B. (1996) 'Thriving in an information age', *Management Today*, August, p. 5.

Oakley, M. (ed.) (1990) *Design Management: A Handbook of Issues and Methods*. Oxford: Blackwell.

Olins, W. (1984) *The Wolf Olin's Guide to Design Management: Mysteries of Design Management Revealed*. London: Design Council.

Sigband, N.B. (1976) *Communication for Management and Business*. New York: Scott Foresman.

Design Management potential at David Clarke Associates

Company:	David Clarke Associates
	1301 Stratford Road
	Hall Green
	Birmingham
	B28 9HP
Business:	Public relations: copywriting, media relations, employee and community relations, crisis management, media monitoring
Auditor:	*Andrea Lee*

Introduction

The audit offers an objective investigation into the marketing of the publication unit at David Clarke Associates. This study took place during a thirteen-week period within the company. It makes references to the marketing of the company as well as the publications division alongside working procedures within the unit. Recommendations on how the situation might be improved are also made with the primary aim being to increase the division's client numbers.

Due to the scope of the investigation and the relatively short time-scale given for its completion, this report offers a brief examination into a potentially open-ended and continual project. Certain areas which are typically studied in marketing audits have had to be overlooked.

The research methodology employed within the study includes:

- Interviews and questionnaires from personnel providing qualitative information regarding existing situations, opinions and perceived needs.
- Objective and critical observation of working procedures and team communication.
- Analysis of company literature.
- Market research conducted through postal questionnaires.
- Research into the profession to which the company belongs.
- General background reading on marketing and public relations.

As an introduction, the nature of the public relations industry in the UK is summarized, with short profiles of significant PR companies operating in the Midlands.

David Clarke Associates (DCA) offers a range of public relations services, advising their clients about PR benefits and undertaking publicity programmes on their behalf. The company has a division that specializes in publications, graphic design and computerized presentations. The majority of clients are from four principal sectors: business to business, industrial and manufacturing, property and construction, consumer and retail. The company has belonged to the Edelman Public Relations UK network of PR consultancies since 1987, enabling it to recommend suppliers nationally, and link with associates worldwide.

There are two account teams at DCA, one dealing with clients in manufacturing, the professions and engineering, and the other handling accounts in business to business, professions and consumer markets. A separate division, David Clarke Publications, specializes in producing publications which are part of the consultancy's public relations services for their clients. The division also supervises the work of design consultancies and other specialists such as photographers, bureaux and printers hired to undertake work that cannot be done in-house.

As might be expected of a public relations company, DCA have a structured marketing strategy for self-promotion, in which they develop their presence through a company logo, a company brochure, advertising campaigns, a web-site, press coverage, a reception display, directory listings, and networking activities.

The company's working methods are explained in detail. The company has an explicit policy for delivering its services in the form of a procedures manual, which ensures that there is consistency in work procedures, service delivery, meeting client needs and improving client satisfaction. The procedures for service delivery, which include financial control and time management, also apply internally for the publications division, ensuring the quality and efficiency of its operation. It is seen as an area for future expansion, as it has a proven record as a design and print business.

The relationship between design and PR within DCA is examined, concluding that publications and graphic design, while not recognized as traditional PR activities, are essential to the delivery of PR services. The retention of the division as an in-house operation is desirable, although the marketing of its services independently of PR services might benefit from being perceived as part of a PR company. This central dilemma is seen as acceptable if design and publication are marketed as a separate division within the company literature.

The publications and graphic design services at David Clarke Associates are often overlooked in the realm of PR. Clients and the potential market are unaware that these can exist as a separate service. New customers need to be targeted as over 90 per cent of the work produced in the publication unit is for current clients as part of their PR programme.

The Public Relations industry

The official definition of public relations (PR) as offered by the Institute of Public Relations (IPR) is: 'The planned and sustained effort to establish and maintain goodwill and mutual understanding between an organisation and its publics' (Howard, 1989). There are two basic forms of PR – corporate and product. Corporate PR is concerned with the presentation of an organization to its target groups in the most favourable light; product PR applies to the presentation of an individual product or group of products.

Market areas

Public relations cover many areas of life. These include: agriculture, the arts, construction, finance, food and drink, fashion, healthcare, leisure, publishing, engineering, telecommunications, insurance and education. The majority of PR consultancies cover a number of these areas, but there are also a growing number of agencies that specialize within a particular sector.

PR activities

In an effort to portray organizations or products in the most favourable light, PR companies perform a number of activities. The general activities offered by PR consultancies are advertising, community relations, copywriting, crisis management programmes, employee relations, exhibitions, government relations and international PR campaigns. Most PR consultancies offer a 'full service' which is an agreed PR programme that may be carried out over a number of years. Other organizations may hire consultancies for single projects of a limited duration.

Industry structure

The structure of the UK public relations industry ranges from many small and medium-sized enterprises to large consultancies, to in-house PR departments in UK companies. Mergers and acquisitions of advertising agencies and graphic design consultancies over recent years are increasing the numbers and size of these larger PR firms. The PR industry is now becoming polarized between the global giants who offer a range of PR services and the small specialist firms serving niche markets.

Number of consultancies

Since the early 1960s the number of consultancies in the UK has grown. According to British Telecom's Yellow Pages, there are roughly 2,660 PR consultancies in the UK. Over half of these are located in London and the SE of England.

Employment

It is hard to judge the number of people directly involved in the PR industry. Along with consultancy employees, there are those who work for internal PR departments for major companies. There are also many indirect workers such as journalists, photographers, graphic designers and printers. However, it is estimated that in 1988 there were around 35,000 people working in the industry (*Business Ratio Plus*, 1994).

Suppliers to the industry

There are many suppliers to the PR industry. These include journalists, photographers, TV and radio stations, graphic designers, printers, press cutting bureaux and media monitoring agencies. Companies who manufacture promotional items, along with corporate hospitality and media training, also lend their services.

Trade associations

The leading trade bodies for the public relations industry are the Institute of Public Relations (IPR) and the Public Relations Consultants Association (PRCA). The IPR is open to public relations practitioners working in consultancies, companies, government and public organizations. To be accepted, these practitioners have to meet high standards of professional practice and have a minimum of five years' experience in the industry. Members are asked to follow a professional code of conduct. This code requires them to abide by the Association's rules and submit to penalties if they fail to do so.

The Association also publishes a journal and newsletter – *Public Relations* – which is available to members and subscribers. The PRCA represents and protects the interests of all its members, which includes groups and individual consultancies. The Association is also involved in training and recently issued a new code of conduct – the PRCA Professional Charter – to encourage high standards in companies involved in public relations.

European trade associations include the Comité Européen des Relations Publiques (CERP) while internationally there are the International Public Relations Associations (IPRA) and the International Committee of Public Relations (ICPR).

Nature of the companies

A variety of companies operate as PR consultants. Some have their origins dating back to the 1960s, while others began during the economic boom of the 1980s. Some operate from one office, while other companies have a number of offices situated around the UK. The size of consultancy also varies from those with four employees, to larger firms employing over 300 members of staff. Most of these larger consultancies are based in London and act on behalf of major businesses in the UK.

Ownership

The majority of the PR consultancies are independent, privately owned companies with the senior members of staff as directors and leading share-holders; Charles Barker, Harrison Cowley and Key Communications make up part of this group. Some consultancies belong to a network of other PR firms, while others are owned by international groups. Many of these international holding companies are advertising agencies. These include Young & Rubicam who own Burson-Marsteller and Cohn & Wolfe; WPP Group who own Hill & Knowlton; and Abbott Mead Vickers, owners of Freud Communications and Fishburn Hedges. With UK companies increasingly providing services worldwide, many acquisitions and mergers are made with international PR, advertising and graphic design companies.

Specialization of markets

The majority of consultancies create PR programmes for a variety of companies. These include banks, supermarkets, solicitors, property surveyors, charities, professional organizations and the utilities. However, some consultancies prefer to specialize with one type of company. Specialists include Medical Action Communications (healthcare), Text 100 (hi-tech) and Stephanie Churchill PR (fashion and beauty).

Specialization among these smaller consultancies has provided competition for the large agencies. This has led many of the larger consultancies to create – through acquisition – what are in effect many small, specialized firms under one roof. These operate as separate businesses in an attempt to provide a total communication package, consisting of PR, advertising, graphic design and market research.

Significant PR companies

The consultancies in this section have been selected for a variety of reasons. Some, despite experiencing increased competition, have dominated the industry for a number of years, while others have been selected for their financial performances over the past five years.

Shandwick Plc

Shandwick Plc is the largest PR group in the UK and is second in the world to Burson-Marsteller. The group has ninety-four offices in twenty-five countries across Europe, North America, South Africa, Asia and the Pacific. It also has affiliate companies in a further twenty-eight countries, bringing the total number of offices worldwide to 110. Shandwick's aim is to expand its global operations by offering international companies a 'one-stop' for their PR needs.

The group is also investing heavily in technology over the next three to five years. In an effort to co-ordinate its systems worldwide Shandwick are introducing Shandnet – a communication system that enables the network companies to talk to each other – and a database that can be used by everyone.

Although none of the international agencies carry the Shandwick name, a two-stage programme, launched across Europe in 1995, has introduced a common infrastructure and understanding throughout the network and pulled all the agencies together. A similar philosophy also has since taken place in the UK. In a bid to create a sense of community among the management of the Shandwick group, agencies were sold and the remaining ones were re-branded with the company name.

With 505 clients in total for the group, major accounts include Tarmac, Midlands TSB Bank, and Shell among many others. Shandwick's dominance is slowly being eroded, however, due to increased competition from smaller consultancies, and fee income fell from £32.6 million in 1990 to £22.4 million in 1995. This only rose again in 1996 due to more work with the Halifax Building Society, British Gas and MasterCard. The drop of income in 1995 is likely to have been due to a controlled loss of around thirty non-profitable clients. Revenue was also hit by the decision of one major client to cut £1.0 million off its PR spend and the continued rise in staff numbers.

The Red Consultancy

Based in London, the Red Consultancy was founded in 1994 by an ex-director of Shandwick Plc. Seen as a specialist in consumer work, the consultancy's twenty-four clients include the Whitbread-owned coffee brand and café chain Costa Coffee, B&Q, Cellnet and Direct Line. Other work comes from Johnson & Johnson on brands ROC, Neutrogena and Johnson's Baby.

With these high profile accounts, The Red Consultancy has emerged as the fastest growing agency of 1996. Fee income has grown 129 per cent from £766,312 in 1995 to £1,754,585. The company has also witnessed the highest growth in employees from the consultancies listed in the *PR Week*'s annual top 150 agency charts – an increase from 18 to 39 (117 per cent).

Key Communications

Key Communications began in Oxfordshire in 1984. With offices in Birmingham and London, the consultancy is now part of an international network of other communications companies and has recently joined with Germany's largest consultancy – Reporter.

In 1995 the company established two new divisions – one dealing with internal communications and Key 3D, a multimedia specialist. Most of the consultancy's income comes from clients in the business to business and consumer sections. Clients include international companies such as Hertz, Disney, Kraft Jacob Suchard and Apricot.

The Midlands office works more with regional companies. These include the solicitors Eversheds and the computer group Kalamazoo. The office has also won a new contract from the NEC group.

With a fee income of £4,180,065 in 1996, up from £1,023,850 in 1991 (a growth of 308 per cent), Key Communications is the best performing UK consultancy over the past five years. Staff levels have increased 282 per cent from 17 to 65 and the company has recorded a 300 per cent growth in clients since 1991.

Nature of the regional companies

A variety of consultancies make up the PR industry in the Midlands. Some are small, single office companies with ten employees, while others are multi-office firms employing over 200 members of staff. Over 120 PR consultancies are based in the West Midlands. Most of these are situated in Birmingham and act on behalf of businesses in the region.

Ownership

The majority of the Midlands' consultancies are privately owned and belong to worldwide networks. However, some are group-owned and others are national and international consultancies who have branch offices in the Midlands. Privately owned consultancies include The Warman Group, David Clarke Associates, Priority Services and Ocean Blue. Those belonging to international networks are Haslimann Taylor, a Shandwick affiliate, Cimma Public Relations, who are part of the International PR Association, and Edson Evers & Associates who belong to the PR Organisations International Network.

Activities

Consultancies in the Midlands offer a full range of services including copywriting, community and employee relations, media relations, graphic design, advertising and market research. Clients for regional companies include the Sports Council and consumer companies such as Bass,

Kellogg's and Kraft Jacob Suchard, along with professional companies like accountants, solicitors and property surveyors.

Work is also produced for smaller professional organizations such as development agencies, the Business Link network, NHS Trusts and regional Training Enterprise Councils (TECs). National Express, Birmingham International Airport and communications companies such as Telewest and Birmingham Cable, also enlist the help of PR consultancies in the region.

Significant regional companies

Willoughby Public Relations

Established in 1992, Willoughby Public Relations is based in the centre of Birmingham and is a subsidiary of St Paul's Holdings. The majority of the company's fee income derives from work in the home sector, that is to say, carpet makers and furnishing. Other market sectors include fast-moving consumer goods, trade commercial property and building products.

Willoughby has plans to move the company into new areas of business. This has led to the appointment of an account director who has experience in the catering market. During July 1997, the home and property division also won three new accounts – the Rugby Group, Sharps and the national BT Property portfolio. The success of the company has made it the fastest growing consultancy in the Midlands over the past five years. Between 1992–6 annual fee income rose from £105,000 to £515,000. This is a growth of 390 per cent and places Willoughby well ahead of their nearest competitor. Staff levels have tripled from seven to twenty, while the number of current clients have also risen from eleven to twenty-five, providing growth rates of 86 per cent and 127 per cent respectively.

Seal Public Relations

Birmingham-based Seal Public Relations is an associate of Seal Advertising, with 50 per cent of its income coming from consumer work and 25 per cent from business to business. The company's experience comes in the food and drink, leisure, manufacturing and the utilities sectors. Listed among their twenty-five accounts are clients such as Carlsberg-Tetley, Allied Domecq Leisure and Swedish manufacturer VBG UK.

In June 1997 Seal were appointed by the West Bromwich Building Society's Community Programme to oversee their media relations, together with the sponsorship of West Bromwich Albion Football Club.

The company has invested in new staff by taking on three new account managers – helped by a rise in annual fee income. Fee income rose between 1995 and 1997 from £534,852 to £695,195 – a growth of 30 per cent. These figures demonstrate that Seal had one of the highest growth rates for a Midlands' consultancy in 1996.

Edson Evers & Associates

Stafford-based Edson Evers began as a public relations consultancy in 1972. While PR remains the company's main area of business, services have expanded over the years to include event management and a separate division that concentrates on graphic design and publications.

Clients include local, national and international organizations from construction, engineering, health, DIY, veterinary and horticultural sectors. Newey & Eyre, the Wolseley Group, Coalite and the Federation of Garden and Leisure Manufacturers comprise some of the names on the client list. With twenty-five clients bringing in a total fee income of £696,076 in 1996, Edson Evers produces the highest fee income per client in the Midlands. Each client earns the consultancy an average of £27,843.

Trends

National

The UK recession had a large impact on the PR industry. Many large corporate clients, who were also encountering difficulties, reduced their budgets by a sizeable amount. In 1992 the fee income of the UK's top ten consultancies fell from £110,878,502 to £98,610,714. Only when financial confidence returned in 1994 did the figure rise to £103,847,180. Income levels have since continued to rise – in 1996 fees generated by these consultancies reached £133,260,249.

Not only did companies reduce their spending on PR during the recession, but some stopped their entire spending. The number of organizations enlisting the help of the top ten consultancies fell from 2,522 to 2,092 during 1991 and 1992. However, this figure rose to 2,982 in 1996, echoing a similar rise in fee income.

To ease the effects of the recession, many PR consultancies had reduced staffing levels. This is echoed by the fall in employees of the top ten consultancies. In 1992 staff levels fell from 1,926 the previous year, however, employment is beginning to rise – staff numbers for 1996 rose to 1,773.

A continued trend is the tendency for employees from established consultancies to leave and set up their own companies. One notable example is Alison Canning – former head of UK operations for Burson-Marsteller. Canning left to start First and 42nd a 'virtual' consultancy whose directors work from home with the aid of new technology.

Areas of PR showing growth are hi-tech, crisis management and healthcare. Growth in the healthcare sector follows a demand from NHS Trusts, together with more pharmaceutical firms beginning to understand the role of PR. The emphasis has also shifted from financial PR towards the consumer and corporate sectors.

Regional

Although the recession witnessed some of the region's consultancies losing a sizeable part of their fee income, total fee levels for the top six consultancies in *PR Week*'s top 150 have continued to rise. The largest rate of growth was between 1995 and 1996 with fee income rising from £3,240,913 to £3,749,756.

The number of staff employed at these consultancies is also rising. Employee levels have now reached more than 100 after being in the eighties for the majority of the 1990s. Client numbers have risen to 202 after falling for many years. However, despite the rise in fee income, employers and clients, Midlands' PR consultancies are falling down the national league tables. The average league table position of these consultancies has fallen from 95, which was the peak in 1992, to 122 in 1996. There is, however, an increase in the number of consultancies situated on the outskirts of the Midlands acquiring business from organizations in the region.

Developments within the industry

Present

Spiralling media costs in advertising have witnessed the rise of PR as a key branding tool. The discipline has been found by marketers to be an inexpensive way of testing a product's market place before advertising is used. With more issues today attracting negative coverage in the media, the areas of society needing a PR strategy is growing. PR now covers religion and consultancies that specialize in the Church are being established.

Developments in technology have also affected the ways in which PR consultancies conduct business. One application has been the use of international televised link-ups via satellite for briefing and news conferences. An increasing number of organizations are also using the Internet, making it easier to communicate internationally.

A further development is the re-branding of PR itself, with many practitioners believing that the term no longer defines the broad service offered. The term 'PR' has picked up many negative connotations, prompting some consultancies to drop the term completely.

Future

The blurring of PR with other elements of marketing will continue, adding more confusion to the profession's current identity crisis. However, PR consultancies of all sizes will develop as industry growth proceeds. The emphasis for the future will be on technology and specialization. Specialist areas of PR that should see growth in the five years (1996–2001) include hi-tech (through the Internet), health (through increased government funding), education, property, employee communications, crisis management and the consumer sector. There should also be an increase in agencies and bodies formed through the new government, and these will need PR services.

The next few years will also witness a rise in the number of 'virtual consultancies, such as First and 42nd, where directors operate from home. The Internet and email will be used more frequently, along with new electronic presentation tools such as CD-ROM, etc.

Due to their existing capabilities, law firms and management consultants will provide competition in certain areas of PR. These include public affairs, lobbying and internal public relations. Competition will also come from design consultancies and internal design departments in larger organizations.

David Clarke Associates

Introduction

The current managing director – David Clarke – established David Clarke Associates in 1986. Previously based in offices in Shirley, Birmingham, the company moved to its current premises at Centre Court in 1987. The company advises their clients in PR and undertakes publicity programmes on their behalf. Some clients require a full service programme that may last a number of years, while others hire the consultancy for *ad hoc* project work lasting only a few months.

These programmes comprise of a number of services including copywriting, media relations, employee and community relations, crisis management and media monitoring. The company also has a division that specializes in publications, graphic design and computerized presentations.

Clients

David Clarke Associates devises PR programmes for over twenty-nine companies and organizations. The majority of these businesses are based in the West Midlands and come from four principal sectors:

- business-to-business;
- industrial and manufacturing;
- property and construction;
- consumer and retail.

They range from private and financial organizations, to stately homes and manufacturers of industrial components. The company's current client list includes:

- Black Country Development Corporation;
- Business Link Sandwell;
- Norwich Union Risk Services;
- Telewest Communications.

The majority of these accounts have been gained during the 1990s, however, some clients have been with the company since 1987.

Employees

There are currently twelve people working at David Clarke Associates. Most are employed full-time, however, four members of staff work on a part-time basis. The company also employs another account executive. Freelance writers and consultants are also used on large projects.

Mission statement

Although no formal mission statement exists for David Clarke Associates, a set of objectives have been devised for the consultancy. These are:

- to offer the best and most advanced public relations service in the Midlands;
- to constantly deliver and never let our clients down;
- to never give our clients the reason to look elsewhere;
- to take personal pride in all that we do;
- to be the best and most profitable PR consultancy in the region . . . and for all to benefit from it.

David Clarke would like to think that the consultancy offers the first three objectives and that they strive to do the last two.

Network

David Clarke Associates is part of the Edelman Public Relations UK network of PR consultancies. The consultancy has been a shareholder in this network since 1987. Being part of the network provides the company with services around the world from its associates. This enables network offices to recommend suppliers and work together on national campaigns on behalf of Edelman's clients.

There are thirteen consultancies in the network that covers all areas of the UK – Belfast, Birmingham, Bristol, Glasgow, Manchester, Newcastle-upon-Tyne, Norwich, Sheffield and Tonbridge. This network is part of a larger worldwide structure, Edelman Public Relations World-wide.

Edelman Public Relations World-wide

Edelman Public Relations World-wide was established in 1967. Based in London and employing over fifty staff, the international network has sixty-seven offices in thirty-one countries. The company is structured into five specialist groups:

- Edelman Medical Communications
- Edelman Financial Communications
- Public Affairs
- Consumer and Trade Marketing Affairs
- Technology and Business Communications.

Each group offers a range of individual and integrated services including brand marketing, employee relations, crisis management and design and print. These services are used in market areas such as consumer and trade marketing, business-to-business, travel and tourism, healthcare and sport.

Organizational structure

Managing director, David Clarke, heads David Clarke Associates. Three other directors support him, these are: Richard Bull (Director); Alison Burrows (Account Director); and Gordon Brindley (Director of Finance). Each director heads their own team of supporting staff (see Figure 4.1). This includes an assistant and either an account manager – or an account executive – in the account teams.

There is also a publication and graphic design division – David Clarke Publications – which is run by Margaret Condon. The computerized presentations are also part of this department.

Account teams

There are two account teams at David Clarke Associates, each working for clients from specific market areas. Richard Bull and Alex Bickers work for clients who operate in manufacturing, the professions and engineering; Alison Burrows and Joanna Yoffey handle accounts in the business-to-business, professions and consumer markets.

Each account team is responsible for carrying out an agreed publicity programme for the client. This may involve issuing press releases; improving employee and community relations; monitoring the press, organizing seminars and building public awareness and generating goodwill for the client.

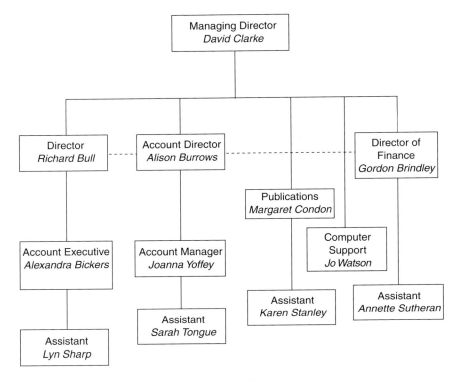

Figure 4.1 Management structure of David Clarke Associates

As account directors, both Richard Bull and Alison Burrows have the job of overseeing the direction of their client's accounts. Their role is a strategic one – looking to the future and acquiring new business. Joanna Yoffey – the account manager for Allison's team – has the job of managing the team's accounts on a daily basis. Alex Bickers, account executive for Richard Bull, also has this role with no manager present in the team.

Computer systems

All account handlers and assistants use IBM PCs. They use Microsoft Office 4, which includes Word 6. Each account team has access to a black and white laser printer. One PC has recently been upgraded to include Windows 95, Office 97, a CD-ROM, and the Internet and email facilities. David Clarke considered that it was appropriate to go onto the Internet in order to create greater options for the work they produce for the clients.

Publications division

The publications unit at David Clarke Associates is part of a separate division of the consultancy – David Clarke Publications, formed in 1988. The division has two members of staff: Margaret Condon (Publications Manager) and Jo Watson (Computerized Presentations). As publications manager, Margaret Condon is responsible for the development of publications and design at David Clarke Associates. This involves the design and production of artwork, negotiating with suppliers, cost control and reviewing and monitoring the work of designers and suppliers.

The unit specializes in producing publications for the consultancy's clients as part of their specified PR programme. These can be internal newsletters for employees or more elaborate customer magazines. However, other work is also created such as brochures, letter headings, advertisements and leaflets.

Production of the publications involves the use of specialists such as photographers, bureaux and printers. Graphic design consultancies are also hired to provide new ideas into the unit and take on work that cannot be produced in-house. Their work is supervised on a regular basis.

Over 90 per cent of the work produced in the department is for the consultancy's existing clients. When Margaret Condon joined the company in 1994, the publications unit had only two or three accounts of its own. She has since tried to win more business and with the one client that she has gained – the West Midlands Industrial Club – she has now established a good working relationship.

Marketing

As David Clarke does not see the company extending its business much outside the region, most marketing is conducted within the West Midlands. The East Midlands are targeted to a lesser degree.

Ideas for company promotion come from staff marketing meetings; these are usually held on a monthly basis. The directors also have brainstorming sessions during board meetings.

A marketing budget is prepared before the beginning of each financial year by David Clarke, Richard Bull and Gordon Brindley. The size of the budget is determined by past expenditure on marketing, fee income for the previous year, salaries and other overheads.

Current methods used by David Clarke Associates to inform potential markets about the company are:

* corporate identity;
* company brochure;
* advertising campaigns;
* publicity;

- web-site;
- reception display;
- directory listings;
- networking.

Corporate identity

The company logo – created in typeface Garamond – is red and black on a white background. It has remained unchanged during the ten years that the company has been established. Each item of stationery – letterheaded paper, compliment slips, etc. – features the logo. All have been designed with similar layouts and colours to create a common style.

Company brochure

The purpose of the brochure is to generate awareness of the company and its services. It highlights:

- the company philosophy;
- the range of services provided by the consultancy;
- the consultancy's understanding of the Midlands and its companies;
- the clients;
- some of the work that has been produced;
- how the company works to professional standards;
- awards that have been won;
- members of staff;
- the Edelman network.

Advertising campaigns

Advertisements for the company are regularly placed on the media page of Saturday's *Birmingham Post*, in the Birmingham Chamber of Commerce magazine and *Finance Midlands*. These adverts take the form of short messages highlighting the benefits that using David Clarke Associates can provide. Although only a small amount of work has been generated as a result of these ads, they have increased awareness of the company.

Publicity

Opportunities for free publicity are often taken by the company. These are usually stories in the local press about work that is currently being produced for a client. David Clarke also writes comments for the media page in the *Birmingham Post* on a Saturday. The company also becomes involved in community projects and has recently helped a local school produce a new prospectus.

Web-site

Since 1996 David Clarke Associates has had its own site on the Internet. The site provides an excellent introduction to the company. It also includes information on the clients, the staff and the services the company has to offer (http://www.david-clarke.co.uk/).

Directory listings

David Clarke Associates is currently listed in a number of directories – both specialist and general. These include:

- BRAD Agencies and Advertisers;
- *Marketing Managers Yearbook*;
- *IPR Handbook*;
- Kelly's Products and Services;
- Yellow Pages (both Birmingham Central and South).

The nature of these listings ranges from one-line entries and block entries to small advertisements. David Clarke has no formal marketing plan laid out for the company, feeling that there are many external factors that could affect the plans. However, his unofficial plan is to 'get a large enough share of the market to dominate the West Midlands'. For this to be achieved, he would like to see all the divisions better promoted.

Networking and entertainment take up the largest part of marketing expenditure. As the majority of new business is gained through recommendation, account handlers have to make sure the company name and reputation are known to a large number of people.

Individual marketing tasks

David Clarke believes that as a company they are bad at allocating marketing tasks and then monitoring their outcomes. However, every fee-earning employee knows that they have a part to play in winning new business. Each set themselves their own marketing tasks as no one employee is solely responsible for winning new accounts or finding new business opportunities.

These tasks include networking and direct mail – mailshots that are distributed to companies and organizations in market areas where the account handlers have experience. These mailshots, which may be montages of previous work, are then followed up with telephone calls. Computerized presentations have been marketed through mailshots – postcards that informed clients and potential clients of the service that is currently available. The service has also been advertised in regional publications.

A PowerPoint presentation in the Reception area highlights what the consultancy is about and some of the work that has been produced for clients. In the short time that it has been there, the response has been favourable.

New business

Information on potential new business is passed on to fee-earners through a list that highlights all of the enquiries they have received that week regarding possible work. It lists the name of the client, who is handling the enquiry and the status of that enquiry. The list was originally produced on a weekly basis, but, due to time constraints, it is now produced every few weeks.

Some of the company's new business enquiries derive from the advertisements or the entries in directories and the Yellow Pages. Edelman or the IPR sends other companies and organizations to David Clarke Associates. However, more than 80 per cent of the company's new business comes from recommendation.

As most of the company's new business comes through recommendation, most marketing activity is directed towards the referral market. These people – who may in the future recommend the consultancy to other organizations – include intermediaries, existing clients and suppliers. This marketing takes the form of informal communication in order to build and maintain good relationships and gain a greater understanding of clients' needs.

The account team undertakes research into the company's market and details of how they are going to answer the brief are highlighted in a proposal document. These proposal documents are set out with the following sections:

- the objectives set by the potential client;
- assessment of the client's expectations;
- introduction to the consultancy;
- working methods;
- previous experience with similar work;
- how the requirements will be met;
- directors and account handlers to work on the account;
- project costings and estimates.

Some companies like to have the written document before a verbal presentation is made.

The account team who will be working on the project – were the company to be chosen – also presents proposals to potential clients. The proposal is delivered via a PowerPoint presentation. Any artwork that is part of the pitch is desktop-published for better presentation and discussed by the account team. After the presentation, the consultancy will leave copies of the consultancy profile and the proposal document if the organization has not already seen it.

Service quality

In order to offer clients a service that meets their needs, frequent meetings with account handlers are established. Meeting reports are also kept so that a record of reviews and the next stages of progress are made. These regular meetings and reports ensure that throughout the duration of the PR programme both the client and the consultancy are kept up-to-date on progress and informed of any problems that may have occurred.

Apart from the regular routine liaison with the clients, account handlers also hold monthly, quarterly and half-yearly meetings. These reviews are an important part of the continued interaction with clients and are used to get feedback from them on the quality of service that they are receiving. This is the consultancy's equivalent of a client satisfaction survey.

It is the account handler on the project who has the most contact with the client. However, clients will also have some form of interaction with the administration staff through telephone conversations, letters and faxes. These employees are aware that they have something to add to the quality of the service that the clients receive. They are encouraged to consistently produce a high standard of work that is free from mistakes; telephones should be answered promptly, as should both written and telephone enquiries.

A procedures manual provides all employees with a framework in which to work. This is to ensure that there is consistency in work procedures and in the layout of correspondence and press releases. The manual also gives clear guidelines expected for service delivery, meeting the needs of the clients and improving client satisfaction.

Publications

When the unit began in 1988 it was marketed as a separate service. The unit had its own stationery and an identity that was separate from that of the company. Marketing activity declined once the manager left and due to a lack of time and finances not much marketing has taken place since.

However, there is now a feeling from Margaret Condon that the unit would now like to make a name for itself and win some accounts of its own rather than just producing work for existing PR clients. She would like to produce work for more regular titles in addition to the annual publications that she works on at the moment.

The only marketing carried out for publications, in the two years that Margaret has been there was mailshots. The mailshots take the form of a targeted letter explaining who they are, what they can offer, and for which companies they have worked. This is sent along with some examples of recent work –something that is appropriate to the targeted company and illustrates the unit's ability to work with large clients or small budgets. Companies and organizations targeted in these mailshots are varied as they are selected from newsletters and publications that she has been sent.

If time allows, these are followed up a week later with telephone calls to get responses from the targeted companies. A record of targeted companies and the outcome is kept in the marketing file. Some enquiries have been made as a result of the mailshots, but no work has directed from them. The company realized that the mailshots were not a successful method of marketing the publications unit. Lack of time allows her to do some marketing only when her workload is slack.

She has a number of ideas that could help raise the profile of the publications unit. These include:

- Contacting educational schemes – perhaps to do with the arts, music or sport – as this would tie in with the work already produced for the West Midlands Club and the Engineering Education Scheme.
- Writing an article on Midlands' design for the media page in the *Birmingham Post.*
- Setting up a design forum with regional design consultancies to discuss why companies are still going to London for their design work.

Margaret Condon also aims to meet the needs of the clients by delivering a quality service. To Condon, this means producing work that is:

- cost-effective;
- of the highest quality;
- delivered on time and within the agreed budget.

The company believes in strong financial control and working within agreed budgets. In order to stay within budget, Condon maintains a careful record of how her time is spent; time sheets are used for this purpose. Expenses on each project are managed on a budget control sheet. As spending figures are always known, action can be taken in advance if an overspend in budget is likely. This means obtaining permission from the client to either shorten the project or increase the budget.

Production schedules are devised for each stage of the project to ensure that the right amount of time is left to complete each stage. Proofing procedures are also in place so that mistakes are avoided before artwork goes off to print.

All copy and artwork is proofread by the account handler before it goes to the client for approval. The client will then come back to the account handler with any amendments. Once the corrections have been made, a print-out of the new version is checked against the amendments highlighted by the client. This process continues until no further amendments are needed. However, some problems have arisen when deadlines have become tight. This has been due to the computer equipment being unable to cope with some of the work that has been produced. On one occasion final layouts for a client to proofread could not be printed because the computer was unable to cope with the size of the file. This particular client had to come into the studio and proofread the copy on screen.

The low memory capacity of the computer also makes it hard to save large documents and process changes to artwork. Condon has had to drop the resolution of images and clear files off the hard disk so that the computer can cope with what has been asked.

Suppliers

Producing quality work and on time is also aided by using suppliers who share the same belief. A number of different suppliers are needed by the consultancy for it to deliver its work. The main ones used by the publication manager are printers, bureaux and design consultancies. Condon chooses many of her suppliers through recommendations from others. Selection criteria cover quality of work, technical expertise, cost, quality control and the ability to deliver work on time. Other suppliers are found through mutual contacts, advertisements and inventive mailers. However, a decision to use them is not made until after an initial meeting with the supplier to see if they meet the selection criteria.

Meetings involve seeing a selection of the supplier's work and discussing their prices and working methods. Sometimes – particularly with the printers – visits will be made to the company in order to see their organizational set-up.

Condon has a number of printers with whom she works. Some printers are selected to print complex colour work; others are chosen specifically to print two-colour newsletters, while some are used for much simpler smaller jobs. Many of these printers, especially the larger companies, work to the quality standard ISO 9000 Part 1. This means that artwork returning from the printers is checked against a recognized quality management system.

The company also hires design consultancies to work on various projects. They are used for their expertise and varying styles of work. Condon would like to extend the list of designers that David Clarke Associates use. This is to enable them to get a wider variety of styles and to stop work becoming stagnant. The consultancy also has to use suppliers that are recommended by the client. Companies such as Centre Exhibitions and Rover have their own list of suppliers – such as printers and bureaux – that they have worked with before. It is up to the publication manager to select a supplier from these lists.

Interaction between design and PR

Every PR programme is controlled by an account director who takes personal responsibility for its success. There is also an account handler who has responsibility for the day-to-day running of the account; making decisions and liaising with others to ensure that all deadlines are achieved.

Following an initial briefing from the client to the account handler, a PR strategy is agreed between the two parties. Budgets are also established for each part of the project so that the account handler knows how much there is available to spend. It is after these meetings that the publication manager is briefed by the account handler about any artwork that needs to be produced. Production schedules are then developed and the publication manager obtains quotations from a number of suitable printers.

Both the account and publication managers work in unison during all stages of the project. With progress and ideas being discussed between the two on a regular basis, creativity is also encouraged by the informal communication structure that encourages impromptu brainstorming sessions. The communication process between the client and the account handler is shown in Figure 4.2. It is rare for the publication manager to have any contact with the clients. Clients are only asked to get in contact with her when the account handler is unavailable.

The account handler presents ideas for artwork to the client during their regular meetings. Account handlers decide whether the publication manager attends these reviews, however, it is rare for her to be present.

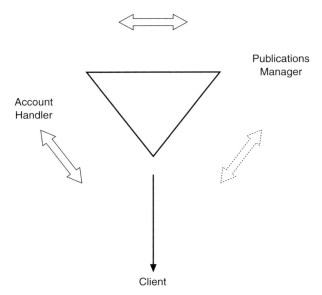

Figure 4.2 The communication process at David Clarke Associates

The account handler passes anything discussed about artwork at these meetings to her at a later date. Artwork may also be sent to the client by the account handler to gain their approval before the next stage of the project can go ahead. A description of the artwork is typed by the publication manager and pasted next to the colour proof.

Problems with communication

A client was budgeted for a low colour proof – normal for the third stage of approval – unaware that he preferred to see high-resolution Kodak prints. This client was used to see high resolution colour proofs at approval stage, as the company who previously produced artwork for him provided them. Another colour proof had to be provided by the bureau, adding further costs and delays to the project. Other misunderstandings have also arisen about the style and content of design work. The publication manager had not been present at any of the meetings with these clients.

Approval

The account handler provides the client with proofs at various stages of the design process. The typical proof stages for a newsletter is:

- black and white laser prints of draft copy;
- black and white laser prints of initial page layouts containing copy;
- colour laser proof. This is supplied to the client before the final work goes to print. These prints are usually of a low resolution. However, sometimes clients request a much higher quality proof such as a Kodak print;
- match-prints. These are handed to the client for colour checking, prior to the final artwork sent off to the printers.

Approval from clients is either written or verbal. Written approval comes from the signing of a match-print, while verbal approval is given to the account handler. He will then give the publication manager permission to proceed. A record of the client's approval is kept. Each project is looked at when it is finished to assess if there were any cost over-runs in the production process.

Professional services and marketing

'The number of professional service organisations is growing. With increased competition and an underlying need for effective promotion, the marketing of professional services has become the subject of a number of texts' (Morgan, 1991; Palmer, 1994; Woodruffe, 1995). These marketing experts agree that there are two ways in which a company can market itself: (1) by informing the market about the services on offer; and (2) by building the company image to clients and the referral market. Professional organizations need to inform the market about the services they offer, simply to communicate their availability to the public who may not be well informed. This could be through advertising, company literature or personal selling.

However, for professional services marketing to be successful, the marketing approach should not only fulfil all the practical aspects of a marketing programme. It must also be based on a philosophy that places the customer first – the emphasis in professional services marketing is on relationships and the 'people' element of the marketing mix. Principal elements of this include:

- relationships with customers;
- referral markets;
- internal markets.

The nature of a professional service – typically performed on a one-to-one basis – can allow a company to tailor its activities to the needs of the client. Therefore, by understanding the client's needs and wants, the service provider can ensure client satisfaction and the building of the company's reputation.

Customer retention is more likely if a strong rapport and a feeling of confidence are developed between the client and the provider. Satisfied customers will not only be retained, but as the level of businesses arising from 'word of mouth' recommendations is very high in professional services, referrals will also be made.

The final element – internal marketing – focuses on building appropriate strategies for customer (after-)care programmes. This is to ensure consistent quality and client satisfaction which can play an important role in making businesses more effective.

Marketing design services

Satisfying the needs of the client and providing a quality service are important elements in the marketing of a design service. There are many ways in which client satisfaction can be developed – most of these form the basics of design management. These principles are:

- realizing the true importance of design to the company;
- having a member of staff on the board who takes a personal and qualified interest in design;
- using design as a management tool to ensure that the best possible design results are achieved;

- making sure that client needs are fully understood before the design process begins;
- taking design out of isolation by having different departments working in tandem on the same project;
- investing in powerful design equipment to ensure that work is produced efficiently;
- introducing quality checking systems so that faults are found before production starts;
- developing long-term relations with suppliers.

Communication will always be a key factor in ensuring client satisfaction, so ways must be found for the client and designer to communicate on a regular basis throughout the whole design process. This not only encourages the development of the client and designer relationship, but will also avoid wasting the budget because the right questions will have been asked in the first place.

Design pitches should provide the designer with the first opportunity to meet the needs of the client. However, in order to make an integrated presentation, the designer and account handler should pitch for business together. Other presentations of design concepts to the client should be made by the designer as they are much more familiar with the work they have produced.

It is more beneficial to undertake these work processes when design is produced in-house. Not only does this make it easier to encourage a greater understanding of client needs, but the account handler can also monitor work on a daily basis and changes requested by clients can be made immediately.

Conclusion

An assessment of how the publications unit at David Clarke Associates is geared for successful marketing can be summarized in terms of a SWOT analysis.

Strengths

- The reputation of the company and its good position in the Midlands' PR industry.
- Experienced specialist employed in-house.
- Good working environment where effective communication is paramount.
- Strong planning in the unit enabling work to be carried out to the highest quality as possible, to the clients' deadlines and within budget.
- Good quality control seeing the careful selection and monitoring of suppliers and supervision of the production processes.

- Good relationship with suppliers.
- Ambition to succeed and expand the unit.
- Satisfied clients who return with more work.

Weaknesses

- The unit has no real recognition in the marketplace.
- Current working practices not allowing relationships to be formed with clients which may lead to more recommendations for the unit.
- Computer equipment in need of upgrading.
- Constant use of bureaux for colour print-out.
- Lack of finances affecting how the unit can be marketed.
- No clearly defined marketing strategy.
- Shortage of personnel.

Opportunities

- To raise the profile of the unit in the same way that David Clarke Associates is recognized in the region.
- To develop relationships with existing clients.
- To strengthen the unit by winning more regular work.
- To enhance service delivery by upgrading current computer equipment.

Threats

- Existing graphic design consultancies.
- Increased competition from PR consultancies adding in-house graphic design and publications to their services in order to provide clients with a complete communications package.
- Increased competition from PR consultancies who are upgrading their existing design facilities.
- In-house design departments producing their own publications.

Recommendations

The following recommendations are based on the observations made throughout this report. They are listed under the areas believed to be the most important in aiding the marketing of the publications unit and encouraging the acquisition of new work.

Marketing

An attempt to provide clients with a complete communications package has led many of the larger PR consultancies to create – through acquisition

– what are in effect many small specialized firms under one roof. Offering advertising, graphic design and market research services, these divisions operate as separate businesses and are marketed as such.

Publications and graphic design are not recognized as traditional PR activities. To inform the market of its services the publications unit needs to be marketed as a separate division. Although the unit is defined as a division of the company – David Clarke Publications – this is mentioned more on an internal basis than an external one.

With the good reputation that the company has it is important not to lose the David Clarke name. If the name of the division was to be changed, the link with David Clarke Associates should be made more apparent.

David Clarke Associates is listed in a variety of specialist directories under the category of 'Public Relations'. As many organizations go to specialists for their design, it is recommended that the publications unit place listings and advertising in specialist design press.

Both *Marketing* magazine and *PR Week* publish listings for industry related service companies. These lists include 'Contract Publishing' and 'Design and Advertising' categories. Specialist design directories include the Creative Handbook. Advertising could also be placed in the regional press and design publications to increase awareness on the new division. The current company brochure and consultancy profile describes publications as a service that can be provided to clients as part of their PR programme.

The identity of the division would be strengthened if a separate section dedicated to publications were included in company material. This section should highlight what the division has to offer; together with the companies and organizations that it has produced work for.

To strengthen the identity of the division further it is also recommended that the division have its own range of stationery using the division's new corporate image. At present company stationery is being used for all correspondence undertaken by the publications manager.

It is understood within the publications unit that past marketing activity has not been successful. As the response to the advertising and marketing of professional service companies is never immediate, the mailshot needs to be something that will be remembered when the service is required. It is recommended that inventive mailshots be produced, as these are more likely to stay in the mind of recipients.

However, some consideration must be made to the type of work required by the recipient. Most of the work produced by the division is commercial and does not allow for a wide creative scope. Telephone calls must also be made to establish the effectiveness of these mailshots.

It is suggested that there be a more structured approach to the selection of these target organizations. A marketing strategy should be drawn up to market to one industrial sector at a time or one type of organization. For example, experience of engineering education schemes – gained from working with the West Midlands Industrial Club and the Engineering Education Scheme – could be used in two ways: (1) to target engineering companies and organizations; and (2) to target educational schemes in other sectors. This would enable publications to gain experience in new sectors.

Improving client satisfaction

Most of the work produced by the publications manager is for clients as part of their PR programme. However, Condon has very little contact with these clients. Top service companies are customer-obsessed. They have a clear understanding of the needs of their customers. Communication between all parties involved in the design process is an important factor in meeting the needs of the client and ensuring satisfaction. Not only is awareness of – and commitment to – the project increased, but the development of the client and designer relationship is also encouraged.

The very first meeting between the publications manager and client should be the briefing for any artwork. Other meetings where artwork is going to be discussed should also involve the publication manager. Having the publications manager and the account handler together will enable each to draw on their own expertise, providing a holistic approach to the client's problem and increasing the overall understanding of their requirements. However, as this is not always practical – artwork only takes up a small amount of most client meetings – the publications manager and client should be given an opportunity to discuss the brief and subsequent artwork at a later date. Meeting the needs of the client and enhancing service quality can only be good marketing for the division.

As over 80 per cent of new business for David Clarke Associates arises through a recommendation, developing the relations and service delivery between the publications manager and the clients may encourage the latter to make referrals. The client will be more likely to recommend her to others if they have worked together beforehand.

Publications and graphic design are two of the most widely used services offered by PR companies. Promotional literature is also in great demand by all market sectors. The suggestions that have been made – although it is not possible to implement them immediately – have been presented with the future growth of the publications unit in mind. It is recognized that some recommendations can only be introduced with time and substantial funding. However, it is considered that financial contributions need to be made in order for the unit to become a profitable part of the business.

Conclusion

All organizations – whether they are manufacturers of fast-moving consumer goods or professional service companies – operate within a marketing environment. A company that is marketing orientated aims to achieve its objectives by anticipating and satisfying the needs and wants of its customers better than the competition. Long-term customer satisfaction is an important goal, as is attracting new customers and retaining them.

For manufacturers of fast-moving consumer goods this means offering products in packaging designs that not only draw attention to the product, but display brand characteristics which consumers feel will meet their needs. Customer satisfaction occurs when these product expectations match their experiences through use. For graphic design services understanding the client and their needs provides customer satisfaction, but also by producing high quality work that meets the client's objectives.

To identify their needs and provide offerings, which will meet them research is important. Marketing research for fast-moving consumer goods companies is essential to find out who is buying the product, how they buy it and their attitudes towards it. For service providers meetings should be held between the service provider and the client to enable work to be reviewed and modified if necessary. However, customer needs may change and it is up to the company or service provider to find out what these changes are. This highlights the importance for marketing research to be ongoing and for client meetings to be held on a regular basis.

Recently there has been a growth in the understanding of the importance of design in both packaging and public relations. Therefore, it is also important for both company types, to have knowledge of the competition and their use of design.

Fast-moving consumer goods manufacturers need to be aware of how other manufacturers are using design to gain attention and to communicate the values of their brands. Research also needs to be conducted to understand the consumer's perception of competing products.

Public relations consultancies need to have an understanding of how other similar consultancies are making use of graphic design: do they have facilities in-house?; what equipment do they use?; do they have work produced externally? Knowledge of other organizations and their use of graphic design services would also be beneficial.

This growth in understanding the importance of design underlines the need for it to be treated with the same importance as other areas of business. Packaging designers should be involved right from the conception of a new package, while graphic designers should attend briefings with clients. This would ensure a broader and deeper understanding of what is involved in the projects and which could be reflected in subsequent design work.

Achievement of customer satisfaction relies on an integrated approach from all areas of business relevant to the project. In the case of packaging design, designers, marketing, advertising, research and production should all work together on a regular basis; for a graphic design service regular communication should be held between the designer, account handler and client.

Review questions

1 Referring to the text, what are the main variables known as the marketing mix?
2 What promotional activities do you consider the most effective for David Clarke Associates?
3 In the service industry, price is one factor to compete upon, can you identify other factors which are equally as important to the client?
4 Discuss the benefits to the organization and to the client through David Clarke Associates being a member of a professional trade association.
5 Discuss the different ways in which PR can significantly contribute to the organization's branding strategy.
6 Referring to the text, what other methods would you suggest, for the company to attract new clients within the West Midlands region?
7 Would the methods that you suggest be appropriate to attract new clients at a national level or not? Discuss the different approaches and why.
8 David Clarke Associates do not have a formal 'mission statement'. Discuss the benefits to both the company employees and clients if they decide to produce one.
9 Offer suggestions for an effective mechanism that monitors the latest developments in the PR industry, that David Clarke Associates could use to maintain competitiveness.
10 Why is it so important that all the stakeholders in the design project be involved at the initial stages of the design process?

Project questions

1 Describe the key changes required to develop David Clarke Associates' mission statement towards providing services exclusively based on design.
2 Devise a short questionnaire that would elicit the important aspects of David Clarke Associates' services which are design based. This may then be adapted to be used with equivalent PR or marketing firms, but centre on client satisfaction.
3 Describe how design may feature in a management plan to obtain new business from advertising rather than recommendation.
4 Find a good quality benchmark service sector example for David

Clarke's management. In particular, the development of publications as an account winner in its own right would be expected.

5   Within 'graphic design' what are the policy options now open to David Clarke Associates? These should be described in terms of IT-based services concentrating on the current core activities of the firm.

References

Business Ratio Plus (1994), Hampton: ICC Information Group.

Howard, W. (1989). *The Practice of Public Relations*, Oxford: Heinemann Professional.

Morgan, N. (1991), *Professional Services Marketing*, Oxford: Butterworth-Heinemann.

Palmer, A. (1994), *Principles of Services Marketing*, New York: McGraw-Hill.

Woodruffe, H. (1995), *Services Marketing*, London: Pitman.

Further reading

Archer, B. (1996) 'Can PR build brands?', *Campaign*, 24 May, p. 41.

Bennett, O. (1996) 'What's Jarvis got that the Archbishop wants?', *The Independent on Sunday*, 14 April.

Birmingham Post (1997) 'Whittmore caters to Willoughby's needs', 31 May, p. 18.

Birmingham Post (1997) 'Seal sports new account', 28 June, p. 18.

Birmingham Post (1997) 'Willoughby extends home interest Division', 19 July, p. 18.

BRAD (1997) *Agencies and Advertisers*, April, London: EMAP Media.

Cooper, R. and Press, M. (1995) *The Design Agenda: A Successful Guide to Design Management*, Wiley, Chichester.

Gofton, K. (1997) 'The top 135' *Marketing Supplement*, 29 May.

PR Week (1992) 'The top 150 PR consultancies', supplement, 30 April.

PR Week (1994) 'The top 150 PR consultancies', supplement, 28 April.

PR Week (1996) 'The top 150 PR consultancies', supplement, 26 April.

PR Week (1997) 'The top 150 PR consultancies', supplement, 2 May.

Smith, W. (1997) 'Catching the eye of the market', *PR Week*, 21 March, pp. 11–12.

Thompson, C. (ed.) (1996) *Public Relations Consultancy 1996: The Public Relations Yearbook*. London: Public Relations Consultants Association.

Branding in the fashion industry
Charlie Allen Menswear

Company:	Charlie Allen Menswear
	186 Upper Street
	Islington
	North London
Business:	Bespoke menswear
Auditor:	*Maria Morse*

Introduction

Branding has become an increasingly important marketing strategy within the fashion industry, used to unite all the designed elements of a company, to communicate an image or identity. Fashion garments and the labels that appear on them communicate messages and implicit meanings. They are interpreted as being symbols of social class or representative of one's lifestyle. Aspiration or association purchases fashion and their brands.

Brands have deeper symbolic dimensions than their visual appearance. Brand labels on garments can influence perceptions of quality, status, fashionability, price and inferences about the person. Perceptions are dependent on whether brands are a designer, national or private label.

An in-depth organizational analysis of a menswear company studies a brand in a 'live' situation. This case study is used to illustrate how to create a strong brand identity and establish that identity as an effective form of communication between the company and its audiences. A combination of market research, customer questionnaires and audit evaluations are used to identify, assess and redevelop the Charlie Allen brand. A brand development strategy provides recommendations over a four-year period. Charlie Allen Menswear operates in a relatively young industrial sector termed the New Tailors. These individuals are both tailors and designers who are striving to establish themselves through various approaches to design. The craftsmanship of bespoke tailoring is discussed, as is the mechanics of designing collections, fashion diffusion and fashion branding.

From reviewing existing research and the present study, it can be concluded that fashion branding can add value to a company and its products leading to perceived quality, loyalty, awareness, diffusion and brand extensions. The brand must be approached from various levels: the visual representation, the company's design elements, the perceptions it instils and the symbolic messages conveyed.

In the past thirty years, the fashion industry has witnessed the emergence, growth and mass adoption of fashion branding. In comparison to research on the branding of consumer durables, research on fashion branding is minimal. Although some of the principles of the former are applicable to the latter, fashion branding and the growth of designer labels have become a phenomenon in their own right. It is one of the various methods companies within the fashion industry have adopted to differentiate themselves in an ever expanding market.

Aim of the case study

This audit aims to provide an in-depth study of a menswear company to investigate the existing use and organizational application of branding and to recommend how the brand can be redeveloped to be made stronger. The overall aim of the audit was to study a brand in a live situation, with a view to providing new research to the area of fashion branding. To validate the need for this research, it must be understood how clothes communicate meaning, and how labels alter the meaning and how branding adds value. Only after these issues are discussed can the recommendations for creating a strong brand be justified.

The Charlie Allen Menswear Company, situated in Islington, North London, is an independent retail outlet, established in 1992. Charlie Allen provides a full bespoke tailoring service and retails men's classic outerwear clothing. It is a small business which retains both family traditions and traditions of the tailoring industry. Charlie Allen Wholesale also operates from the same address, and both companies are limited and owned by Charlie Allen. The main problem within the company was that it has been communicating messages implicitly to its audiences. Although they have been totally ineffective, it does mean that this lack of control has led to the company transmitting confused messages.

The objectives of the case study related to the present activities of the company and were to assess the impact on design undertaken and design elements. Also to conduct external market research that will enable the company to increase its knowledge about the environment it operates in.

Methodology

Information collected by observation included the general daily activities of the company and the interaction between the organization and consumers. It had been intended to employ observational techniques to create data charts, but this became somewhat impractical. There was neither enough staff nor consumers to discover specific behavioural categories.

Observation became paramount to understand the various design processes and to analyse the present identity of the company.

Content analysis was the technique used for sampling and analysing communications with the company and its audiences. A press analysis and a geo-demographic map were created. Systematic analysis allowed a lot of information to be condensed into a quantitative objective format from which conclusions were drawn. This information is combined with secondary information on social and market trends, thus enabling the construction of lifestyle and competitor comparisons.

Interviews were employed to collect information from key individuals: Charlie Allen, the Managing Director of Charlie Allen Menswear and his peers (other tailors in that sector). Interviews were structured but with open-ended questions to allow the interviewee to elaborate at will. Three interviews were conducted with Charlie Allen to establish company operations, developments and future strategies. The interview technique started as formal and structured but adapted an unstructured informal style.

The main source of quantitative information came from a postal questionnaire issued to customers, which used a combination of fixed and open-ended questions. It also included summated ratings and the semantic differential where respondents are asked to mark a scale or provide rating scores. These questions deduced the attitudes of consumers and assess their requirements. A subsequent pilot questionnaire was issued to a professional organization to compare customer requirements. Figure 5.1 shows the outline of the audit.

Fashion branding

This section forms the basis for the in-depth organizational analysis contained within the main body of the work. It is both an explanation of the theoretical approaches which describe fashion as communication and the importance of fashion branding. A literature review of experimental research suggests actual value the brand can offer.

A brand is a name, term, sign, symbol or design, or a combination of them intended to identify the goods or services of one seller or a group of sellers (Kotler, 1994). Branding of any nature is used as an effective marketing technique. It is the overall presentation of a company and its product offer.

Kotler (1994) suggests that a brand is a seller's promise to consistently deliver a specific set of features, benefits and services to customers. But a brand is an even more complex symbol that can convey up to six levels of meaning. The positive elements of the Charlie Allen brand will be described succinctly according to these six levels of meaning as defined by Kotler:

- Attributes: expensive, exclusive well-made products. Modern but classic. Durable, comfortable and thoughtful in design.

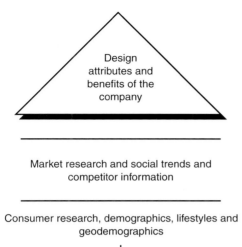

Market research and social trends and
competitor information

Consumer research, demographics, lifestyles and
geodemographics

Management Direction and Vision
Short-term objectives
Raise company profile
Create a strong brand identity
Increase customer awareness

Long-term objectives
Direct manufacturing
Increase the percentage of revenue from ready to wear
Expansion of 1–2 shops in strategic locations
Diffusion

Figure 5.1 Outline of the audit

- Benefits: the functional benefits are that garments are constructed to last years and styled to outlast more than one season. The emotional benefits are that clothes will give a feeling of wealth, affluence, importance and admiration. A feeling of pleasure and high self-esteem.
- Values: classic quality, artistic in thought and traditional.
- Culture: an English culture based on tradition, the monarchy, a class system and pride in history and craftsmanship. Also a business culture.
- Personality: the brand projects a certain personality. If the brand were a person it would suggest an English aristocrat. If it were an object it would suggest a classic painting or a marble statue. If it were an animal it would be a Gyr Falcon, an impressive bird, the largest of the falcons, which is able to survive in cold climates.
- Use: the brand conveys a certain user type. An educated professional

male of 39, established in his career. In control of his business, he displays his class and social status through expensive clothes and possessions. But he always remains modest. He is a family man and a firm believer in tradition.

This illustrates that a brand is more than a name and a symbol, it conveys messages on all dimensions. Some of these levels of meanings can be used to promote the brand to give it depth and differentiation. The attributes, culture, emotional benefits and personality dimensions will be considered in the brand strategy. The brand's strength seems to be most evident in these areas, as deduced from the evaluation. But this has yet to be legitimized by the customer questionnaire.

Origins of fashion branding

The origination of fashion branding cannot be explained any clearer than it already has by Chenoune (1993, p. 307):

> In a world of media type and increasing abstract social relationships, it became more than ever important to remain present and visible. Inner city kids began spray painting their signatures everywhere and graffiti 'tags' was inundating the New York subway in 1972. By the 1980's this craze ... had spread ... The strategy of high visibility was adopted by the fashion industry too. On streets already saturated with logos, signs, billboards, images and words, brand names began invading the previously overlooked advertising space of clothing. Garment makers scrawled their signature, seal or emblem on clothing like space-hungry 'taggers'.
>
> Following in the footsteps of Gaston Louis Vuitton who in 1896 put the initials LV on his firm's luggage to distinguish it from imitations, as well as in those of tennis player René Lacoste who in 1933 marketed the 'alligator' shirts he had been wearing on the tennis court since 1927, Pierre Cardin decided in the 1960's to cash in on his own name by signing his neckties. Twenty years later the phenomenon had taken on the scope of a fad, a fashion war.

Now the most exploited technique in fashion marketing is diffusion. Diffusion ranges are sub-ranges designers' launch to run alongside their existing collections. Diffusion may be used to make garments more accessible (to more market segments). Concessions are made in price, quality and exclusivity. Consumers pay extra for the designer name on the garment, rather than the garments actual value. Brands outlive their creators, which is particularly relevant for fashion houses led by one designer. A brand is a promise of the products benefits. According to Feldwick (1991) brands do the following:

- are a guarantee of authenticity;
- are a promise of performance and reliability;
- give the value of reassurance;
- cause a transformation of experience through abstraction. For example, Charles Revlon sells hope through his cosmetics.

Fashion as a form of non-verbal communication

Globally, people adorn themselves with fabric or material termed clothing, dress and/or fashion. The extent to which this occurs is contextual and relative to time and place.

Lurie (1992) refers to clothing as being synonymous with language. Like language, clothing can be broken down. Semiotics has tried to do this, by breaking down clothing into various meanings. The semiotic approach identifies everything as a sign, representative of something else. In the symbolic realm of dress and appearance however, a 'meaning' tends to be simultaneously both more ambiguous and more differentiated than in other expressive realms (Davis, 1992).

The initial intent of clothing was a functional device, but because clothes are so visible, they have become material objects that are relevant to everyday life. Clothes help us to organize and make sense of our social experiences (Kaiser, 1990). They are now complex symbols, which communicate both what we are, and the influences which have made us. Whether consciously or unconsciously, people communicate messages about what they wear. The various determinants that can be communicated by fashion are:

- cultural: culture, sub-culture and social class;
- social: reference groups, family, roles and status's;
- personal: age, occupation, economic circumstances, personality and self-concept;
- psychological: beliefs and attitudes (Kotler, 1994. p. 2).

These determinants cannot be represented in isolation because they are so closely inter-related.

Not all clothing and dress constitute fashion. Clothing is any tangible or material object connected to the human body (Kaiser, 1990). Dress includes the total presentation of all coverings and ornamentation worn on the human body, including the use of clothing, accessories, hairstyling, cosmetics, facial hair and tattoos (Sproles and Burns, 1994). Fashion is a social process in which new styles are created, introduced and then popularly accepted by a large group of people at a particular time (Kaiser, 1990). Social psychologists believe that the distinction between clothing, dress and the use of fashion lies predominantly in Western societies.

Barnard (1996) writes that individuals must posses two social tendencies for fashion to be present – the desire to be part of a larger whole society and to be considered to be apart from that larger whole. These are expressed through group identity and individuality. In non-western societies, individuality is subjugated to the values and beliefs of wider society.

Fashion changes rapidly, whereas dress is fixed. For example, national costume remains constant over time, therefore it cannot be considered fashion. Dress represents continuity. Fashion represents change and the desire to want change.

Fashion and class stratification have been linked by many academics. Barnard (1996) and Kaiser (1990) viewed fashion change as the result of a class struggle for social superiority. Class leadership, he considered, was displayed through conspicuous consumption: tangible evidence of the cost of one's apparel, indicating an ability to spend freely on clothes.

Many have believed that fashion is used by the ruling classes to differentiate their privileged position. The lower classes imitate these styles, expressing their aspiration to improve their social status. When the ruling classes see their fashion has been adopted by people they wish to distinguish themselves from, they change their styles, causing a change in the fashion process. Modern social codes allow the immediately subordinate group to emulate the tastes and preferences of the social class above (Partington, 1992).

The purchase of haute couture is an example of conspicuous consumption. It symbolizes the wearer's wealth and ability to afford waste (as high fashion is only such for a short period of time). It is a method used to differentiate upper-class positioning, as only the rich can afford designer one-off garments.

Classic and traditional clothing seems to suggest the wearer want things to remain the same. By definition, classic means ageless. The existence of classic and traditional clothing in a fashion conscious society means these garments can become fashionable and subject to change, but they often sustain their cycles a lot longer.

It may just be the case that social class is the most decoded message of fashion communication, by those who are able to interpret them. The emphasis on social class was probably more important when these theories originated. There were not as many diverse cultural groups present in western societies then as there are now. Culture (including social class) as a whole now seems to predominate. Market segments within all social groups have fashion leaders. The mass media is targeted at market segments, so the flow of information and influence is primarily within, rather than across, social class groups (Partington, 1992).

The existence of sub-cultures and street fashion proves that fashion leaders can come from those other than the ruling classes. Some would describe this as conspicuous counter-consumption: status seeking by deliberately choosing alternatives to status fashion symbol, by making pretence of those fashion items. But many street styles have been used for the themes and influences of designers' collections, before trickling down the fashion process.

Mass market theory and sub-cultures may be aided by the fact a lot of groups are not even considered part of any social class definition. So belonging to another group or market segment has become important, as too, has the visual expressions of them.

It seems that conflicting arguments can be defined in terms of aspiration and association. Certain people use clothing to communicate a desire to aspire to better things. Others wear clothing, which they associate with as being representative of their lifestyle.

These messages delivered by clothes are further transformed by fashion branding. Not only does it convey messages sent by the wearer, but it identifies the designer and symbol as well.

> It is not difficult to understand that even when garments are covered in words, as brand names or slogans for example, there is still a level of non verbal communication that exceeds the literal meaning of those slogans or brand names.
>
> (Barnard, 1996)

Research into fashion branding aims to establish the reasons why branded garments are purchased. Most research is concerned with the symbolic dimension of fashion brands and what they mean to consumers and their purchasing decisions.

When consumers purchase clothes, their evaluation is subject to sets of subtle cues; intrinsic cues inherent to the product which are physical characteristics and extrinsic cues, which are product related but not part of the physical product. For example, fabric type and style are intrinsic, while price, brand name and the image of the retail outlet are extrinsic.

The definitions of different brand types are listed below:

Designer label: Items that carry an external brand mark such as a designer name, symbol or logo, that has the purpose affiliating the garment with a famous designer in order to create a basis for status and price differentiation (Baugh and Davis, 1989).

Name brand: Well-known recognized brands that many stores carry, e.g. Levi's (Morganosky, 1990).

National brand: A name brand that is established nationally, e.g. Burberry's in the UK.

Private brand: Goods that are produced exclusively for one retailer and carry the store's name, e.g. Warehouse.

Store brand: Similar to a private brand but usually refers to a private brand associated to a lower status store.

Brand names can alter perceptions about intrinsic and extrinsic qualities or how these qualities affect the perception of the brand. When researching fashion branding, many authors base their work within a theoretical framework. One such framework is congruity theory. The theory is based on the idea that if a person has two related thoughts that are inconsistent, they will strive for consistency by changing one or both thoughts.

Forsythe (1991) used congruity theory to examine the impact of brand name and actual product characteristics on consumer's evaluations of product quality and price. Three identical shirts were given a private, designer and national brand label, then presented to shoppers in a retail complex. The designer brand was perceived to be significantly more expensive than national and private brands. Brand-conscious shoppers attributed higher prices than quality conscious shoppers.

Baugh and Davis (1989) used the theory to look at how brand perceptions are influenced by store image. Three identical knitted shirts were given either a designer label, a private label from a prestige store, a private label from a low prestige store or a controlled no label. The designer shirt was perceived as having significant status characteristics.

The shirt with the designer label was viewed as having favourable styling regardless of the store it came from, whereas the shirt with the private label from the high image store was rated as having more favourable styling characteristics than the shirt with the private label from the low image store.

Quality has become an important value component of fashion branding. Do brands mean quality assurance of the physical product, or is it a perception in the mind of the consumer? Huddleston *et al.* (1993) describe the brand-conscious shopper as being brand orientated and knowledgeable of brand names with a tendency to lean towards these products when purchasing apparel. When they surveyed 303 people, quality proneness (a desire for quality when selecting apparel) was the strongest predictor of brand orientation. The desire for quality is directly related to a tendency to purchase brands.

This supports other research that has established a relationship between branding and consumer's perception of quality, see Davis (1992). Shoppers were asked to rate and purchase one of four white blouses (consistent across general construction and attributes style) which varied according to the care label, fabric, neck label, price, the store it was from and the brand label. From the designer, name brand and private labels, the designer label was rated highest in quality and fashionability. The two main reasons for this were because of the fabric content and designer's label (Calvin Klein). However, most shoppers said they would purchase the private label because of the fabric and price.

Results also suggest that men associate quality with a moderately priced well-known label: 'Overall, the most important findings were that subjects who were familiar with all the labels perceived a difference in quality, while subjects who were unfamiliar with the labels accurately perceived no difference' (Behling and Wilch, 1988). It would appear that the perception of quality is affected by brand names even when the actual physical quality of garments in experiments are identical, but this does not appear to be dependent on brand awareness. Davis (1992) suggests that quality is influenced by any brand label rather than a specific type. His study provided evidence that perceptions of quality were higher for a garment with either a designer label or non-designer label in comparison to a non-labelled designer label.

Quality is positively influenced by the presence of a brand name. Fashionability and higher status can be attributed to designer labels, so too can a higher price. Lennon (1986), like Forsythe (1991) believed that people expect to pay more for a designer label. Lennon found that junior high school students would spend more on designer jeans in comparison to non-designer jeans. She believed this was due to classical conditioning i.e. a repeated association between designer labels and spending.

Just as clothes can send messages about us, so too can brands. The type of brand we choose to wear can influence how we are perceived by others. Correspondent inference theory attempts to account for an observer's inferences about what another individual was trying to achieve by a particular action. In Workman's (1988) study, subjects were asked to provide their impressions of a person based on the labelled jeans they owned. The owners of store brand jeans were attributed with negative inferences such as being less fashionable, less popular and having poorer personalities, whereas owners of designer labels were attributed with positive inferences.

The majority of research was conducted in the USA. Taking the last point for example, it is doubtful that the British have such negative perceptions of all private/store labels due to the composition of 'our' high street. Lewis and Hawksley (1990) noticed that: 'A variety of new companies have emerged in the high street with labels aimed at carefully defined market segments, differentiating themselves on the basis of image.' Products which customers symbolize as similar to their self-concept will serve to reinforce it (ibid.). This supports the idea of brand purchases by lifestyle association. When customers strive to move their actual self-concept towards their ideal self, purchase is motivated by aspiration.

Moore (1995) provides an in-depth approach to own branding in the UK and highlights the differences in the significance of the private label in the UK. Research assess the private label from the retailer's perspective, examining the process of brand creation and development, explained in terms of a two-dimensional development:

1   Utilitarian dimension (physical garment) includes:
    (i) Influence of high fashion design.

    (ii) Competitor activity.

    (iii) Social trends.

2   Symbolic dimension includes:

    (i) Consumer research.

    (ii) Product branding devices (e.g. name and packaging).

    (iii) Branding the whole shopping experience (e.g. interiors).

    (iv) Market positioning through mass media: 'The successful fashion own brand has a powerful symbolic dimension, which conveys lifestyle messages to the consumer, who in turn appropriates these and uses them as a means of self-expression within their social context' (Moore, 1995).

Morgado (1993) looks at the semiotics of animal trademark emblems on fashion apparel. The four emblems selected were Munsingwear's penguin, Gloria Vanderbilt's swan, Izod Lacoste's alligator, and Ralph Lauren's polo pony. The emblems are interpreted as an icon, index and symbol, the propositions are that:

- The animal icons signify human dominion over the natural world.
- Some emblems serve as social gatekeepers, which can only be interpreted by those with prior knowledge. For example, to understand the Ralph Lauren polo player on a garment, one would either have to be familiar with polo or have seen printed advertisements.
- Each symbol refers to particular positions on the fashion hierarchy. Each emblem is marketed to a particular socio-economic and lifestyle groups.
- Ralph Lauren's polo player has become positioned as 'the penultimate American status symbol' signifying an aristocratic and traditional lifestyle of elegance, taste and wealth. Although it 'ignores the traditional role of fashionable clothing as a means for the aristocrat to distance himself visually from the serf for the specific purpose of maintaining control' (Morgado, 1990). It does continue to be a weapon of oppression, causing feelings of discomfort and inferiority in those who do not wear it nor understand it. Even the way in which the mallet is held by the polo player symbolizes power.
- The trademark symbolizes living legends – the designers. The polo figure easily lends itself to an interpretation of Ralph Lauren's personal transformation from Ralph Lifshitz, the son of a painter, who was raised in the Bronx. The emblem symbolizes characters (designers) who have made larger-than-life accomplishments. 'Their lives, their activities, and their success stories provide the culture's most pervasive behavioural models' (ibid.).

There can be no doubt the private brands and name brand fashion items are purchased by association to a carefully marketed lifestyle based on a more balanced equilibrium of customer/company values.

It can also be concluded that designer label garments are either worn to indicate one's existing high social position or an aspiration to move up the social strata. But the wearer has to feel some affiliation with the designer or the designer's values far more than with other brand types. They all have their distinctive trademark of creative talents or style that differentiate the brand – symbolized as an emblem.

The literature review highlights the fact that brands, as extrinsic cues, provide value through how they are perceived. The most important of these are differentiation, quality, status, fashionability and price.

The menswear fashion industry

Charlie Allen Menswear Company operates in two interrelated sectors: ready-to-wear and bespoke. A considerable amount of bespoke tailors operate, the most recognized area being Savile Row which is home to long-established companies such as Gieves & Hawkes. But it is a group within the industry commonly referred to as the 'New Tailors' to which Charlie Allen belongs. They are a 'new breed of designers concentrating on the traditional tailoring techniques of Savile Row' (Williams, 1996a), (see Figure 5.2).

First, it is important to appreciate the wider sphere of the industry in which the New Tailors operate, and to recognize that while they share these associations, the sector types are distinct and separate, often with variations in their customer base.

The New Tailors want the national recognition of British designers, but also aspire to the status of the international designers. Some international designers produce haute couture collections, all produce ready-to-wear (RTW). Most designers develop perfumes, aftershaves, and cosmetics, and accessories that provide financial support for larger more expensive ventures.

A good example is the Ralph Lauren brand, established in 1972. His name is universally recognized. His company turnover in the UK (Ralph Lauren Ltd) was £6,687,145 in 1995. His concept is classic old-world charm. He sees sport as classic and timeless 'in a clean contemporary sense'. The name sells clothing, fragrances, CDs, luggage and home furnishings. Diffusion ranges for clothing are as follows:

- Purple Label ($1,200–$2,500 for a suit)
- Blue Label ($800–$1,500)
- Polo Sport (casual classics)/fragrances
- RRL (jeans)
- Polo jeans

Paul Smith 'heads an empire worth £54m (Yusuf, 1993) and 'he is now the biggest selling European designer in Japan ... he has over 150 Japanese

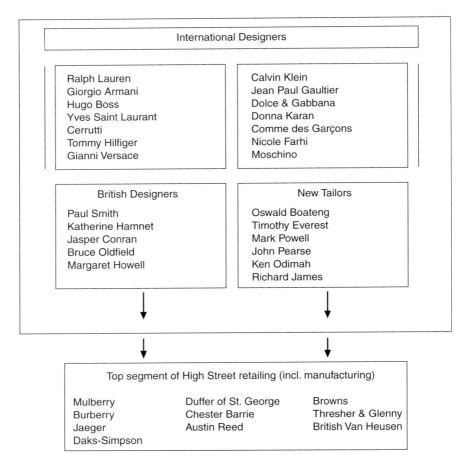

Figure 5.2 The main players in the fashion industry

outlets' (Jones, 1996). He expanded twenty-five years ago and now produces menswear, womenswear, and children's swimwear.

> As well as shops in Japan, there are now six shops in London, one in
> Nottingham, one in Paris and another in New York. Plus a couple in
> Singapore and a few more in Hong Kong. The eighties made Smith –
> his flair for idiosyncratic yet traditional Menswear coinciding with a
> boom in men's retailing; not only that, but as the eighties blossomed
> so did design as a cultural force.
>
> (Jones, 1996)

The New Tailors have the financial capacity to compete in this sector but
the British designers are more established. Figures indicate that turnover

in general has increased greatly, giving the New Tailors a chance to become established and grow in a sector where market demand appears to be on the increase.

The top segment of high street retailing offers more affordable classics and often a greater range of accessories. These shops are more accessible to consumers with numerous outlets on the high street. While they are not 'designer names', the company name is easily recognizable as a national brand. Some are suppliers to Charlie Allen Menswear, while others represent an outlet opportunity.

The New Tailors

The New Tailors are names and expertise behind their successful companies (all based in London). Unlike traditional tailors they design collections and appear to be more active within the fashion industry. The New Tailors are:

- Oswald Boateng
- John Pearse
- Timothy Everest
- Mark Powell
- Ken Odinah
- Richard James

This sector is characterized by relatively new, small businesses with growth potential. Table 5.1 is a taxonomy of their companies

Oswald Boateng

Boateng, arguably is the most discussed name in the New Tailors sector. He is self-taught, working for Tommy Nutter prior to working from home at Portobello Road in 1991. His first fashion show was in Paris Summer 1994. 'The immediate demand for ready-to-wear was from Japan and only since last winter (1995/6) has the collection been available to European buyers and is currently being sold in Liberty' (Williams, 1996b).

His main focus is to produce collections that resemble tailored garments, referred to as bespoke couture: a fusion of design and traditional tailoring. He sees his company responsibilities as being a creator, but is also aware of the business requirements. He designs collections and co-ordinates marketing while his assistant takes care of production. Design and its management are undertaken by he himself, his assistant and his business partner.

Table 5.1 The New Tailors: their prices and markets

	Oswald Boateng	John Pearse	Timothy Everest	Mark Powell	Ken Odinah	Richard James
Location	Savile Row	Soho	Spital-fields	Soho	Fulham	Savile Row
Opened	1995	1988	1993	1996	1995	1992
Retailing	1991	1966	1993	1985	1988	1992
No. of designers	One	None	One	None	None	None
Time taken to produce bespoke suit	8 weeks	4–5 weeks	6 weeks	3–4 weeks	4–5 weeks	6 weeks
Price of bespoke suit	£1,400 to £2,000	£900	£800+	£750 to £1,000	£650 to £900	£975
Price of 'ready to wear' suit	£600 to £750	£500+	£550	£500 to £600	£399	£550 to £685
Exports to	France and Japan	Japan	France and Japan	Europe, Japan and the USA	Europe and Japan	France, Japan, USA and Hong Kong

John Pearse

After being a Savile Row apprentice for two years, Pearse opened an outlet in Kings Road 1996, after having various premises, is now established in Mead Street, Soho. He is possibly the most established of all the New Tailors. Pearse goes on to say in an interview 'that he had wanted to be a designer but had ended up being a business man'. He describes his responsibilities as everything, although he does have an assistant who takes care of some of the responsibilities.

He is currently aiming to license his name in Japan as part of an export deal, but a search found a company name similar to his in Japan, so it may not be possible. He then goes on to say that it is not worth registering his clothes under another name as 'it is the name that sells the garment' (ibid.).

Timothy Everest

Everest moved from Wales to London, where he worked for Tommy Nutter in Savile Row, learning how to cut and construct garments. He did freelance work for four years prior to opening his retail outlet in 1993. He started the business with no financial help and trade picked-up within eight months. He views himself as an entrepreneur and a front man for the business. He would like to design more, but sees this as impossible because he must be more rounded.

The company structure consists of a board of directors, nine staff and forty outworkers all in a flat hierarchy. The aim is to keep him and the company as two separate entities. Over time more responsibilities will be handed to his assistant/manager. Everest now sees 70 per cent of clients himself, but this will have to be reduced to 50 per cent to enable effective management. When working on a collection, review meetings are held daily, otherwise meetings are scheduled monthly.

Timothy applies a three-stage development theory to his business: (1) the panic zone; (2) the stretch zone; and (3) the coping zone. For example, the first time a customer complaint is received, a company panics. After a few times, the company stretches to accommodate this change.

His objectives are to discover potential new markets, to develop and advise the brand and set up workshops out of London with the old work-force system of manual assembly.

Table 5.2 is a comparison of Everest's financial performance (1994) with Charlie Allen Menswear.

Mark Powell

Powell taught himself bespoke tailoring while working as a hairdresser and clothes shop manager. He has had various Soho-based premises since 1985 and moved in 1996 to his present location in Newburg Street. He designs the garments and client fittings, but does not make the garments.

Powell believes firmly that his product offer to be a complete lifestyle and that is how his brand will be marketed; he designs everything from clothing to accessories and footwear. The year 1996 has witnessed Powell paying close attention to the brand, and it was simply a coincidence that the advert opportunity occurred at the same time. He aims to establish the name first for three to four years and also develop the women's side of the business.

He has always used his current logo, but has recently restructured the logo for Japanese markets. 'It is good testing ground because over there is where they are already thinking about putting your name on perfume, socks, everything.'

Table 5.2 Comparison of the financial performance of Charlie Allen Menswear and Timothy Everest in 1994

	Charlie Allen (£)	*Timothy Everest (£)*
Turnover	115,724	416,480
Cost of sales	72,682	303,180
Less expenses	104,597	135,174
Deficit carried forward	−61,556	−21,874

Source: Companies House

Powell has just sold his latest collections to Barney's of New York. He is now looking to expand his ready-to-wear in London department stores. 'I want to develop the ready-to-wear a lot more, because obviously once the company's profile increases, the name and credibility are going to have so much more to it. Enabling us to charge more for individual (bespoke) commissions'.

Ken Odimah

Odimah's background is advertising and publishing. His mother, who is a designer, taught him how to cut. He joined Tom Gilbey in 1987 and founded his own label in 1988. Now based in Fulham, he does not have the high business rates that his counterparts have to pay in central London, so his operating costs are lower which allows him to reduce his pricing.

He provides consultation and fittings for clients in their own home. This allows him to go through his customer's wardrobe, providing a colour and style analysis. He will also deliver the end product and re-visit for any repairs that may be required. Odimah will then provide an initial sketch for his clients and then amend it to their own requirements. If the client brings a picture of the suit wanted, he will scan it into the computer using the customer's face and altering any details.

He believes tailoring will become a thing of the past, only affordable to the elite. Alterations will become more commonplace, so a company must seek to provide a complete service. This is also why he is developing 'ready bespoke,' part hand-tailored garments in a selection of styles and suggested fabrics, ready in seven days.

Now looking to Japan, he is considering direct manufacturing as an alternative to licensing agreement.

Richard James

Having graduated with a degree in Graphic Design, he worked his way up to a buyer at Browns. In the 1980s, seeing a market demand for a certain type of clothing, he self-funded his Paris collections. Now James differentiates by designing specific fabrics and ordering small runs from mills. He quickly points out that 'We order enough fabric to make twenty suits. When we run out we do not repeat, enabling us to offer exclusive products.'

The future

All the New Tailors saw 1997 as a time to move forward with new strategies to obtain more market share. What this means for Charlie Allen Menswear is that these competitors are becoming an increasing threat. Rather than being reactive, or benchmarking, the company must actively seek to differentiate. For example, Charlie Allen expressed a desire to produce semi-bespoke, expanding the sizing range of ready-to-wear. The market offer for this service would have to be more innovate than his competitors, if the company was to achieve a competitive edge. Table 5.3 shows the characteristics of the New Tailors.

Charlie Allen Menswear Company Ltd

To understand the mechanics of the company it is necessary to gain an insight into the background of Charlie Allen. It is because of his capabilities as a tailor, designer and manager that the company exists.

Charlie Allen has fifteen years' experience in the bespoke and tailoring market. He is a third-generation tailor, taught the trade by his father. Charlie Allen (Managing Director) comes from a West Indian family, where he is one of ten children. His father who has been a tailor since the age of 13, has taught all his children the craft. He has an MA in Menswear from the RCA (Royal College of Art). The sale of his collection to Jones prompted the creation of Charlie Allen Ltd in 1982. Allen began his career wholesaling to Italians, French and Americans from a small studio/factory in Cross Street, Islington. His collections have featured on the catwalks of Paris, New York and Japan. He has worked in Hong Kong, Singapore and Japan.

In 1984 Allen had a new partnership with the OMC group. They provided him with premises in Golden Square (off Regent Street) to wholesale his Menswear. During 1984 Allen landed a licensing deal with the leading Japanese Suit House (Koyo Clothing). By 1985 they were producing four collections per year. New contracts were established with Moss Bros. and Blades, Savile Row. The partnership dissolved in 1986.

Table 5.3 Product characteristics of the New Tailors

Tailor	Product characteristics
Oswald Boateng	Angled pockets to enhance shape
	Use of colour
John Pearse	'Individuality'
	Hand-painted ties
Timothy Everest	'Very Savile Row'
	Pattern is probably my signature
	Sharp silhouettes, humorous use of pattern and colour
Mark Powell	Attention to detail (collars and cuffs)
	High waisted trousers and inverted back pleats
	Kipper ties
	(Gangster/Edwardian)
Ken Odimah	Pencil-cut – 1700s' element
	1950s' waisting/1960s' tailoring
	Unusual fabrics
Richard James	Quality and modern spirit
	Usage of special fabrics

Between 1986 and 1989 Allen engaged in a legal battle with OMC in an attempt to win back his name and trademark. He was unable to work as an individual without it. He provided consultancy work to clients such as Next and Katherine Hamnett.

During 1990–2, Allen became course leader of Fashion Menswear at the RCA. This period saw him win back his trademark and locate his current premises, Allen is quick to point out that:

> I just had to pay the trademark owner for doing the work for me ... When I got it back I found this space here [Upper Street, Islington] that was run-down so badly that nobody wanted it ... but we spent far too much doing the shop-up; it cost 35k to make the shop look the way it is.
>
> (Interview, Charlie Allen, 1996)

Charlie Allen Menswear Company, 186 Upper Street, Islington was registered in December 1992. Section 3(a) of the memorandum states that the company is established 'to carry on the business of a gentleman's fashion shop and as gentlemen's outfitters, and tailors'. The business can be succinctly described as a retail outlet producing collections for retail, wholesale and offering a bespoke tailoring service. In addition, clothes and accessories are bought in.

Charlie Allen Wholesale (established 1993) operates from the same address, but is not trading sufficiently to be considered as a separate entity where design and management issues are concerned. In February 1995, a new partner bought out the other shareholders, but a year later he left the company, leaving Allen with financial difficulties.

The Charlie Allen signature is a trademark, although the company is no longer recognized as Charlie Allen Menswear, the trademark can still be used. Allen now trades as a new company (Charlie Allen Menswear). After carefully considering various investment proposals, Allen has a new business partner – Simon Tailor.

Organizational structure of the company

Allen's initial business plan for Charlie Allen Menswear contained a proposed organization structure (Figure 5.3). By comparison, Figure 5.4 illustrates the type of organizational structure operating at present.

The majority of communications involving decisions about work are processed through the managing director. Goffee and Scase (1995) suggest this is a typical entrepreneurial structure, influenced by culture, family values and the size of the company.

In comparison to the original structure, some tasks have now become the responsibility of the managing director. Allen now assumes the roles of commercial director, sales manager and design executive. Although a PR

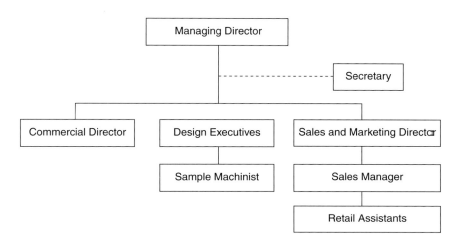

Figure 5.3 Proposed organizational structure at Charlie Allen Menswear

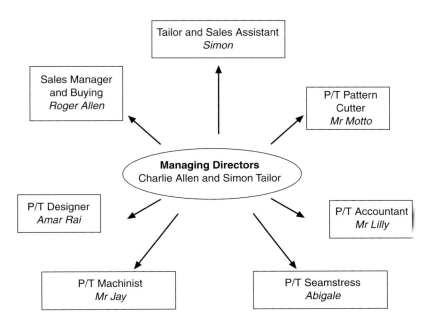

Figure 5.4 Present organizational structure at Charlie Allen Menswear

company is used occasionally, the sales and marketing responsibilities are almost non-existent.

> People with creative talents usually have little desire to exercise managerial control over others. They are more inclined to be more interested in exercising their personal talents to deliver professionally orientated quality services to their clients and to enjoy personal recognition. Accordingly, they regard their employers as providers of resources, financial, technical and human – which they can use for the purposes of personal goals. There is likely to be little management depth in these businesses and underdeveloped strategic capabilities because of the prevalence of 'professional' or scientific values. There are unlikely to be business plans; expansion is likely to be haphazard and customer driven. Growth, as a result is the outcome of a reactive response to market demand, rather than of *proactive* strategy.
>
> (Goffee and Scase, 1995)

Roger Allen, as well as being retail manager and buyer, is also responsible for merchandising the shop and creating the innovative window displays that the company is renowned for.

Operating and financial overview

Bespoke represent 60–70 per cent of the business. Bespoke fabric and trimmings can be bought when needed, whereas collections require at least £40,000 prior to commencement. In-house ranges require initial cash but not as much (approximately £5,000 depending on the range). In addition, bespoke customers pay a deposit before the garment is made.

Due to start-up capital and the expense of the collections, cash flow has become a growing concern. Financial data show that while wholesale operations were able to achieve a profit margin in 1994, retail was not. Total liabilities exceed total assets because cost levels are too high (such as administration and cost of sales).

By 1996, Charlie Allen Menswear went into voluntary receivership, but is now trading again with little effect to bespoke, where customer loyalty is high, retail operations need focus. When recommending any strategy for change, there should be particular sensitivity to cash flow.

Company mission

The original business plan (1988) did not provide any clear directional mission. What was documented was the lack of British designers within an international framework, a niche that Allen could encapsulate. The product offer was referred to as a quality high-class menswear. Attaining quality is an objective that has remained. Allen points out that:

The emphasis is on quality, not a statement as such, not like wearing bright colours, it's more like wearing things that feel good because they are well made. A lot of people do not understand why it feels good, and what I do is explain to them that it feels good because the fabric is expensive. You can wear this jacket unlined because the wool does not itch you and the way it is constructed is light, so that you can wear it all year round. A lot of the garments I design are to be worn all year round . . . so my particular hand writing is comfort, casual, smart, etc. What I am trying to do is design modern classics.

(Interview with Charlie Allen, 1996)

Because his products are expensive, another mission is that they are 'wearable in five years' time'. Allen believes to create and re-design that look, you have to be focused.

The retail manager, Roger Allen's description of the product offer is that styling is very simple and classic. Clothing can be worn all year round. 'It's the quality of the garments that makes Charlie Allen . . . classic, old English, traditional suiting with a slight modern twist.' To summarize, the (verbal) company mission, ready-to-wear menswear and accessories must be

- modern classics;
- high quality;
- casual but smart;
- comfortable;
- classic, old English, traditional suiting with a slight modern twist.

The bespoke offer is products and services to meet the customer's requirements – the customer has commissioned a piece of work which the company has the skills and expertise to create. Figure 5.5 illustrates how, by incorporating the company's problems and long- and short-term objectives, the mission can be translated into a brand identity programme.

Product design

Bespoke tailoring

Bespoke tailoring is the oldest form of making clothes. By tradition, the most requested bespoke garment is the suit.

It is a team job where your client says, right, I want to look like James Bond, I want to feel good, I want to be structured – I have got sloping shoulders, I have got a very bad stance, I want to look smart, I want to look upright. And what bespoke is all about is building a suit to make that person not only feel good mentally, but physically look good and for all their defects makes them look good.

(Interview with Charlie Allen, 1996)

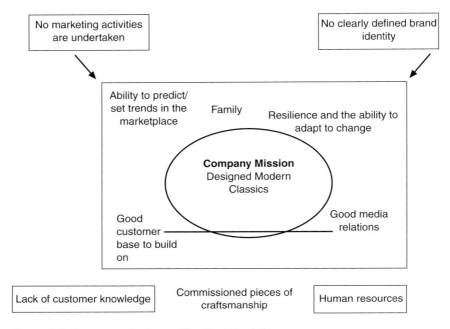

Figure 5.5 Company mission at Charlie Allen Menswear

Tailoring is a skilled craft that differs from the practice of design. Tailors must understand cloth and its application and be able to construct tailored garments.

A garment is a commissioned piece of work to meet the customer requirements. Suits from Charlie Allen Menswear retail at between £850–£1,500, depending on the fabric costs per metre. Because fabric is bought as and when it is required, bespoke tailoring means products are supplied just-in-time, with only the minimum amount of stock. The process takes an average of four weeks and is about personal service and care. Most of the customers who use the company expect to receive service from Charlie Allen.

Consultancy

The rear of the premises is used for bespoke consultations and fittings. The customer is seated and offered refreshments before Charlie will ask a series of questions. (It will be presumed that the hypothetical fitting is for a suit, although any garment can be ordered.) The following questions will help Allen determine how much the client is prepared to spend, etc.:

- What occasion do you want to wear this suit for? Must it last a long time?

- Are you hard-wearing on your suits?
- How many suits do you have?

If the client is getting married, the suit will have to be special but will not necessarily last. For this, fabrics such as silk and cashmere may be suggested, they are precious but generally not hard-wearing.

The customer's measurements are then taken and documented on a work ticket. For example, 'If the top pocket is ten inches down from the shoulder, the pockets on the waist should be three inches below the waist, or nine inches from the hem of the jacket' (Allen, 1996). The length of the jacket should end where the hand cups.

The style is discussed, and many customers come in with ideas from magazines. There are literally thousands of style combinations to choose from. The client will then choose the main fabric and the lining from sample books. Wool is the most popular fabric for suiting.

In the consultation, Allen will ask the client to try on a ready-to-wear jacket to see how it fits, and it highlights the imperfection easily. A customer may play sport and have one arm longer than the other or muscular legs, therefore this will enable the finished garment to be adapted to the particular client.

There is usually a period of two weeks between the consultation and first fitting in which time the shell of the jacket is constructed. Canvases, padding and quilting are used to form the shape of the jacket. The contents for a fully tailored jacket are shown in Table 5.4.

First fitting

The customer tries on the shell of the jacket. It is checked for balance, if it hangs straight, and any other observations. It is easy to alter the jacket at this stage as it is tacked together. Posture such as a round back may make the jacket gape at the shoulder blades, and this would be adjusted by

Table 5.4 The contents of a fully tailored jacket

Contents	*Amount*
Wool canvas	1 metre (single breasted)
	1.20 metres (double breasted)
Pocketing	2.2 inches
Hair cloth	17 inches
Domette	15 inches
Linen	9 inches
Collar canvas	5 inches, bias cut (undercollar melton)
Shoulder pads	
Sleeve lining	30 inches
Sleeve head-wadding	18 inches (double)
Lining fabric	1.5 metres for a jacket, 0.5 metre for trousers

lifting the collar to its correct height and marking the new position. Now the jacket can be finished. The buttons' position are marked and the overlap of the jacket.

Second fitting

This is usually the stage where the customer will try on the completely finished suit, and the trouser hem may be altered. The second fitting is only needed if there was a major alteration identified in the first fitting. It is really for the tailor and customer to check the finishing touches.

Between the first fitting and when the customer returns to collect the suit, it is sewn together by a tailor or seamstress. The lining is hand-stitched in. The edges, hem, buttons and holes are also hand sewn. The whole jacket will naturally form to the shape of the customer's body using his body heat over time.

Ready-to-wear collections

The structure of the fashion market is illustrated in Figure 5.6. Allen produces collections termed either ready-to-wear or designer wear, or prêt-à-porter. Garments are highly priced. Designs are produced in limited numbers and the quality must be of a high standard. There are two main collections a year (plus mid-seasons). The collections may be shown on the catwalks of London, Paris, Milan and New York.

In the 1980s and early 1990s, Allen was producing two collections a year to show on the international catwalks. The design process for a collection is outlined in Figure 5.7. The stages are as follows:

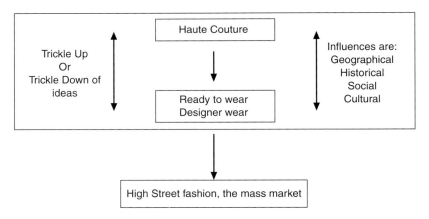

Figure 5.6 The fashion industry

Source: Adapted from Sorensen (1995)

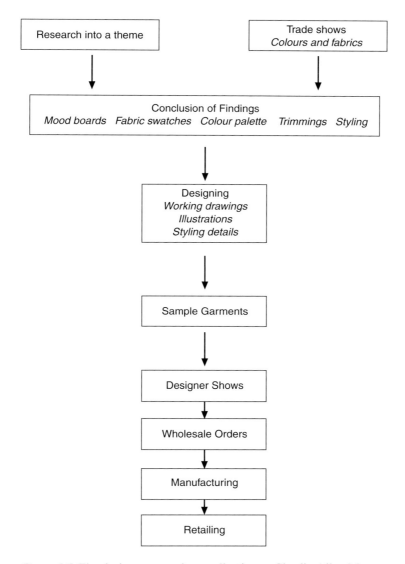

Figure 5.7 The design process for a collection at Charlie Allen Menswear

- The initial theme or story for the collection. Themes have to be innovative and somewhat original as what these designers create will
  trickle down to the high street.
- The International Wool Secretariat, ICI, the Silk Board, the Cotton
  Board all provide predictions for colours and fabrics they think will
  sell next season. The colour palette should be decided upon before the
  fabric show is visited. How much per metre of cloth the designer can

spend depends on that particular collection, cash flow, sponsorship and the designer's preference.

- Mood boards/Story boards. Usually numerous A1 or A2 boards convey the collection's themes, images, fabrics and colour palette. It becomes a reference point while designing. It visually pulls all the research together.
- Designing. Sketches working drawings and/or illustrations are made. Because of the type and size of the company, Allen does not need to produce specification drawings. He collaborates with his pattern cutter to ensure designs are interpreted correctly. Clothes may be modelled on the stand (tailoring dummy) in which case a toile (a prototype of a half-garment used to construct a pattern) is used to create a pattern or a block (standard pattern) may be adapted. A calico garment is constructed from the pattern to assess its function, aesthetics and styling.
- The sample garment or final garment is made. This is the garment the model will wear down the catwalk and orders will be made from and further manufacturing will be based on.
- The fashion show will require more than just the garments as it is a marketing event. Within the industry it is usual for companies to have sponsorship from other companies. Courtaulds Fibres sponsored Allen's 1994–5 Autumn/Winter collection. This allows Allen to reduce his costs and the sponsor to gain publicity. At the show, buyers will order designs they like. It is also where the designer either receives good or bad publicity, depending on the quality of work at the show.
- Manufacturing and retailing of collections. When a suitable price is negotiated with a manufacturing company, the range goes into production. Fabric is re-ordered in bulk. Orders are delivered or shipped out. Allen will not retail his collection in-store until orders are received and prices are standardized. As a consequence, this will ensure that the supplying company does not undercut their customers.

The company has to have a significant amount of cash to participate in designer shows (see Table 5.5). To research and stage a collection costs over £10,000. To show the collection together costs £10,000, plus another £10,000 to produce customer orders. There will be no return on investment on the initial collection for about a year. After six months, work begins on the next collection. Before any profit is made a cash flow sum of £40,000–£50,000 is needed. Due to the large amount of money required and to increase the choice to customers in the retail outlet, small collections are put together in-store. Usually in-store ranges are planned four to six months in advance. The timescale of a collection can take up to a year (see Table 5.6).

Wholesale collections are similarly conducted. Cost is worked out by fabric per metre, the actual cloth consumption, patterns, buttons, trimmings and how long the garment takes to make or how much the factory

Table 5.5 Requirements for Charlie Allen Autumn/Winter 1994–5 collection

The Collection (54 garments shown)	Budget
Fabric 100 metres @ £10.00 per metre (average)	£1,000
4 models for the fashion show @ £650 per model	£2,600
4 models for fittings @ £100	£400.00
Sound, light and seating	£1,000
Styling	£750.00
Hair and make-up	£400.00
Accessories	£250.00
Hospitality based on 100 people	£1,000
Invitations	£500.00
Total	**£7,900**

Table 5.6 A collection plan produced by East Central Studios

Timescale	Collection tasks	Estimated costs
Oct–Nov 1997	Research and Development for Autumn/ Winter 1998/9 Collection	£10,000
March 1998	Paris Catwalk A/W 1998/9 Show	£10,000
April 1998	R&D for Summer 1999	£10,000
March–Sept 1998	Orders and Production	£10,000
By Sept 1998	Wholesale orders out and in-store retailing	
October 1998	Next designers' show s/s 1999	£10,000
Oct–Nov 1998	Return on Investment	

charges. As a general rule, the mark-up is 100 per cent for wholesale and 250 per cent for retail.

Buying

Buying operates for Autumn/Winter and Spring/Summer like the ready-to-wear. Items must fit in with the season's theme. New suppliers are researched from trade magazines, trade shows, suppliers' phone calls and word of mouth (other designers).

A budget is set for each supplier depending on the season's requirements. Suppliers are kept depending on the sales performance of previous merchandise and whether the product is classed as trendy or classic as the former has a higher turnover but a shorter lifecycle. Suppliers who have remained constant over time include John Smedley, N-Peal, Burlington and Creed & Harris.

Technology

The company attempted to integrate CAD/CAM into the bespoke side of the business to automate the process of tailoring. The idea was that a shift towards technology would enable the company to offer the service on a larger, less expensive scale. Two systems were introduced.

The range of sizes is wider than off-the-peg suits, but not as precise as traditional manual methods. There are forty-one different jacket sizes available without vents or with one or two vents, and in twenty-eight different finishes available on the Scabal Iota system. The CAD/CAM system brings up the nearest pattern match from its database and adjusts the pattern on the Gerber system. Regardless of how vast the database is, it still is somewhat limited and inflexible in comparison to traditional tailoring practices.

In contrast, fabric technology helped to increase the company's market position and status in the industry. Courtaulds Fibres sponsored Charlie Allen Menswear Winter 1994–5 collection by providing the fabric Tencel. The collection marked the re-launch of Charlie Allen's ready-to-wear collections and his return to commercial fashion. The association between the two companies ensured an increase in press coverage, which was beneficial to both parties. The technological, environmental and functional aspects of Tencel produced in classic designs were popular but for a company which only produces limited designs the research and uses of technologically advanced fabrics are costly.

Identifying and evaluating the Charlie Allen brand

The primary aim of organizational analysis is to illustrate how market research can be used to create a strong brand identity for Charlie Allen and to establish that identity as an effective form of communication between the company and its respective audience. The audience for Charlie Allen Menswear is shown in Table 5.7.

The aims are communicated to by the various designed elements of the company. What these elements (or channels of communication) are is relative. 'In a market characterised by products with little generic differentiation, the fashion own brand has emerged as the cornerstone of marketing

Table 5.7 The audience and aims of Charlie Allen Menswear

Audience	Aims
Customers	To instil loyalty
General public	Enhance awareness of the company and products
The media	Communicate new strategy and performance/increase awareness
Financial	Communicate new strategy
The industry	Differentiate products and services from that of competitors
Local community	Communicate commitment to growth
Internal	Set an agenda and common objectives – team work
Influential groups	Show commitment to the environment
Government	Communicate commitment to growth and global markets

strategies' (Moore, 1995). Wilson suggests (1982) brand image can be broken down further into:

- current image – how audiences see the company;
- mirror image – how the company sees itself;
- wish image – the way the company would like to be seen.

Figure 5.8 shows how a brand identity programme is created.
   The Charlie Allen brand will be identified by:

- explaining motivation and design policy;
- identifying how the company would like to be seen (the wish image) established from the company mission and philosophy;
- investigating the design elements of the company and what they communicate (involves observing the mirror images);
- auditing design elements on an evaluation scale based on the wish image;
- describing the brand according to six levels of meaning;

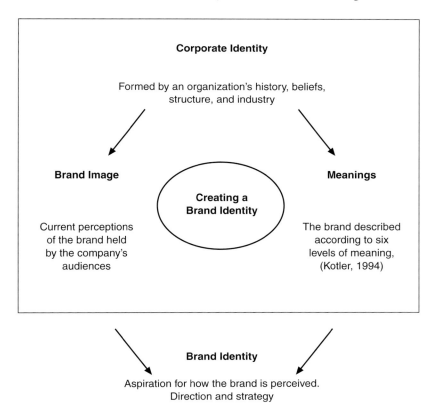

Figure 5.8 Creating a brand identity programme

- comparing competitors' brands (names, symbols and logos) and finding common elements and characteristics of the industry;
- the Charlie Allen sample logo;
- conclusion of findings and recommendations.

Purchasing motivation and design policy

Design communicates messages about the company to its audiences. Audiences must be able to decode these messages with minimum effort and this is achieved by a strong coherent and consistent brand identity. An effective design policy, which describes the context and constraints within which a company carried out design work can ensure this. It describes in design terms how customers' needs and wants are being met.

Design policy at Charlie Allen Menswear is not documented, nor is their design process. Because the company has a typical entrepreneurial structure, little is formalized. The managing director rarely has time to communicate the policy verbally, therefore they cannot communicate it to customers or ensure that work meets set standards. Design policy must be formalized and standards set to measure the effectiveness of design if the company is to move forward.

The wish image

The company's specific mission, or the purpose for the company's existence is:

- to design modern classics;
- to create aesthetic garments of unmistakable quality;
- to ensure the company conveys comfort (in its clothing and environment);
- to ensure the company conveys quality;
- to provide traditional skills and expertise;
- to support and exhibit art.

After investigating the style and content of design communication, it can be audited against these objectives.

Design communication

Charlie Allen Menswear has only paid twice to advertise their bespoke design service. Characteristic of the tailoring industry, little paid advertising is done. Any publicity or promotion is the result of articles in the press, particularly fashion magazines. The main results of a press analysis are outlined in Tables 5.8 and 5.9. Samples of fifty articles were selected, representative of all press coverage about Charlie Allen and the company.

Table 5.8 Analysis of press coverage of Charlie Allen Menswear

Article content	Amount
Charlie Allen and student success	3
Collection at Jones	3
Fashion	11
Fashion shows	6
Styling	4
Bespoke Tailors	2
Famous men in Charlie's clothes	3
Black businessmen	2
Career in general	3
Courtaulds, Tencel and Charlie Allen	9

Table 5.9 Coverage by periodical of Charlie Allen Menswear

Coverage by periodical	Amount
Menswear	16
Daily Mail/Mail on Sunday	5
Daily Telegraph	3
Guardian	2
GQ	1
The Face	1
FHM	1
Times	1
Independent	1
Financial Times	1
Evening Standard	1
Pride	1
Japanese Magazines	2
Others	14

The majority of the articles occurred between 1984–6 (new collections and career launch) and 1994–5 (Charlie's comeback and use of Tencel). Rather than slow steady coverage over a period of time, press coverage occurred in two curves of saturation and then declined. Due to this, the company aims to associate itself with tradition, classic and quality, and coverage has to be constant to establish the company over time.

Press coverage resumed in greater emphasis in 1996, largely due to the New Tailors movement when tailoring became fashionable. This can be used to launch a new strategy, after which, marketing issues need to be addressed and press relations monitored. Other forms of promotion used by the company are postcards with pictures of the shop or the work of local artists. They simply reinforce the visual concept of the company.

The most popular and regularly attended trade show attended by Allen is the Clothes Show where sales can be doubled or tripled. It is also effective in raising customer and press awareness.

Sufficient product levels are fundamental to promotion. With the acquisition of a new partner, the company aims to increase stock levels to clear existing debts and trade at a profit before addressing promotion in greater depth. Therefore promotion is a long-term aim that precedes the brand's development. As part of the design audit, a press release was put together for the company. This was to replace the existing three incomplete press releases and to illustrate how promotion can be used to present one clear message.

Passing trade

At just under six square miles, Islington is one of the smallest boroughs in London, with a population of 164,000. It is characterized by contrast, vitality and modern cultural diversity. Upper Street is home to the Business Design Centre (BDC) which separates two distinct shopping areas. On one side towards Angel, there is the high street – multiple chains, which are easily recognizable. On the other, towards Highbury and Islington there are independent retail outlets – very high in design content and product price. Charlie Allen is situated in the latter part at 186 Upper Street.

Renowned for its innovative window displays, the company changes them every 1–2 weeks. The windows of the shop front are curved with a tiled path. The window display area has a polished wooden floor with a backdrop of mirrors. Often done in conjunction with a company called Urban Roots, examples of displays include a window full of daffodils in spring, with a merchandised mannequin in the centre. Sometimes the window display is a piece of artwork combined with merchandise, such as the yes/no heads and two wooden/mechanical heads, shaking and nodding. Not only does this promote local art but also provides local artists with a place to sell their work.

Customer service

The bespoke service is as it was fifty years ago – the customer is made to feel important with personal attention and advice. Allen understands fully his craft, enabling him to provide an impeccable consultancy service to bespoke customers. The only problem is enabling customers to visualize a 3D-product prior to its construction.

Once the customer has the suit, it is more or less guaranteed for two years. Allen will even press the suit after its first dry-clean, out of courtesy. Repairs are part of the service. Merchandise can be exchanged if unsuitable, but there is no formal policy on returns and no set complaints procedures.

Assessing general service is also fundamental, as this is an asset which can differentiate a company from their competitors. Below are some questions that the company may need to ask about their general standard of service:

- Is the telephone answered in 3–4 rings?
- Is there somewhere for clients to rest?
- Are the staff attentive?
- Are products guaranteed?
- Are customers served immediately?
- Are individual complaints handled effectively and efficiently?
- Are refreshments offered to bespoke customers?

It would also be advantageous for the company to have a complaints book to log all complaints, so they could be prevented from recurring. This will help the company assess in the short term what customers expect. 'However, it must be remembered that for every customer who is dissatisfied and complains, there are many who are equally dissatisfied yet, for reasons best known to themselves, they say nothing' (Lepparc and Molyneux, 1994).

Products as objects

Fabrics and patterns are sent to manufacturers who make a sample garment before the line goes into full production. Generally, fifty garments at a time is regarded the maximum, possibly in five styles. Allen himself checks quality control. It is a general check of the cut-make-trim (CMT).

Although visual defects are checked manually, garments or cloth are not checked for quality assurance. Performance characteristics are neither checked nor presented to the customer as a measure of quality. These include:

- shrinkage (BS 5807);
- colourfastness (BS 1006);
- dry cleaning/washing (BS 4961);
- durability and maintenance (BS 5807);
- other care characteristics;
- fire resistance.

It is not suggested that the company attempts to comply with British or European Standards. BS 5750 (ISO 9001) is often difficult in its application for companies, particularly of this size, to comply with. However, there is nothing to prevent the company producing its own standard based on BS/ISO 9000.

Products use

Clothing does what it is designed to (i.e. meet physiological requirements) and is easy to use by its very nature. Clothes are high in durability and are either maintained by mainly dry cleaning or machine washing. Care labels could be more informative. Comfort is the result of how the garment 'feels'. This is achieved by the use of quality fabrics and by producing well-cut garments.

The logo

The current logo, designed by Kall Kwik, has existed since the retail outlet opened in 1992. The 'Charlie Allen' name is reversed in a racing green rectangle. The font is Times New Roman, in large capitals. Although it is both classic and yet traditional, it does not represent the entire elements of the (wish image) company mission.

The logo appears on the letterhead, business cards, invoices, bags and leaflets. Other corporate elements that the logo does not appear on are the external signage and woven labels. There are two different woven labels used.

Observations on the logo are:

- The same paper type is not used throughout.
- On the bag the logo is enlarged. Because the bag is brown, the symbol takes on a slightly different appearance.
- Compliments slips and envelopes with the logo are not used (fax paper and PR paper are other considerations).
- Signage, packaging, labels and paper do not fit together as one image.
- The logo is not responsible for the company's identity – it represents it. The problem is in the foundations of the company so the logo simply represents this.
- The graphic logo is similar in colour and shape to that of a company called Racing Green.

Comparing competitors' brands

Graphical representation of international designer logos can be divided into:

- Names – the name of the designer (or company if there is no predominant designer) which symbolizes personal, as well as company values. For example, Calvin Klein and Yves Saint Laurent. Names are often abbreviated (e.g. CK and YSL), sometimes as an alternative graphic symbol, other times to represent a diffusion line.
- Colour blocking – the best example is Tommy Hilfiger. His logo uses navy blue, red and white, the colours of the USA flag, which, to most,

is a symbol of quality. The symbol, together with the designer, suggests quality and pride in American cultural values.

•   Symbols are used to represent the company, and these have risen in popularity because only those 'in the know' can translate the symbolic message. Examples:

Burberry	Knight on a horse with a joust and flag
Mulberry	A tree
Margaret Howell	The walkers (a silhouette of 2 people)
Duffer of St. George	A crest
Armani	Abstract eagle
Ralph Lauren	(1) USA flag with RL
	(2) Coat of arms with RL
	(3) Polo player on a horse

When people know your name, they come back. When I started in 1967, there were no designers in America. Well, Pierre Cardin possibly, but he was French. Men would not wear a name: they would wear a brand. So instead of putting a name on my clothes, I used a polo player. It connotated sophisticated, sport … stylish people … Then three or four years later, when designers became popular, I added my name to it.

(Dunn, 1996)

Allen's direct competitors use the following:

Timothy Everest	Name
John Pearse	Name
Ken Odimah	Graphic logo (due to change)
Mark Powell	Name and crest/shield
Oswald Boateng	Name and tailoring stand; alone, with wings or with a snake

What is most important is that a brand must gain recognition over time and establish itself to gain the maximum amount of credibility.

The design brief

There will be many organizations where there is no formal structure for either introducing or maintaining an identity programme. In such companies it is necessary to create a corporate identity formally, so that it can be introduced and disseminated throughout the organization. The work of creating an identity can be conveniently divided into the following phases:

1   Investigation and analysis leading to development of design brief.

2   Creation of a new visual identity incorporating, where appropriate, name changes and visual ideas based on the organization's agreed personality, strategy and structure.
3   Launch and introduction of the programme.
4   Implementation of identity across all areas of the organization in product environment and communications (Olins, 1990).

The whole visual identity for Charlie Allen Menswear must focus on the mission statement and portraying the customer's lifestyle. It is also import-ant for the visual identity to appear to be established. It is therefore rec-ommended that the visual identity focuses on an existing work of art – symbolizing the elements for the company logo. The company would need to research sculptures/statues in the public arena to see which ones rep-resent:

- affluence;
- modern classics;
- visually aesthetic elements;
- pleasure;
- traditional values;
- art.

By selecting an artistic work from a public place, it will already be recog-nizable and established. Graphic designers or artists will translate it from something classic to modern classic by its modern reinterpretation.

   It is important that the chosen sculpture is reinterpreted as a work of art such as a painting before it is symbolized into a graphic logo. It may be advantageous for the company to employ both an artist and graphic designer for the project.

Elements of a design brief

Background

This would include the company and customer profile, market and struc-ture. It would focus on the company mission as the problem. All this information could be condensed from the audit.

The problem

How to represent the company mission and customer lifestyle successfully. Acknowledging that research has shown the existing logo/symbols to be ineffective in communicating with customers and other audiences.

Project scope and objectives

The solution will be a visual logo comprising a symbol and the company name. Design is expected to communicate the elements of the company mission and suggest a distinct lifestyle. The overall aim is to visualize the promise the company has made to the consumer.

Statement of requirements

- A series of paintings/drawings of the sculpture the company has chosen to represent it.
- A final artistic representation.
- A series of logos comprising the company's name and symbol (cf the artists' representation of the chosen sculpture).
- Final bromide of the new logo.

Design objectives – aesthetics

Clarification of things to be expressed in abstract terms: affluence, classic (modern classic), quality, pleasure, tradition and art. The design work should represent the affluent lifestyle of professionals – the existing customer. While retaining a traditional feel, slightly reminiscent of 1940s' England, the design work should also represent modern classics The designs should aim to evoke pleasure from the senses of sight and touch.

Design guidelines and specifications

These are standards to which the symbol must be designed. First, the existing signature trademark should be considered in some of the design solutions presented. Second, there should be a maximum of three colours used in any one design.

Contractual elements

The company will make four payments on completion of each of the statement of requirements. An agreed sum will be paid rather than an hourly rate. The company will automatically receive all design rights and copyright ownership of all design work.

Constraints and priorities

The name Charlie Allen should not be abbreviated to CA, but can be abbreviated to C. Allen.

Design criteria

It must be possible to reproduce the logo on a variety of materials (from metal to woven labels) without the loss of visual clarity. Designers should consider what the design will look like on buttons, to fragrance bottles.

Organizations and authorities

The final design should be registered as a trademark.

Processes

- Company brief and consultancy brief – agreed contract.
- 1st meeting and initial brief including the company is choice of sculpture.
- 2nd meeting and set of paintings/drawings for the selection process.
- 3rd meeting and final painting/drawing – briefing for the logo.
- 4th meeting and design options/solutions for the logo.
- Focus groups and testing to help make the final decision.
- 5th meeting and company's final choice with specified alterations.
- Final design work and project completion.

Completion requirements

The company will expect a bromide with measurements, colour codes, font types, sizes and weights, showing exact dimensions and printing techniques; plus, all development work.

The audit

Auditing design and service

The scale was constructed by taking key words from the company mission, finding associated words and meanings, then devising questions to assess if these qualities exist within design elements (see Table 5.10).

The evaluation results highlighted in Figure 5.9 suggest the following:

- Bespoke customer service, visual merchandising and the logo are not as strong as the other design elements.
- The interiors, window display and products are the company's strengths. These need to be maintained and constantly improved through innovation.
- The weaker business element seem so because they are generally not original or as innovative as the stronger areas. They do not represent the wish image as the other areas do. In order for a redeveloped corporate identity to be effective, these areas must be improved.

Table 5.10 Evaluating design scale

Rating scale	No 0	Rarely 1	Sometimes 2	Often 3	Yes 4	
Quality	Window display	Interiors	Product design	Corporate identity	Bespoke service	Visual merchandising
Is it of the highest standard the company could achieve?	4	3	3	1	2	2
Is it ever validated?	3	4	3	1	3	2
Does it conform to users' needs?	3	4	3	1	3	2
Is its design ever reviewed?	4	1	3	1	1	3
Is its presentation distinctive?	4	4	2	2	2	2
Have any employees been formally trained to maintain it?	4	2	4	0	4	1
Is design coherent?	4	4	3	0	3	2
Total of a possible 24	23	18	18	5	15	12
Modern classic						
Is design ageless?	2	4	3	3	3	0
Is design definitive?	3	4	3	2	1	2
Is design traditional?	2	4	3	3	3	2
Are there elements and characteristics of the present?	4	4	4	0	3	4
Is design open to modern reinterpretation?	3	4	3	1	3	2
Is design consistent?	2	4	3	0	4	2
Does its design seem established?	2	4	3	3	2	2
Is it original?	4	4	3	1	0	1
Total out of a possible 32	22	32	25	13	19	15
Pleasure and comfort Does design gratify the senses; sight, sound and touch?	4	3	2	1	1	1
Can its design be enjoyed?	4	3	4	2	3	2
Is satisfaction derived from ideas?	3	4	3	1	2	2
Is its design relative to the customers' lifestyle?	3	4	4	3	4	3
Are customers' esteem needs met?	4	3	4	1	3	2
Can design put customers at ease both physically and mentally?	2	3	3	1	4	2
Does design appear to be a luxury?	4	4	4	0	4	2
Does it suggest wealth/affluence?	4	4	3	3	3	3
Total out of a possible 32	28	28	27	12	24	17
Overall totals out of a possible 88	73	78	70	30	58	44

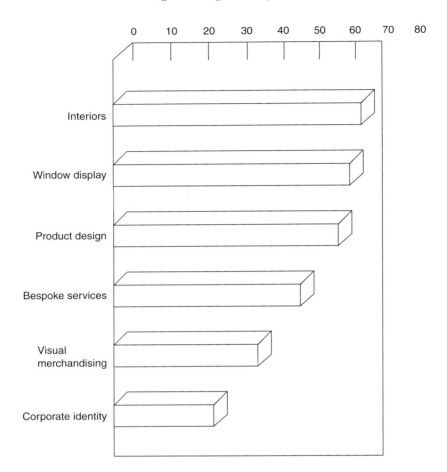

Figure 5.9 How the design elements performed on the evaluation scale

• Visual merchandising, bespoke customer service and the logo need to be works of art – original in thought, visually suggesting classic quality while evoking pleasure and comfort to the observer.

The bespoke customer questionnaire

A questionnaire was administered to assist the company develop its customer knowledge and to establish what the brand image is. Consumer research evaluates the existing brand image. It can be used to measure design capability as only the customer can sufficiently evaluate what they want with what they are receiving.

A postal questionnaire was issued to ninety-two bespoke customers, who had tailored garments made between 1994–6. This sample was selected from company files and thirty-seven questionnaires were returned. Some factors need to be considered when assessing results:

- A certain 'type' of customer may not have returned the questionnaire, e.g. those unhappy with the service. Another reason may have been the length of the questionnaire.
- There were some limitations with question design. A question should have asked how customers initially found out about the company.
- The rating scale described the logo in terms of 'the bag' where the graphic appears largest. Some bespoke customers had not seen it.

The questionnaire measures the customer base and their opinions, therefore the overall results are considered valid and significant to any recommendations made. In this instance, significance can only be measured by the meaningfulness of results. It cannot be verified by inferential statistics because the sample size is too small.

Customer profile statistics

Table 5.11 outlines the customer, who can typically be described as married, between 30–39 and in the socio-economic groups A and B. A high proportion are artists and designers which corresponds with how the company would like to be seen, that is to say as having a strong association with the arts.

Press information has highlighted that the New Tailors have contributed to making bespoke tailoring fashionable. With this comes the possibility of new markets, which Table 5.11 highlights are not being exploited.

Table 5.11 Customer profile statistics

Ethnic group	(%)	Socio-economic status (AB*)	(%)
White	86	Managerial	25
Black (Caribbean, African and mixed)	14	Professional	30.5
		Artists and designers	33.5
		Technical	11
Customer age		Marital status	
19–29	8	Single	22
30–39	68	With partner	11
40–49	8	Engaged	3
50–59	8	Married	59
60 and over	8	Divorced	5

Customer lifestyle

Some 64 per cent of customers read style magazines, highlighting that men have become more fashion conscious and 61 per cent of customers enjoy shopping implying that 39 per cent need buying motivation from design. The majority of customers do not let anyone else purchase their clothes even though only 8 per cent are single.

Their favourite leisure activities include walking, training, swimming and running. Walking being the most popular pastime, this is a consideration for garment designing and footwear stocks. Contrary to social trends information connected to this market segment, the majority would prefer to visit the cinema than the theatre.

Customer characteristics

Quality of clothing is the most important characteristic for customers, which often leads to word-of-mouth recommendations – free publicity. This is illustrated in Table 5.12.

What is apparent is that not one customer believed the company's pricing point is reasonable. Quality should be of value, therefore the customer should believe that the price is good for the quality that they are receiving. Since 78 per cent of customers said they would be using the company again, it suggests the pricing point is not a dominant problem but does need attention. Therefore pricing should either be maintained over time or reduced for promotional techniques.

Over 50 per cent of garments were purchased for work or a work-related event. The company assumed that a large percentage of revenue came from weddings, this may be true, but statistics show work as a primary reason. This could be translated to extending trading hours to Sunday, therefore being more convenient for his customers. Some 89 per cent of customers wear their garments often or occasionally. This is a significant total considering in some cases the purchase was over two years ago.

The two product design elements customers were happy with the most were the cut of the garment and the design detailing (design lines, pockets, buttons, etc.).

Table 5.12 Reasons why customers chose Charlie Allen Menswear

Reason	(%)
Quality of clothing	43
Recommended by a friend/relative	26
Reasonable price	0
Convenient location	9.5
Appearance of the shop	9.5
An advert	7
Knows Charlie Allen	5

The two main reasons why customers have bespoke clothing made is because of the quality of bespoke; and because it is hard to find ready-to-wear suits that fit well. These are the elements that should transcend into collections and in-store ranges. Expanding the sizing range over time can solve the last point.

Some 24 per cent of customers use other tailors and 53 per cent do not purchase ready-to-wear from Charlie Allen's, and that suggests selective loyalty. The latter figure is cause for some concern, in particular. The top three stores for ready-to-wear purchases are:

- Paul Smith, a British designer;
- Marks & Spencer for quality and value;
- Armani, an international designer renowned for his suits.

These companies are distinctive and established for different attributes and features. It seems to suggest that because Charlie Allen's ready-to-wear is neither distinctive or established and has not been able to define its attributes – customers for ready-to-wear are being lost.

Customer service

Over half of his customers are happy with the service, but some concerns were expressed where garments were not ready for the agreed date promised and there were functional problems with garments. Cross-tabulation shows that of the 27 per cent of the customers who thought the service could have been far better, half would be using the company again and half were unsure. This suggests that although it is recognized that bad service is not intentional, it does affect possible repeat purchase. Over a period of time, this figure could significantly damage turnover. The first objective is to establish a channel of communication about service and a complaints system.

Some 78 per cent of customers will be using the company again, of which 22 per cent were unsure. What is positive is that no customers said that they definitely would not be using the company again, which means that those unsure can be motivated to purchase.

Brand image

Some 72 per cent of customers do not mind people knowing where they got their clothes from but 47 per cent do mind if the brand name is on the outside of a garment (see Table 5.13). This highlights some significant figures since it was assumed that with trends in the fashion industry, external labelling would be more popular. Overall, 53 per cent of customers were not opposed to brand labelling. The majority preferred labelling to be kept discreet. Any brand strategy must take this into account. By

Table 5.13 Opinions on brand labelling

Do you mind if the brand label is on the outside of a garment?	*(%)*
Yes	47
No, if discreet	44
No	3
Don't mind	6

putting a label on the outside of a garment, the company could lose 45 per cent of its potential customers.

Some 97 per cent of customers like the current image, 3 per cent did not mind. No one was either opposed to it or thought it needed changing. It can be concluded that the overall image is effective and the company's attention must now be directed to details.

The design areas which customers show as giving cause for concern are the merchandising of clothing, then the graphical elements – trademark and logo. It can be concluded they are not coherent enough in what they are trying to communicate, as it was possible for all elements to achieve maximum points equally. Customers need to be incorporated into any design decisions made by being given the opportunity to comment.

Compared to the evaluation scale based on the wish image, customers place clothing quality in higher regard than the window display. Merchandising is thought to be less effective than the logo. But there is a general consensus that merchandising and the corporate/brand identity need attention. The questionnaire provides evidence that supports the evaluation scale.

Targeting new customers

Every product class has the potential of attracting buyers who are unaware of the product (Kotler, 1994). Attracting new customers and heightening customer awareness can eventually increase market share. For a small business, its location and areas close in proximity may hold potential customers. For Allen, potential lies in those that either live or work within Islington and surrounding areas. The 1991 Census Information for the London Borough of Islington reveals the following statistics:

* 81 per cent of the population are white, 10.6 per cent are black.
* 21.7 per cent are aged between 25–34.
* 25 per cent of the borough's population are in the socio-economic groups A–B.
* The majority of residents work in the banking/finance industry.

The last point led to a pilot questionnaire being issued to a large banking institution to assess awareness of the company.

The census information indicated that there are 40,007 people (about 25 per cent) within the same socio-economic groups of Allen's clientele (A and B). But this information does not tell how they can be reached or if they are viable markets. However, the postcode targeter of Great Britain divides Britain into postcodes. Each postcode area is then sub-divided into population figures, twelve lifestages and affluence categories.

The postcode areas all indicated index numbers over 100. The targeter states that if the index is over 100 (the national average), that sector has a higher than average amount of members in that category. In this case the category – socio-economic group A–B is cross-tabulated with the lifestage that most of that category is in. The postcode area N1 is inserted as a comparison because that is where the company is situated (see Table 5.14).

Based on the customer profile described in the questionnaire results, the potential for Charlie Allen lies in the lifestage category 3: Adults 25–34 without dependent children under 16 (lifestage 3). When Table 5.14 is analysed in conjunction with the geo-demographic map of bespoke customers, most of the existing customers are in the postcode areas N1 (fifty-one customers) and N5 (twenty-four customers).

While N1 is beginning to target customers, N5 does not seem to be using its full potential. Because the index number is over 100 (the national average) and the main lifestage indices is 3, this is a significant sector. All areas of N5 and N6 could be successfully targeted by direct mailing. Names and addresses can be obtained from list builders.

The City (EC1) holds potential customers from people that work in the area. A geo-demographic map needs to be constructed of companies in the City to enable marketing strategies to be developed. Although direct

Table 5.14 Postcodes, socio-economic groups and lifestyle

Geographic location	Indices for the socio-economic groups A–B	Lifestage indices*
N1	153	3
N3	200	1
N5	126	3
N5	116	3
N6	209	3
N6	215	3
N6	202	3
N10	203	3
N12	270	10
N20	260	10

Source: The postcode targeter of Great Britain.

Notes:
*The lifestages listed in column 3:
 1 Aged 16–24 without dependent children under 16
 3 Aged 25–34 without dependent children under 16
10 55–retirement age working or retired

mailing is not a traditional method of advertising for the company, it is more cost effective than advertising in style magazines.

The Royal Bank of Scotland pilot questionnaire

A pilot questionnaire was issued to the Royal Bank of Scotland (Unit Trust & Product Development departments), which is also on Upper Street, Islington, in close proximity to the company. This was to assess awareness about the company and use of bespoke tailoring. The main findings were:

- 93 per cent of the employees questioned wear suits instead of smart separates.
- 38 per cent of the sample have had bespoke garments made. However, this figure had no significant association with income. Bespoke users' income brackets varied from £15,000–£29,999. Which indicates that expanded markets should possibly be targeted by profession/status and not income.
- The majority of the sample spends between £20–£39 on a shirt for work, slightly more money is spent on a shirt for social occasions, £40–£59 being the average. In line with the company's pricing points, this suggests small purchases such as shirts are the best ways to attract customers and motivate them to spend more.
- 7 per cent of respondents were opposed to external labelling, the majority preferring discreet labelling.
- 93 per cent of respondents have never heard of Charlie Allen, which is within walking distance. This was the most significant figure as it is evidence of an extreme lack of consumer awareness.

Recommendations

The audit has assessed how resources match with the requirements. The foundation of these requirements is stated in the company mission, which has been translated by the research into an overall strategy. The audit recommends a schedule of activities to be actioned over four years: design strategy should be towards brand development and the schedule of activities should have strategy implications. The strategy must take the following into account: the timescale, budget, resources and amount of change, although the actual budget will have to be agreed upon by management themselves. The strategy should be re-assessed annually upon the monitoring of activities and projects. This is important because of the rate of change characteristic of the industry.

In order for any strategy to be successful within the company, Allen needs to delegate responsibilities to enable him concentrate on the management of design. The reformed practices and procedures need to be documented. Design work needs to be documented, duplicated and copy-righted. Individual projects need to be documented as with written contracts.

Needless to say, this has strict legal implications but it will also allow the company to adapt to change and growth. As management control is decentralized, the vision should be slowly implemented into the company's culture and personality in an organized fashion.

By having a procedures manual there would be no confusion about company expectations and direction internally, which can then be projected outward to external audiences through the Charlie Allen brand.

Figure 5.10 illustrates how the information researched in the main body of the audit led to the formulation of the brand development strategy. This is based on a combination of the brand identifying and projecting the lifestyle that a consumer may wish to express (Cooper and Press, 1995) and the lifestyle the company wishes to offer. The two should be very closely interrelated. Market research and consumer research have revealed what trends that are happening, what consumers do and buy and what they think they want. The design conclusions from this research should transcend those expectations offering new options for their wants and needs. By differentiating from what already exists in the market/industry, the company will create an advantage for itself on which to build.

Table 5.15 is a schedule of activities and projects which need to be completed to develop the brand. A strategy cannot simply suggest a redeveloped visual identity, associated company elements must be addressed. It has a series of recommendations over a four-year period, parts are interrelated, therefore timing is crucial. For example, promotional direct mailing cannot commence until the redeveloped brand logo/designer label is completed. This cannot be completed without customer feedback and testing. Recommendations for change take into consideration the size of the company and budget restrictions. However, this is only a preliminary schedule. A more detailed plan will be needed as projects are undertaken and budgets are allocated.

The main priority of this strategy is to create a visual identity as this represents the company – symbolizing all the things discussed. The logo and company name can literally make or break a company. This is particularly true of the fashion industry. Many problems arise in designing a logo because of poor communication between what the company wants and what the designer thinks the company wants.

Range extensions

Rather than trying to diffuse bespoke or trying to offer a faster turnaround time as competitors do, it may be easier to educate the younger consumer to wait for quality. Reverting back to traditional methods may be fashionable again.

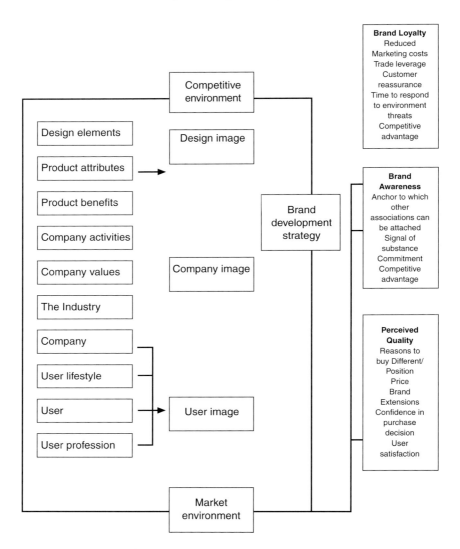

Figure 5.10 Formulation of the brand development strategy

Source: Adapted from Safari (1996), Aaker (1991)

   Made-to-measure shirts cost the company £40–£50 to produce and cost the consumer anything from £90–£120. Research shows that ready-to-wear shirts with designer labels such as Ralph Lauren and YSL retail at £100–£200 which means a bespoke shirt is cheaper in comparison.

   The company can offer a personally designed shirt in any fabric, except leather. If promotion concentrates on advertising the design input the consumer has – the cut and fit, and bespoke quality – these product attributes

Table 5.15 Schedule of activities to develop the brand

	Action now	1997	1997	1998	1998	1999	1999	2000	2000
Creating a visual brand identity	Choosing designers to undertake work. Finalizing the design brief	Design work, focus group testing and final project requirements	Launch and implementation and the new visual identity	Monitoring and management of the brand and its representation on all company material	Assessment of the messages it transmits to and receives from its audiences	Redevelop design work for brand extension ranges (year 2000) and international markets	Considering what the logo will appear on, but also the overall corporate visual image		
Customer service improvements	Customer complaints log. Format should separate bespoke and ready to wear	Complaints procedure – who and how will problems be dealt with	Service/ loyalty cards which allow bespoke customers 2 free pressings	Formal returns and refunds policy to be documented for internal and external use	This should include information on customers rights, etc.	Quality control procedures to be set in place and formally documented		The key to quality service is to document that form company guidelines	Procedures have been documented over time – a manual should be established
Visual merchandising and restructuring	Re-assessment of the current format. Staff and client feedback	The addition of fixtures and fittings. Lighting improvements	Periodical distinctive in-store merchandise displays	Art collection schedule constructed and implemented to correspond with in-store displays		→ Merchandising considerations for the new store, based on existing company image		These could possibly be adapted	

Table 5.15 continued

	Action now	1997	1997	1998	1998	1999	1999	2000	2000
Product development	Focus on building good-will relations with suppliers for the bespoke shirt project	Development and production of an in-store collection	The construction of 3 specialized shirting ranges: classic, contemporary and opulents	Also pay attention to trouser and tie designs	Formalize design procedures. Set up a direct manufacturing base	International collections	Start to expand the range of sizes	Design accessory range of brand extensions →	
Diffusion			The use of the logo on garment fastenings and discreet external labels.	←—— Establishing the brand ——→		Brand extension planning – development of a fragrance to be launched 2001		Start to diffuse the name by developing cheaper ranges with semi-discreet labelling	
Promotion	Keep a visual log of window displays. Create customer database	Select a PA responsible for project management and PR work	Promotion of bespoke shirts to a wider audience. Promote London collection	Concentrate on press coverage and editorials	Periodicals price incentives and loyalty incentives	The promotion of Charlie Allen's return to the catwalk	Advertise the company in London underground stations	A stronger advertising campaign as extending and diffusing the brand begins	Use famous clients and artists who personify the brand and lifestyle
Expanded markets	Open Sundays for some bespoke fittings and admin work	Production of a geo-demographic map of businesses	Direct mailing to N5 and N6 districts	Develop selective concessions in department stores	Export products to Japan and Hong Kong	Expansion into America	Increase concessions in London ready for next launch	Opening of the Charlie Allen ready-to-wear outlet in London	Islington premises reserved for bespoke only

and benefits will outweigh the four weeks' waiting time (which could be reduced as business improves).

It is suggested that shirt ranges are divided into three distinct ranges to coincide with expansion of stock. This is to give design direction and to meet with customer requirements. Shirts can accompany suits or separates, making up the basics of a man's wardrobe.

Whereas suits, jackets and trousers are designed in-house, shirts are designed and bought in. This may be the reason why the overall range seems to lack both distinction and direction. The customer does not know what 'type' of shirt to consistently expect from the company.

It is suggested that ranges are divided into three distinct types:

- Classics: traditional styles with modern styling designed for business and formal occasions. This would include considerable amounts of white fabrics, stripes and classic colours and include both button and traditional cuffs. Distinction would be translated through classic design lines and fabric quality. Prices starting at £40.
- Contemporary: season's colours are the main feature in fabrics which are original/technological. These are intended for casual wear. This range may include a discreet label on the centre back yoke but should not include labels on the front breast. This is because this type of labelling is commonplace. Price range would generally start at £70
- Opulents: the use of patterned fabrics, linings and unusual fabrics are the focus of this range. Shirts should 'feel' expensive. Design will particularly focus on variations in pockets, cuff, collar types and size. These will be more flamboyant in design for special occasions. The aim of this range is to provide products with a strong artistic element to tie in with the company mission. This will be a smaller range with prices starting at £100.

The company should look to expand sizes only after an annual assessment of the range's sale performance and customer feedback.

The company has successfully made trouser designs distinctive through the cut, fabrics and design lines. Over time sizes need to be expanded. The merchandising of trousers need to be re-designed as their design benefits are often lost among shirts and jackets on rails. The company should aim for more press coverage of trousers in particular, as they are a strong product.

Displays and shop layout

The overall shop layout needs reassessment in terms of product merchandising. It's important for merchandise to be displayed in the centre of the store to break up the linear appearance of the shop. In-store displays need to be as innovative as the window displays, clothing needs to be more visual. Specific recommendations for merchandising depends on the allocated budget and the effect refurbishment would have on daily retailing.

Conclusion

The research contained within this section provides an in-sight into a relatively new industrial sector: the New Tailors. For them, branding has become an important device to differentiate themselves, as many of their business elements are similar. It is used to create positive perceptions in the mind of their various audiences.

The audit also provides information about the working mechanics of a brand within a company. The openness and honesty of Charlie Allen Menswear allowed an in-depth look into how fashion branding works. The analysis enabled the brand to be described, assessed and re-developed, providing qualitative information to the subject. This was from the combined perspectives of the company and its customers, whereas existing research is typically from one perspective. The aim was to show how the interaction of perceptions affected the brand.

The study supports existing literature, in that the brand has to be a combination of company and consumer values. An associated or aspirational lifestyle combined with the company is the ideal brand identity. The aim of the brand development strategy was to enable the brand to present itself as offering something different from competitors and to attempt to attract new customers. Within a business setting, as proven here, branding adds value. This is fundamental if it is to be of any use.

The literature review verifies the value a brand can give to products and the company. Allen's original brand was identified through auditing the organization and its design, and the customer questionnaire was associated with some of these attributes, but these were not fully exploited to their full potential or marketed as a consistent and coherent brand. The analysis was similar to that of Moore (1995) in that findings could have been divided into both utilitarian and symbolic dimensions.

Recommendations decided that the company should focus and market the brand as a designer label (rather than a national label). Any brand, as other studies have illustrated, can bring perceived quality, but it would seem that the designer label instils the most positive perceptions: status, fashionability and positive inferences. Another benefit for the company at least is that people expect to pay more for designer labels.

It was important that the four-year plan aims to increase brand awareness, as it has been significantly related to perceived quality. But the product had to be of a high standard initially for this to work. Although positive perceptions are instilled by branding, these are created by a combination of all intrinsic, extrinsic, tangible and intangible elements.

Brand symbols have become increasingly visual in the past twenty years. External labelling has, in part, been influenced by diffusion. The diffusion for the Allen designer label was not recommended until the fourth year, when the brand was established.

Diffusion allows the lower classes to emulate the upper classes. It would appear the extent to which there is external labelling on a garment is directly related to how 'diffused' it is. This is supported by the fact that the upper class clientele of Charlie Allen only approve of discreet labelling, if any at all.

The recommended design brief and brand testing allow for the careful monitoring of design work for the visual identity, suggesting what should be used to visually represent the company. The suggestions for the symbol were intended to be exclusive, representing the company mission: affluence, modern classics, the visually aesthetic, quality, pleasure, tradition and art. It was recommended that an existing sculpture be represented as a 'work of art' painting. This painting would be graphically represented to symbolize the brand.

There is no doubt that the brand and its symbol are representative of the company's upper-class customer. The pricing points, classic garments, bespoke tailoring service and interiors all indicate this. The brand is fashion for the privileged people with a certain income or people aware of what bespoke is.

Classic and traditional suggest continuity, but 'modern classics' and other findings within the company suggest that if the company's fashions are for the upper classes, it is for a newly defined upper class, which would probably would not express itself as a class but rather a social or cultural group.

It could be said that fashion (modern classics) and art, which are embedded in the company mission, signify the desire for the company to change or redevelop itself from something old and traditional. Therefore, Charlie Allen's bespoke tailoring, fashions and brand symbolize both continuity and change simultaneously: tradition taking on a transformation. By association or aspiration, customers want to convey these messages and meanings in an aesthetic manner. They are aware of their origin, but want to transform themselves into something better, not necessarily higher.

The organizational analysis gave an in-depth insight into a fashion brand. Understanding fashion branding can provide manufacturers, retailers, marketers and designers with the ability to ascertain the future direction of the fashion industry. Fashion branding will become increasingly important to the customers to eliminate risk and as a symbol of reassurance. For companies this means increased awareness, loyalty, perceived quality and the chance to diffuse or create extensions of product offers.

Alternatives to experimental methodological research are needed on:

- fashion branding in the UK;
- relating the brand to human belongings, aesthetic and esteem needs;
- longitudinal studies of how fashion brands develop over time;
- looking at the brand diffusion process of designer wear.

Although the present study could have been a little more scientific in its approach, it does highlight a modest and potentially significant industrial sector. The audit has the potential to make Charlie Allen an internationally renowned designer in the future.

Review questions

1 Charlie Allen is a prominent member of the 'New Tailors' in the UK today, can you name the other six?
2 The Charlie Allen brand is focused primarily on the Managing Director and owner of the company. What possible drawbacks can you foresee when the company expands or adopts a new management style?
3 What are the most commonly used promotional tools employed by Charlie Allen? Are they successful enough to maintain and attract new clients?
4 What are the advantages of market segmentation? Would mass marketing be appropriate for Charlie Allen?
5 Charlie Allen has a clear business mission statement. How does this help him when developing his branding strategy?
6 What are the advantages and disadvantages of branding?
7 Why is it difficult to develop a product range with lasting success in the fashion industry?
8 What significant external forces in the marketplace influence present and potential client needs?
9 Is price the only factor in attracting clients in the bespoke tailoring marketplace? Can you identify and discuss other factors involved?
10 How important is it for Charlie Allen to design an interior that reflects the ethos of his approach to tailoring? Discuss in more detail the role of branded interiors, perhaps identifying major retailers who rely heavily on branding.

Project questions

1 Devise a non-visual description of the Charlie Allen brand alongside a new suitable logo. In particular, identifying the Charlie Allen brand to new customers may require new policies. Consider particularly the 'design elements' shown in Table 5.10.
2 In consideration of Charlie Allen's current press coverage, what key policies now need to be put in place to maintain the market position as well as develop the company towards younger clients?
3 The audit attempts to match marketing theories with policies in design. Develop a marketing plan for the company which takes into account design potential and the theoretical description of consumers and their lifestyle and location.

4   Devise a short questionnaire for customers. This should concentrate on current lifestyle and design issues but be capable of being used annually. This may be then transferred to a collaborative piece of research with an equivalent to Charlie Allen Menswear.
5   Specify an IT-based style brief descriptor which would enable a new customer of Charlie Allen to negotiate an order.

References

Aaker, A.D. (1991) *Managing Brand Equity. Capitalising on the Value of a Brand Name*, New York: The Free Press.

Barnard, D. (1996) *Fashion as Communication*, London: Routledge.

Baugh, D.F. and Davis, L.L. (1989) 'The effect of store image on consumers' perceptions of designer and private label clothing', *Clothing and Textiles Research Journal*, 7 (3), p. 15.

Behling, D. and Wilch, J. (1988) 'Perceptions of branded clothing by male consumers', *Clothing and Textiles Research Journal*, 6 (2), p. 46.

Chenoune, F. (1993) *A History of Men's Fashion*, Paris: Flammarion.

Cooper, R. and Press, M. (1995) *The Design Agenda*, Chichester: John Wiley & Sons.

Davis, F. (1992) *Fashion, Culture and Identity*, Chicago: University of Chicago Press.

Dunn, B. (1996) 'Lauren to himself', *GQ*, April, p. 157.

Feldwick, P. (1991) 'Defining a brand', in D. Cowley (ed.) *Understanding Brands*, London: Kogan Page, pp. 19–28.

Forsythe, S.M. (1991) 'Effect of private, designer and national brand names on shoppers' perception of apparel quality and price', *Clothing & Textiles Research Journal*, 9 (2), 1–6.

Goffee, R. and Scase, R. (1995) *Corporate Realities*, London: Routledge.

Huddleston, P., Cassill, N. and Hamilton, L. (1993) 'Apparel selection criteria as predictors of brand orientation', *Clothing & Textiles Research Journal*, 12 (1), 51–6.

Ind, N. (1990) *The Corporate Image*, London: Kogan Page.

Jones, D. (1996) 'Paul Smith', *Arena*, March, p. 134.

Kaiser, S. (1990) *The Social Psychology of Clothing: Symbolic Appearances in Context*, 2nd edition New York: Macmillan.

Kotler, P. (1994) *Marketing Management: Analysis, Planning, Implementation and Control*, 8th edition London: Prentice-Hall.

Lennon, S.J. (1986) 'Adolescent attitudes towards designers jeans', *Adolescence*, 21 (82), 475–82.

Leppard, J. and Molyneux, L. (1994) *Auditing your Consumer Service*, London: Routledge.

Lewis, B.R. and Hawksley, A.W. (1990) 'Gaining a competitive advantage in fashion retailing', *International Journal of Retail and Distribution Management*, 18 (4), 21.

Lurie, A. (1992) *The Language of Clothes*, London: Bloomsbury.

Memorandum of Association (Appendix B) p1, Section 3(a), Companies House. Charlie Allen Menswear – Company Business Plan, Draft 2.1.

Moganosky, M.A. (1990) 'Store and brand type influences on the perception of apparel quality: a congruity theory approach', *Clothing and Textiles Research Journal*, 9 (1), p. 46.

Moore, C.M. (1995) 'From rags to riches – creating and benefiting from the fashion own brand', *International Journal of Retail & Distribution Management*, 23 (9), 23.

Morgado, M.A. (1990) 'Animal trademark emblems on fashion apparel: a semiotics interpretation', (Part 2, Applied Semiotics) *Clothing and Textile Research Journal*, 11 (3), 36.

Olins, W. (1990) 'Corporate identity', in M. Oakley (ed.) *Design Management: A Handbook of Issues and Methods*, Oxford: Blackwell.

Partington, A. (1992) 'Popular fashion and working class affluence', in J. Ash and E. Wilson (eds) *Chic Thrills: A Fashion Reader*, London: Pandora Press.

Safavi, F. (1996) 'Winning the battle of corporate/brand images: an image focused model for selection of names and logo's', *Journal of Brand Management*, 3 (6), 382.

Sorensen, C. (1995) 'The fashion market and the marketing environment', in M. Easy (ed.) *Fashion Marketing*, Oxford: Blackwell Science.

Sproles, G. and Burns, L.D. (1994) *Changing Appearances: Understanding Dress in Contemporary Society*, New York: Fairchild, p. 7.

UK Marketing Guides (1995) *Postcode Targeter of Great Britain: A Guide to Postcode Sector Marketing*, (vols 1 and 2), London: HarperCollins.

Williams, J. (1996a) 'In the marketplace with the New Tailors', *He Lines*, June, 25, 45.

Williams, J. (1996b) 'Oswald Boateng', *He Lines*, June, 25, p. 26.

Wilson, (1982), *Marketing Audit Checklists*, Maidenhead, Berks: McGraw-Hill.

Workman, J.E. (1988) 'Trait inferences based on perceived ownership of designer, brand name or store brand jeans', *Clothing & Textile Research Journal*, 6 (2), 23–9.

Yusuf, N. (1993) 'Continental Drift', *Sunday Times*, 13 June.

Further reading

Atkinson, S. (1995) 'Designing and marketing fashion products', in M. Easy (ed.) *Fashion Marketing*, Oxford: Blackwell Science.

Coolican, H. (1990) *Research Methods and Statistics in Psychology*, London: Hodder & Stoughton, pp. 98–100.

FAME – Financial Analysis Made Easy (1996).

Keynote report: *Clothing Retailing* (1994).

Lydiate, H. (1991) *Visual Arts and Crafts Guide to the New Laws of Copyright and Moral Rights*, London: Britannia Publications.

Mintel report: 'Men's outerwear', April 1993, p. 5.

Mintel report: 'Men's outerwear', April 1996, p. 21

Odiatu, A. (1995) 'Charlie Allen: back to basics', *Pride Magazine*, February–March, p. 58.

CASE STUDY 6

Managing design at Skopos

Company:	Skopos Design Ltd.
	Providence Mills
	Ecolsheaton
	Dewsbury
	WF12 8HT
Business:	Printed furnishing fabrics, wall coverings, interior accessories and furniture
Auditor:	*David Williamson*

Introduction

This case study is a communications audit in a company that has grown significantly to £25m turnover and a staff of 500 in twenty-four years. At the briefing for the researcher, it was suggested that there were communication 'problems' between the design department and other Skopos departments, and the company welcomed the audit.

The model of design process used by the company is a linear model that emphasizes the project management milestones: the communications audit concentrates on communications to manage the process. The research was divided into four areas: taking a snapshot of the company culture, highlighting questions that need to be addressed, gaining an insight into the attitudes, likes and dislikes of Skopos staff, and defining a basis for further audit research.

The company culture was described using a version of the method described by Hamilton (1987), to compile a Task, Relationship and Organization (TRO) chart. The method reveals a preference for Relationship Culture (a concern for personal interaction of people as people – interpersonal warmth or coldness), Task Culture (reflects the organization's concern for physical and measurable production output), or Organization Culture (reflects concern for the administrative function within an organization). This sample summary suggests that the company climate is relatively stable, with 'top-down' management style limiting interdepartmental communication and consultation with general staff.

Interviews with each member of Design Department staff were conducted to elicit evaluations of communication channels and source, destination and content of communications. Without exception, staff reported regular communication problems with other departments, but were satisfied with communications within the department.

Following the Design Department interviews, a list of key individuals with whom Design Department has the most contact was drawn up as potential respondents for a questionnaire compiled after considering a number of communication audit systems (ICA, Hamilton, LTT, OCD). The results are discussed question by question: in summary, while there was general agreement that there were communication problems, they were usually perceived as being the fault of someone else.

A network and content analysis provided quantitative data on communications traffic: this revealed the key role of the Design Director as a channel for information flow, sending, receiving and filtering information in such volume that a bottleneck could be created. Further interviews with Design Department staff revealed that despite the positively perceived elements such as face-to-face communication, friendliness and first-name terms, there was a feeling that some information was not getting through.

In other departments, it was perceived that Design Department was 'too distant', and that information passed through a senior member often can reach its destination in an incomplete state. On the positive side, there was revealed a desire for more interdepartmental meetings in order to improve what was perceived as an acceptable state of affairs.

Overall, Skopos can be regarded as a traditionally hierarchical company, with a top-down decision-making structure. This mitigated against efficiency for Design Department staff needing clarification or chasing work in other departments. The perception of Design, as being distant was not helped by the physical separation of the department from the others. The comprehensive recommendations are grouped for immediate, short-term and long-term consideration.

During the ten-week placement the auditor was based in the Skopos design studio which was useful in that it allowed the auditor to observe first-hand the working environment of the Design Department and the interaction that takes place within it. The auditor was allowed free access to all levels of staff within the department. Likewise, the auditor was given free access to communicate with individuals in other departments, either in person or via the telephone. A major drawback was that computer access was severely limited although this had initially been guaranteed. Overall, Skopos staff were generally approachable and co-operative. In all cases it was expressed to the auditor that the subject of the audit was appropriate and that findings would be welcomed.

Company profile

History

Skopos has grown into an organization currently employing approximately 500 staff and expecting annual turnover to be in the region of £25 million. The company was founded in 1973 by three art students in their first year after leaving the local Batley School of Art. The first designs were large-scale bold patterns printed by hand and were to prove popular for curtains in schools and public buildings. As the company grew, larger premises were sought and in 1976 rented accommodation was found in Batley and investment was made in two 50-metre printing tables. This allowed the company to print more colours and thus was able to produce designs and fabrics to suit a wider audience such as hotels, hospitals and the brewery trade.

In 1980 Skopos obtained its first export orders which coincided with a further move into larger premises at Earlsheaton in Dewsbury. At the same time the company replaced the hand-printing tables with automatic printers extending the colour range even further. Throughout the 1980s Skopos gradually added to their fabric ranges to include wall coverings, accessories and furniture. There are now sixteen UK retail outlets for Skopos products including showrooms in Paris and Atlanta and agents in most European countries, the Middle East and Australia.

Company philosophy

Skopos began as a design-led business and continues to see design as central to the ongoing success of the company. Stephen Battye, the Managing Director and founder member states:

> From the beginning, the Skopos team wanted to design and print innovative furnishing fabrics. The philosophy of the past twenty years has been to create the best possible designs, backed by service, and will continue to stand us in good stead for the future.
>
> (Battye, 1993, p. 2)

Skopos products and services

The range of products made by Skopos include: customized designs and colourways, Jacquard woven upholstery fabric, printed cottons, wallpapers, carpets, designs – florals to geometrics, polycotton bedspreads, upholstered furniture and pelmets/tiebacks.

The manufacturing processes at Skopos include: development printing, zimmer printing, computerized colour mixing, silk screen production, dyeing, colour prediction systems, cloth desizing and bleeding, foam application for pyrovatex and soil tests, inspection, washing and sterning.

The services available include: interior consultancy, design studio, cutting/sewing, curtain making, samples, quotation, scheme boards, installation, roadshows and educational visits.

Educational links

Skopos operates an Educational Support Programme to local schools and further afield by providing them with free boxes of fabric that can be used for collage work, sewing and quilting. In addition, school visits to Skopos are encouraged and provision is often made to concentrate on specific areas that might relate to school projects. Periodic placements are also offered to students from varying disciplines in higher education, particularly in the Design Department. This arrangement is seen to be mutually beneficial in that the student gains experience of how an in-house design studio operates and in return the company benefits from the new ideas and techniques the student brings.

The organization structure

Skopos has four Directors: Stephen Battye, Managing Director; Ivan Goldsmith, Design Director; Mark Astall, Operations Director; and Kathie Lee, Retail Director. The organization is broken down into the following main departments: Design, Production, Technical Services, Stores, Sales, Shipping, Retail, Accounts and General Administration (see Figure 6.1).

The brief

To conduct a communication audit on behalf of the Skopos Design Department and provide recommendations for improving communication between the Design Department and other departments.

The brief was formulated in negotiation with Ivan Goldsmith, Director and Head of Design at Skopos, and Brian Dickie, the design studio manager. Although it was difficult to be specific, the auditor was advised that there existed communication 'problems' between the Design Department and other Skopos departments and it was advised that any findings and recommendations that could be provided by the audit research would be welcomed.

The Design Department

Location and staff

The design studio is located on the top floor of Providence Mills overlooking the Skopos complex but is not physically joined to any other depart-

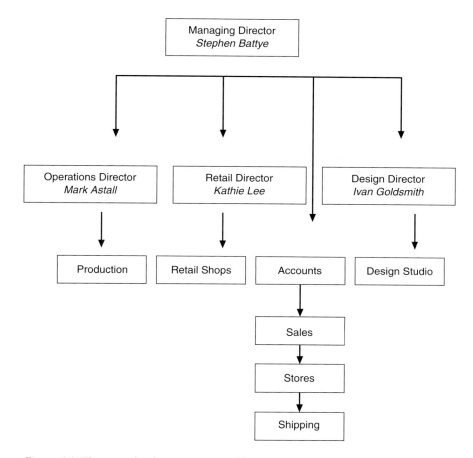

Figure 6.1 The organization structure at Skopos

ment. This is in contrast to most other departments who are located nearer to each other and are thus more conducive to person-to-person communication. The design studio is open plan. Each designer has their own workspace and telephone. Personal computers are restricted to the design director, the senior graphics designer and the design secretary.

There are thirteen members of staff in the Skopos Design Department, ten of whom are sited in the design studio itself.

- Ivan Goldsmith: Director and Head of Design;
- Brian Dickie: Design Studio Manager, Education Liaison;
- Fiona Shopland: Senior Designer, Surface Pattern, Forecasting;
- Deborah Franklin: Senior Designer, Separations and Colourways;
- Deborah Wheeler: Textile Designer, Co-ordinates;

- Karen Randall: Designer, Surface Pattern;
- Kate Jubb: Graphic Designer, Advertising, Company Literature;
- Elizabeth Higgins: Project Development Manager, Marketing, Exhibitions;
- Susan Snowden: Presentation Artist;
- Jennie Fawcett: Design Secretary.

Off site personnel are:

- Julie Cowan: Screen Printer;
- Sandra Burton: Print Development;
- Muriel Borthwick: Samples.

Job profile

The tasks and responsibilities for Design Department staff can be varied and are not exclusive to the individual's job title alone. For example, a surface pattern designer will also be called upon to assist in other design tasks when required such as research or exhibition set-up. A senior designer is even more likely to be multi-tasked – meetings with clients, forecasting collections, research exhibition design and photography – this is in addition to general clerical duties. The extent to which the Design Department staff are called upon to undertake other tasks will vary according to the time of year or if there is a need to have orders or collections finished to a specific deadline.

The design process

The design process at Skopos will usually commence with a written brief compiled by the Design Director in consultation with sales and marketing staff who will have reported on market trends and requests from clients. At each stage of the process the Design Director will have constant one-to-one contact with members of the team assigned to the project (see Figure 6.2).

Should a client require a new design, known as a 'special', then the Design Department will, with the exception of initial brief and final approval, adhere to the same design process as that outlined in Figure 6.2. Should the cost be prohibitive, negotiations are entered into between the Design Director and the client to see if existing Skopos designs can be amended or given a different colourway to meet the client's needs. In such cases, research, artwork and initial separation will not usually be undertaken, thus reducing the cost to the client.

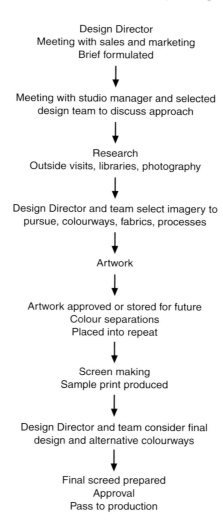

Design Director
Meeting with sales and marketing
Brief formulated

Meeting with studio manager and selected
design team to discuss approach

Research
Outside visits, libraries, photography

Design Director and team select imagery to
pursue, colourways, fabrics, processes

Artwork

Artwork approved or stored for future
Colour separations
Placed into repeat

Screen making
Sample print produced

Design Director and team consider final
design and alternative colourways

Final screed prepared
Approval
Pass to production

Figure 6.2 Internal brief procedure

Company culture

Skopos is an organization led by a board of four directors and formal communication is filtered downwards through the organization structure. In this respect the organizational structure may be regarded as hierachal and somewhat 'traditional' in that all major decision-making and work approval are made through department heads.

A communication audit of the entire organization would necessitate investigation of the formal and informal channels of communication for all departments and may initially require a communication auditor to undertake research into the 'culture' of the company so as to provide a basis for further research. For a medium-sized company such as Skopos, this type of research would involve targeting several people from each department, somewhere in the region of thirty, in order to obtain an accurate insight.

Although the focus of this communication audit is primarily Design Department based, it was still relevant to conduct research, albeit on a smaller scale, in order to obtain a better understanding of the organization. Research was undertaken to provide:

- an objective idea of company culture;
- questions that need to be addressed;
- an insight into the attitudes, likes and dislikes of Skopos staff;
- basis for further audit research.

A quick method of obtaining a 'snapshot' of a company's 'culture' is described by Hamilton (1987) whereby a representative focus group totalling six people are targeted for research. The method was adapted to provide data enabling a TRO (Task, Relationship, Organization) chart to be compiled. A TRO chart visually highlights disparity between personal views and perceived organization views on company culture and attitudes towards working methods. The method reveals preference for:

Relationship Culture   A concern for personal interaction of people as people. Interpersonal warmth or coldness.

Task Culture   Reflects the organization's concern for physical and measurable production output.

Organization Culture   Reflects concern for the administrative function within an organization.

The TRO method required the focus group to consist of:

- six people;
- an equal gender mix;
- each in a different department;
- each of different status.

The focus group selected at Skopos were:

1 A senior executive   Ivan Goldsmith (Director)
2 General admin   Joan Townend (Receptionist)
3 Mid-rank managerial   Ernie Cadamateri (Stores)
4 A technician   Anne Squire
5 A production worker   Michael Callaghan (Screens)
6 A designer   Sue Snowden (Pattern Books)

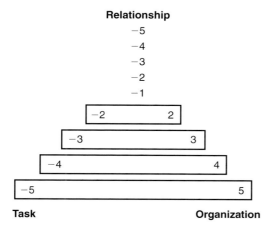

Figure 6.3 TRO chart

The focus group was each given a confidential TRO questionnaire to complete and return to the auditor. Data provided by the TRO questionnaire were analysed and from these a TRO chart was produced, as shown in Figure 6.3.

Interpretation of the TRO chart

The 'own perception' triangle represents the individual's own personal perception of the company culture. The 'organization' triangle represents how the individual believes the company perceives the organization. On the scale (5) relates to the greatest preference.

It is interesting to note that data analysis reveals an exact match for 'organization', but disparity exists where the respondent's own preference towards a relationship-based organization is greater than that of the perceived organizational view. Conversely, the perceived organization concern for production output is greater than the respondent's view. Generally, the less the two triangles overlap, the greater the conflict between the individual and the organization and it may be probable that individuals are experiencing a certain amount of stress at work. This would not appear to be the case from this sample, which for the purposes of this section will be presumed to be representative. The small amount of disparity that exists here can, to some degree, be expected in that production and output are likely to be of greater concern to the organization and working relationships of greater concern to the individual. Questions with the greatest disparity were:

What is made and done is more important than how it is achieved.
Own score 16   Organization score 24

Seniority is an important determinant in promotion.
> Own score 15   Organization score 22

To work effectively it is only necessary that people know what they must do.
> Own score 10   Organization score 21

On the basis of this sample focus group, this report finds that the company climate at Skopos can be said to be:

- relatively stable;
- led from the top – a 'traditional' hierarchical management;
- proof that communication and decision-making are filtered downwards through department heads;
- offering limited access to information outside own department;
- offering limited autonomy for general staff – little consultation.

These points provided a basis upon which to approach further stages of the audit.

Survey questionnaire

Methodology – focus groups

Time and resources dictated that a large-scale questionnaire survey of all Skopos Providence Mills employees would be impractical and in most cases not relevant. Interview 1 with Design Department staff identified the departments and individuals with which Design had the most frequent contact and a list of potential respondents was compiled and confirmed by the Design Director and Studio Manager (see Table 6.1). From this, key individuals with whom Design has the most contact was compiled and cross-checked with Design staff to confirm all relevant individuals had been included.

Table 6.1 Frequency of communication with Design Department

Department	Frequency of communication
Directors	Very rare other than Head of Design
General Admin	Rare, restricted to Reception
Retail, Maintenance	Rare
Accounts	Rare
Shipping, Processing	Rare
Alexandra Mills	Rare, with exception of Planning Dept
Sales	Frequent contact
Stores	Frequent contact
Production	Frequent contact

Information required

To ensure that the data which would be obtained from (1) the Design Department and (2) other departments, could be easily compared, the survey questionnaire asked both sets of identified respondents the same questions but tailored the wording accordingly so as to make it relevant to either (1) or (2). The next stage considered what information would be required from the respondents. The information required by the auditor was:

- By what channels do Design/other depts receive information?
- By what channels do they send information?
- An idea of the quantity of information.
- An idea of the content and quality of information.
- The channels through which they prefer to send and receive information.
- How is communication perceived in their own department?
- Take account of points raised in TRO study e.g. management response to staff suggestions.
- Suggestions for improvements – examples.
- Demographic data.
- Other areas not foreseen.

The respondent was given the following information:

- a reminder of the purpose of the study;
- that their assistance is valued;
- what they state may be actioned upon;
- all details would remain confidential.

Communication audit systems

A number of communication audit systems were considered when compiling the form and content of the questionnaire.

The ICA system

The International Communication Audit System is a survey questionnaire that has over 130 items, approximately 120 of which relate to staff perception of organizational communication.

Strength

- It is highly detailed and covers many areas.

Weaknesses

- It is designed for entire organization communication.

- It is difficult to administer because it takes a long time.
- It has many non-relevant areas.

Hamilton questionnaire

This is provided by Hamilton (1987).

Strengths

- Focus on channels of sending/receiving information.
- It is relatively short.
- It is easy to follow.
- It could easily be adapted for Skopos Communication Audit.

Weakness

- No allowance is made for respondents to express opinions or make suggestions.

LTT questionnaire

This is a questionnaire incorporating a Likert-scale grid system.

Strengths

- It is short and comprehensive.
- It allows respondent to make suggestions.

Weaknesses

- It has many non-relevant areas.
- Emphasis on receiving information.
- It is too simplistic.

The OCD system

This system was developed by Wiio (1978) and is an 18-point questionnaire.

Strengths

- It is short and easy to complete.
- It allows for opinions/suggestions.
- It could be easily adapted.

Weaknesses

- Emphasis on receiving information.
- It has many non-relevant areas.

Distribution

The finalized Survey Questionnaire was developed by adopting the most useful elements relevant to the audit. The questionnaire was compiled to include a Likert-scale and space allowing respondents to express opirions and make suggestions. Areas arising from the TRO study and Interview 1 were addressed in a number of questions.

Results of survey questionnaire

In total, thirty-two questionnaires were issued and received. The question-naires were analysed and data was converted into percentages. A brief interpretation of the data accompanies each question.

Q1 The instructions I receive from the Design Department/other depart-ments about what to do are usually clear.

Results

	Both (%)	Design (%)	Other Depts (%)
1 Agree strongly	18.75	7.62	26.31
	34.37	30.67	42.07
2	15.62	23.07	15.76
3 Neutral	39.75	38.46	36.84
4	25.00	30.76	21.05
5 Disagree strongly	0	0	0

Only 1 in 5 of the respondents for both Design and other departments agreed strongly that instructions were usually clear. Over a third were neutral, and 1 in 4 disagreed. The data reveal that the Design Department is less satisfied with the clarity of instructions it receives.

Q2 The quantity of information I receive from Design/other depart-ments is usually adequate for me to do my job properly.

Results

	Both (%)	Design (%)	Other Depts (%)
1 Agree strongly	3.12	0	5.26
	34.5	23.07	42.1
2	31.25	23.07	36.84
3 Neutral	25.00	38.46	15.78
4	40.6	38.46	42.1
5 Disagree strongly	3.1	0	5.26

The table for both shows that over a third of respondents found the quality of information inadequate, another third adequate, and 1 in every 4 were neutral. Other departments were eventually split in showing a preference at 42.1 per cent. The Design Department veered towards the quantity of information being received as insufficient although no preference for agreeing or disagreeing strongly was given.

Q3   Information I receive from Design/other departments usually arrives in time for me to do my job.

Results

	Both (%)	*Design (%)*	*Other Depts (%)*
1 Agree strongly	6.25	0	10.52
2	28.12	30.76	26.30
3 Neutral	34.37	30.76	36.84
4	28.12	23.07	31.57
5 Disagree strongly	9.30	15.38	5.20

Both Design and other departments generally felt that information should arrive sooner although nearly a third agreed it arrived on time. The notable difference was that the Design Department showed no strong agreement that information arrived on time to complete the task at hand.

Q4   The style in which Design/other departments convey information to me is appropriate.

Results

	Both (%)	*Design (%)*	*Other Depts (%)*
1 Agree strongly	6.25	0	10.52
	40.62	38.46	42.09
2	34.37	38.46	31.37
3 Neutral	37.50	38.46	36.84
4	21.87	23.07	21.05
	21.87	23.07	21.05
5 Disagree strongly	0	0	0

Similarities exist whereby an average 40.39 per cent agreed that the style of conveying information was appropriate, an average of 22 per cent who disagreed and an average of 37.6 per cent who were neutral. Neither showed any strong disagreement and only the Design Department stated it did not strongly agree that the style used was appropriate.

Q5   I can usually provide the necessary information enabling Design/other departments to do their job.

Results

	Both (%)	Design (%)	Other Depts (%)
1 Agree strongly	25.00	38.46	15.78
	84.37	92.30	78.93
2	59.37	53.84	63.15
3 Neutral	15.26	7.60	21.05
4	0	0	0
5 Disagree strongly	0	0	0

Both the Design Department and other departments agreed that they were able to provide the necessary information. Without exception, none of the respondents felt that they could not usually provide the necessary information and only 1 in 8 were neutral on the subject. Separately, the Design Department at 92.30 per cent believed it was more competent at providing information.

Q6 I am usually consulted on subjects about which I have information and expertise.

Results

	Both (%)	Design (%)	Other Depts (%)
1 Agree strongly	18.75	23.07	15.78
	65.62	46.14	78.93
2	46.87	23.07	63.15
3 Neutral	31.25	46.15	21.05
4	3.10	7.60	0
5 Disagree strongly	0	0	0

Almost 7 in every 10 respondents agreed that they were usually consulted. Taken separately, the Design Department data shows that they were consulted less at just under 5 in every 10 compared to 8 out of 10 in other departments.

Q7 The channels of communication between myself and the Design Department/other departments are usually as shown.

Results: Design Department

Order of importance	Telephone (%)	Face-to-face (%)	Written (%)	Meetings (%)
1	61.53	15.30	23.07	0
2	23.07	61.53	15.3	0
3	15.30	23.07	61.53	0
4	0	0	0	100

Results: other departments

Order of importance	Telephone (%)	Face-to-face (%)	Written (%)	Meetings (%)
1	36.84	36.84	21.05	5.26
2	36.84	21.05	31.57	10.52
3	21.05	31.57	36.84	10.52
4	5.26	10.52	10.52	73.68

Respondents for both Design and other departments stated that nearly half their communication was sent and received via the telephone followed by face-to-face, written and meetings. More than 8 out of every 10 felt that meetings were the least important. Viewed separately, the telephone was seen as more important by Design than other departments at 61.53 per cent compared to 36.84 per cent. In contrast, face-to-face communication by other departments was more than double that of Design and a greater importance was given to obtaining information through meetings. The Design Department stated unanimously that meetings were the channels through which they receive least information.

Q8   The channels of communication I prefer to use are as shown.

Results: Design Department

Order of importance	Telephone (%)	Face-to-face (%)	Written (%)	Meetings (%)
1	15.38	69.23	15.38	0
2	38.46	30.76	23.07	0
3	30.76	0	30.76	38.46
4	15.38	0	30.76	61.52

Results: other departments

Order of importance	Telephone (%)	Face-to-face (%)	Written (%)	Meetings (%)
1	21.05	73.68	0	5.26
2	47.36	15.78	21.05	10.52
3	21.05	5.26	63.15	5.26
4	10.52	5.26	15.78	78.94

Thus, 7 out of 10 respondents for both Design and other departments placed greatest preference on face-to-face communication, and 7 out of 10 see meetings as the least preferred channel of communication. Written and telephone communication is preferred less by those using it. Taken separately, the Design Department uses the telephone four times more than it is preferred, and conversely, prefers face-to-face communication over four times more than is actually used. Other departments display a greater dislike for written communication, and although meetings are least favoured, there is a greater preference for them in comparison.

Q9 Most of my information comes to me from my immediate superior.

Results

	Both (%)	*Design (%)*	*Other Depts (%)*
1 Agree strongly	15.26	23.07	10.52
	28.12	38.45	21.04
2	12.50	15.38	10.52
3 Neutral	25.00	38.46	15.78
4	25.00	7.69	36.84
	46.87	23.07	63.15
5 Disagree strongly	21.87	15.38	26.31

In both Design and other departments, over a quarter of respondents stated they received most of their information from their immediate superior in contrast to half who did not. In comparison, nearly 4 out of every 10 in the Design Department usually received information this way compared to 2 out of 10 in other departments.

Q10 Most of the information I get comes from my co-workers.

Results

	Both (%)	*Design (%)*	*Other Depts (%)*
1 Agree strongly	3.12	0	5.26
	24.99	15.38	31.57
2	21.87	15.38	26.31
3 Neutral	37.50	38.46	36.84
4	25.00	38.46	15.78
	37.50	46.15	31.57
5 Disagree strongly	12.50	7.69	15.78

Almost a quarter of respondents receive information from their co-workers and over a third do not. Taken separately, information received from co-workers in other departments is double that of the Design Department.

Q11 Most of my information comes from people who report to me.

Results

	Both (%)	Design (%)	Other Depts (%)
1 Agree strongly	3.12	7.69	0
	12.49	15.38	10.52
2	9.37	7.69	10.52
3 Neutral	15.62	15.38	15.78
4	37.50	38.46	36.84
	71.87	69.22	73.68
5 Disagree strongly	34.37	30.76	36.84

Approximately 1 in every 10 agree that they receive information through people reporting to them compared to 7 out of 10 who do not. The figures for the Design Department and other departments are similar when looked at separately in that approximately only 1 in 10 agrees that they receive information in this way.

Q12 Generally speaking, communication in my department is good.

Results

	Both (%)	Design (%)	Other Depts (%)
1 Agree strongly	31.25	7.69	47.36
	50.00	15.38	73.57
2	18.75	7.69	26.31
3 Neutral	12.50	15.38	10.52
4	25.00	38.46	15.78
	37.5	69.22	15.78
5 Disagree strongly	12.5	30.76	0

There was a general split when combining the data for Design and other departments. Half agreed that communication was good in their own department while over a third disagreed. A greater difference is seen when the tables are observed separately in the upper and lower limits. In other departments, 7 in every 10 agreed communication was generally good in their own department with no strong disagreement. By contrast, 7 in every 10 in the Design Department disagreed that communication was good in their own department.

Q13 Generally speaking, I find senior management take action on suggestions I make.

Results

	Both (%)	Design (%)	Other Depts (%)
1 Agree strongly	3.12	0	5.26
	28.12	53.84	10.52
2	25.00	53.84	5.26
3 Neutral	43.75	30.76	52.63
4	25.00	15.38	31.57
	28.12	15.38	36.83
5 Disagree strongly	3.12	0	5.26

In both Design and other departments combined there is an equal split in those who agree and those who disagree, nearly half were neutral on the subject. Greater differences are revealed when observed separately. Only 1 in every 10 respondents from other departments agreed that management took action compared to over half in the Design Department.

Q14 Generally speaking, I am satisfied with my job.

Results

	Both (%)	Design (%)	Other Depts (%)
1 Agree strongly	6.45	0	10.52
	51.61	46.15	52.62
2	45.16	46.15	42.10
3 Neutral	25.80	23.07	26.31
4	16.12	15.38	15.78
	19.34	15.38	26.25
5 Disagree strongly	3.22	0	5.26
No response: 15.40			

Over half of the respondents were satisfied with their job, a quarter were neutral and 1 in 5 were dissatisfied. The Design Department showed no strong views at either end of the scale.

Q15 I have a good understanding of the working methods of Design/other departments.

Results

	Both (%)	Design (%)	Other Depts (%)
1 Agree strongly	15.60	7.60	21.05
	43.72	46.06	42.10
2	28.12	38.46	21.05
3 Neutral	28.12	38.46	21.05
4	28.12	15.38	36.84
	28.12	15.38	36.84
5 Disagree strongly	0	0	0

For both Design and other departments, none of the respondents felt strongly that they did not understand the working methods. Viewed separately, the data show the Design Department believed they had a better understanding of the working methods of other departments.

Questions 17–20 prompted respondents to express their own attitudes and opinions about how they send and receive information. Analysis revealed that many of the views given were shared by others. The main points arising were condensed and are presented below.

Q16 What is particularly bad about communication with Design/other departments?

- Lack of information on request forms.
- Laziness in written briefs.
- Being taken for granted.
- Over-complication of certain information.
- Telephone infrequently answered.
- Unaware of job duties/responsibilities for certain people.
- Lack of information for special colourways.
- Sales often need to be re-contacted to clarify information.
- Trial room and schemeboard request forms often incomplete by Sales.
- Production often fail to advise change in make-up procedures.
- General ignorance of complexity of design work.
- Little time allowed to complete job satisfactorily.
- Awaiting senior approval often holds job up.
- Mistakes made as messages often sent to wrong people.
- People unwilling to help if not their immediate concern.

Q17 What is particularly good about communication with Design/other departments?

- Face-to-face contact when it occurs.
- Internal mail helps with site locations.
- Most people have their own telephone extension.
- Long-term employees – on first name basis.
- Most contact on same site.
- Fabric orders now more efficient.

Q18 If you have any suggestions which you feel might improve the way you communicate either with the Design Department or other departments, please state.

- Have colour samples/swatches and briefs given for each job.
- To have suggestions considered.
- Network extended for email facility.

- Clarification of people's responsibilities in other departments.
- Avoid leaving work information until the last minute.

Q19 Other areas you think are relevant to this audit?

- Need for general improvement in the communication chain.
- Good communication starts from the top.

Summary of questionnaire results

There was a general agreement among respondents that communication is in need of improvement. Questions 1–9 on the questionnaire, which referred to how respondents send and receive information, often reveal disparity of opinion. The fact that certain questions provoked either strong agreement or disagreement is an indicator that problems exist which need to be addressed. In some examples as many as one third agreed strongly and another third disagreed strongly to the same question, suggesting perhaps that there is conflict in what is perceived as effective or ineffective communication. Interestingly, Question 6 highlights the individual's self-perception as a communicator by asking whether the respondent is usually able to provide information. An average of 85 per cent believed they could usually provide information, none were in disagreement, and this corresponds with earlier findings in Interview 1 that poor communication is often seen by the individual as a problem not relevant to them but to others in another department.

The telephone is the most frequently used channel of communication, meetings the least, and face-to-face the channel most preferred. The sources of most information are either received through a superior or a co-worker. Channels of communication are referred to in more depth later.

On the subject of management taking action upon suggestions, most respondents remained neutral. Asked if they were satisfied with their job, half said they were, 1 in 5 said they were not, and 15 per cent gave no response. These were the only non-responses given between questions 1–16 and this indicates that the respondent felt the question was either not relevant or had a personal reason for not providing an opinion.

Responses given in questions 17 and 18 – positive/negative communication with other departments – can be condensed under a number of main headings:

- Incomplete information sent and received by both Design and other departments.
- Failure of information to arrive in adequate time.
- Information sent to or through the wrong people.
- Little consultation.
- Poor communication seen as another person's 'problem'.

Differences

In areas such as clarity, quantity, style and timing of information receiving, the Design Department was generally less satisfied than the other departments with whom they have most frequent contact. The telephone is the major communication tool for the Design Department whereas in other departments the telephone and face-to-face communication are evenly weighted. In both cases face-to-face communication is the preferred channel. The report speculates that face-to-face communication is made more possible by some of the other departments in that they are physically situated closer to each other, whereas Design, detached from the main body of the Skopos complex chooses to rely more on telephone and written communication.

The Design Department is also more likely to receive information through a superior, most often the Design Director, and it was generally agreed by Design that management was responsive to suggestions put forward – this contrasts with only 1 in 10 in other departments. Only 15 per cent of Design Department respondents thought communication in their own department was good, 69 per cent were in disagreement. These figures are in contrast to the information initially received from Interview 1 where the consensus of opinion was that communication in the Design Department was good. The confidentiality of the questionnaire may have been a reason for this difference although this is only speculation. This point is addressed in Interview 2. In contrast, 74 per cent of respondents in other departments agreed their own internal communication was good with only 15 per cent in disagreement.

Communication analysis

This section looks at network and content analysis, i.e. the flow of information and the content of that information. At this stage in the communication audit it was necessary to examine the frequency of communication between Design and other departments, obtain data on the length of time taken to communicate certain types of information and gain some idea of the content of information usually sent. For the purposes of this audit a network analysis and content analysis were combined and the focus group was restricted to the Design Department. The analysis aimed to identify:

- bottlenecks in information flow;
- their length of time and frequency;
- all sources with whom design communicates;
- whether information needs are real or perceived;
- common problems;
- clarity and style of content;

- channels used;
- areas for further research.

Methodology

The period during which the communication audit was conducted coincided with a peak holiday period at the company and as such the network and content analysis had to be restricted to nine members of the Design Department. To partly counter this, the analysis was conducted over a three-day, rather than a two-day period as was originally planned. Each member of the department was briefed on the requirements of the analysis and was asked to complete the analysis sheet between 8.30 a.m. and 5.30 p.m. each day during the period listing all incidents of work-related communication. The analysis sheet devised for this procedure asked those completing it to state:

- Time of the communication – a.m. or p.m.
- The department/other source with whom communication took place.
- The name of the person with whom communication took place.
- Who initiated the communication.
- The duration of the communication to the nearest minute.
- The channel of communication.
- What was involved.
- Was the communication usual/routine.

At the end of the analysis period staff were asked to state on a 1–5 scale whether communication had been above, typical or below routine for each separate day.

Results

Analysis found that during the three-day period the nine members of the focus group had 256 instances of work-related communication either internally, with other Skopos departments, or with external sources such as suppliers, clients, educational enquiries, etc. The findings were as follows:

Time of day

In the mornings there were 126 instances of communication and in the afternoon there were 127 instances of communication. The results show an equal distribution of communication both in the morning and afternoon.

Initiating communication

Excluding communication that took place internally in the Design Department, analysis shows the following results (see Table 6.2).

Restating this data, the results show communication equally initiated by Design and external sources. In contrast, the results show that the Design Department initiated communication with other Skopos departments by more than a third.

Table 6.3 shows that over 40 per cent of all Design Department communication is with itself, followed by Sales, Clients, Stores, etc. Further analysis reveals that communication between Design and Accounts, Shipping, Reception and the MD is restricted primarily to the Design Director.

Total time – units of time

Analysis reveals that during the three nine-hour day period the nine members of the focus group spent a total of 34 hours and 26 minutes exchanging work-related information. Collapsing this data provides an

Table 6.2 Initiating communication

Communication initiated	Number
By Design to other Skopos departments	74
By Design to external sources	18
Total	92
By other Skopos departments to Design	45
By external sources to Design	15
	60
Total	152

Table 6.3 Frequency of communication between departments

	No. of instances	As a % of total
Design Studio	115	44.97
Sales	39	15.23
Stores	18	7.03
Retail	14	5.46
Production	12	4.68
Samples	10	3.90
Accounts	7	2.73
Shipping	5	1.95
Reception	3	1.17
MD	2	0.78
Clients and Suppliers	27	10.54
Gen Enquiries	4	1.56
Total	256	100.00

average of 11 hours and 42 minutes per day or 1 hour 18 minutes per day per person.

The most notable difference is the amount of time the Design Director is involved in sending and receiving information.

Total time spent by Design Director   14 hours 58 mins
Total time by remainder of focus group   19 hours 28 mins

Collapsing this data, an average of 50 minutes per day is spent by 8 members of the focus group and $3\frac{1}{2}$ hours by the Design Director. In order to illustrate how the time was allocated, the number of communication instances were allocated to time units as shown in Table 6.4.

Channel and contact

Analysis was made to identify communication exchanges which involved direct face-to-face communication and telephone communication. There were 116 occurrences of telephone communication and 140 occurrences of face-to-face communication, making a total of 256.

Further analysis reveals that face-to-face communication is collapsed as shown in Table 6.5. It is evident that the majority of face-to-face communication is restricted primarily to the Design Department itself.

Table 6.4 Time spent exchanging work-related information

Time unit	Number
Up to 5 minutes	197
Up to 10 minutes	28
Up to 20 minutes	10
20 minutes to 1 hour	14
1 hour and over	7
Total	256

Table 6.5 Face-to-face communication occurrences

Department	Number
Internal (Design)	113
Sales	7
Stores	5
Accounts	5
External	4
Screens	2
Shipping	1
MD	1
Systems	1
Samples	1
Retail	1

Table 6.6 Telephone communication occurrences

Department	Number
Sales	32
External	27
Stores	13
Retail	13
Production	12
Samples	9
Shipping	4
Reception	3
Accounts	2
Design	2
MD	1

Table 6.6 reveals an analysis of telephone communication.

Again, these results confirm the general view of respondents in Interview 1 that communication is restricted to a few key Skopos departments.

Content

The focus group were asked to indicate what was involved in their communication exchanges, whether this involved writing/form writing and whether this was usual or unusual. In the majority of cases the information supplied was brief. However, a number of common communication 'problems' were discovered which reflect points arising from the survey questionnaire:

• Design often needs to re-confirm written information due to omissions e.g. trial room request forms, special design/colour request forms, etc.
• Urgent requests from other departments arrive close to a deadline e.g. sample priority lists, scheme board request.

Typical day

At the end of each day of the analysis period each member of the focus group was asked to state on a 1–5 scale if they felt their communication for that day had been above routine, typical routine or below routine. The results of the three-day period are seen in Figure 6.4.

The results indicate communication was below typical routine during the analysis period. The results may be presumed to be reasonably accurate in that the audit was conducted during a 'quiet' period of the company year.

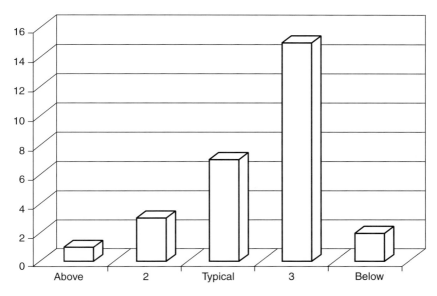

Figure 6.4 Communication – respondent views for a typical day

Summary

By combining the data provided by the communication analysis sheets with the direct observation undertaken by the auditor, one is able to make a few general conclusions. It is stressed that the following conclusions only claim to be 'typical' of communication for the Design Department for the period during which the exercise was conducted.

First, the results show an equal number of communication exchanges in both the morning and afternoon, leading one to conclude that communication is evenly distributed throughout the day. Further analysis of data was unable to detect a pattern of communication frequency by time of day such as: more person-to-person communication in the morning/more telephone communication in the afternoon, etc. This noted, direct observation identified a number of 'quiet' telephone periods during the day. These were:

- early morning – up to approx 10.30 a.m.
- lunchtime – approx 12.30–2.00 p.m.
- late afternoon – 5.00 p.m. onwards.

The results also show that the Design Department initiated more communication with other Skopos departments by almost a third. Analysis of sheets completed by the focus group reveal several instances of the Design

Department having to re-confirm information received from other departments. This was one of the major points highlighted in Interview 1 and in the survey questionnaire results and this may account for the higher number. Again due to the limited amount of information given on content by the focus group, the latter point is only conjecture. The content section of the analysis sheets confirm that certain departments, Stores, Production and particularly Sales, are the ones with which Design often needs to contact to re-confirm information. Similarly, the results show that the greatest frequency of communication is with the Sales Department followed by Stores, Retail, Production and Samples, and that the telephone is the most used channel of communication.

It is interesting to note the amount of time individuals spend each day engaged purely in sending and receiving work-related information – on average 50 minutes for 8 members of the focus group and $3\frac{1}{2}$ hours for the Design Director. These time figures eat into a relatively large part of the designer's creative day, especially for the Design Director. This may be accounted for in that the Design Director is situated in the middle of the department's communication network. Although members of the design team have autonomy to communicate with other departments it is, per the analysis sheets, the Design Director who will act as the filter for much of the information received into the department from other Skopos departments, senior management, clients and suppliers. This can be represented in a simplified conceptual network diagram in Figure 6.5.

In consideration of the amount of time the Design Director devotes to sending, receiving, and filtering information to the department it could be speculated that the Design Director may be overloaded and there may be a bottleneck in the communication process. This is addressed in Interview 2. It was also noted from the analysis sheets and through direct observation that the method of passing on information to the department is usually conducted on an individual one-to-one basis. A spatial interpretation shows that this method is made easier by the physical layout of the design studio. The central siting of the Design Director's office is conducive for contact with all members of the department. During the ten-

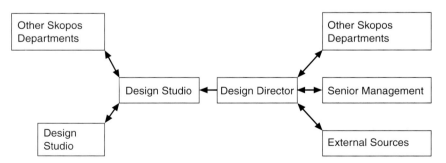

Figure 6.5 Design Department's communication network

week audit placement at the company no meeting, formal or informal, with all Design Department members was observed. This was confirmed in Interview 2.

The results further show that over three-quarters of all communication exchanges during the period usually lasted for less than five minutes, particularly with the other eight members of the focus group. Where it was possible to observe face-to-face exchanges both internally and with other departments in this time unit, it was observed that messages were often short, non-complex and sometimes involved an exchange of a written/visual artefact. As no email facility exists, this procedure is obviously necessary, especially in priority cases. The physical 'movement' around the Skopos complex to obtain or pass on information was seen by respondents as a time-consuming exercise in the survey questionnaire.

Finally, as the analysis period was considered to be below typical routine one can speculate that outwith a 'quiet' company period, and with a full complement of staff, the number of communication exchanges is likely to increase and the average time per individual would also increase.

Interview 1

Interviews were conducted on a one-to-one basis with each member of the Design Department to partly determine the content of the survey questionnaire. It was necessary at this initial stage of the audit to obtain an overview of:

- the departments with whom the Design Department communicates;
- the channels through which they communicate;
- the content of communication;
- the frequency of communication;
- communication within the Design Department;
- good/negative aspects of communication at Skopos;
- personal communication 'problems';
- areas for improvement;
- other areas.

Results

Interview sheets were completed and analysed. Without exception, all members of the Design Department stated they experienced regular communication problems. Interestingly, in the majority of cases, poor communication was not seen as a problem belonging to individuals in the Design Department, rather, it was other Skopos departments who were generally perceived to be poor senders and receivers of information. Respondents veered towards the anecdotal in support of these claims.

Overall, communication in the Design Department itself was seen as good. The main recurrent themes arising from the initial interviews were:

- Most communication problems are with other departments, particularly Sales, Stores and Production.
- Incomplete information is often received from these and other departments.
- Confirming correct information distracts from job at hand and is a time-wasting exercise.
- More 'appropriate' ways of sending information could be used but are not.

The views provided by the interviewees were referred to when compiling the content of the audit survey questionnaire. It was evident at this stage in the audit that the Design Department had frequent contact with some departments and very little with others.

Interview 2

Interviews were conducted on a one-to-one basis with the design studio staff including the Design Director. A technology assessment interview was conducted simultaneously and is covered later. The interview in this section was a follow-up to the survey questionnaire and communication analysis and the rationale behind it was:

- to obtain feedback on the survey questionnaire and communication analysis. To make Design Department staff aware that they were not the only individuals experiencing communication problems by providing them with selected examples;
- to prompt interviewees into making constructive suggestions as to how communication problems might be resolved – on a personal level or on a departmental level;
- to elicit new facts.

Results

On average only 15 per cent of Design Department staff thought that communication in their department was good. This view, given confidentially, was in conflict with the views expressed in Interview 1. Interview 2 asked interviewees to respond to this apparent conflict in opinion by asking: 'Is it good?' Replies given were:

- Generally yes, but the Design Director could pass on more information.
- Still good on a one-to-one basis – staff are friendly.

- Not aware colleagues were having difficulties in quite the same way.
- Ivory tower view would be an acceptable criticism.
- Communication was worse many years ago and heading that way again.

Interviewees were informed of some of the views provided by other Skopos departments with which they have most frequent contact. With these views in mind, interviewees were prompted to give further suggestions as to why communication problems might exist. Replies given were as follows:

Sales

- Seem to demand the most.
- Sales lead times too short but understandable because of client pressure.
- Often complete forms incorrectly – time spent clarifying details.

Stores

- Problems with fabric orders.
- AS400 system often incorrectly used.

Production

- Personality problems with head of production.
- Often fail on details.
- Screens often have to be made at the last minute.

Interviewees were then asked to provide suggestions for improvement:

- All special design request forms should be fully completed.
- A need for some type of IT to improve information sent from department to department.
- Set a 'standard' way of doing things.
- A list of who does what would be useful.

Summary

Disparity would appear to exist within the Design Department with regard to what is perceived as being 'good' communication. Previously it was noted that design staff cite elements such as friendliness, first-name basis, Design Director's helpfulness and face-to-face communication as examples in support of communication being good within the department. The points arising from Interview 2 indicate that, regardless of these positive elements, there is in fact a certain amount of information desired from the Design

Director which is not being received. Interviewees failed to provide specific examples but stated that they often felt that they were not always provided with 'the full picture', and would like to be consulted more often. The Design Director saw these points to be fair criticism and fully acknowledged that due to the bulk and variety of information being received into his office there was always the likelihood of omitting information in the filtering process. Asked whether regular meetings would help remedy the situation, the Design Director agreed that they probably would. Interdepartmental meetings for staff have been extremely rare and meetings for full Design Department staff have not been held for many years.

No significant new areas were exposed when asked to provide further examples of the communication problems experienced. Many of the examples given have already been noted and reinforce the fact that most communication problems are restricted to a few key departments. Similarly, the suggestions given for improvement mirror those previously supplied in the survey questionnaire.

Interviews with other departments

At this stage in the audit process it was necessary to conduct interviews with the other Skopos departments with which Design communicates. The rationale behind these interviews is related to obtaining feedback and prompting individuals to provide suggestions for improvement. The time factor dictated that it was not possible to conduct interviews and informal discussions with all the staff in other departments. As such, the interviews focused upon those who had been identified as respondents for the survey questionnaire. Structured interviews were conducted with the heads of the departments with which Design is seen to have most communication problems and informal discussions were held with other staff.

Production

Interview with Head of Production

The general view expressed by the Head of Production was that Design was 'too distant' and that the department as a whole was viewed by many, not just Production, as suffering from 'ivory tower syndrome'. It was also stated that the majority of information between Production and Design went through the Design Director and it was often felt as though the Design Director was not fully communicating ideas to the department.

Informal discussions

Informal discussions with Production staff echoed many of the sentiments put forward by the Department Head:

- Design needs to improve face-to-face contact.
- Design not fully aware of the methods and procedures of Production.
- Design often needs to be re-contacted to clarify messages.

Stores

Interview with Head of Stores

The Head of Stores stated that over the years the communication between his department and Design had been allowed to deteriorate. It was claimed that people had perhaps become complacent with the communication process and that people will usually wait until a crisis arises before taking any definite action. The Head of Stores was careful to explain that communication often ran smoothly but there was great scope for improvement. Unless someone were to initiate change and have this supported by management, then the status quo would remain. Another concern was that the Design Department did not fully appreciate how the Stores Department worked, and because of this, mistakes were often made. It was acknowledged that Stores were, in part, equally ignorant of many of the working methods of the Design Department.

Informal discussions

The main concerns arising from informal discussions with Stores staff were:

- Design infrequently informed Stores of new ranges.
- There is often incomplete information to complete job at hand.
- Design need advice on using AS400 fabric order system.

Sales

Informal discussions were held with the majority of the Sales team. Many of the examples of communication problems given veered towards the anecdotal and were often only one-off cases. The Sales team did, however, acknowledge that poor communication was a two-sided affair and were fully aware that Design often had to contact them to clarify details and deal with requests at short notice. It was stated that the nature of sales work made this inevitable as they needed to respond to clients' needs and deadlines. Asked to provide a solution, the majority stated that meetings would allows Sales staff to pass on information directly rather than relying on word of mouth or sending memos. Such meetings need only be short and need only occur a few times a year. As with Production and Stores, the Sales Department were of the opinion that Design did not fully understand their working methods. Meetings would afford both sides the opportunity to explain what they were doing, why they were doing it, and what would be required from the other department. Other areas arising were:

- Telephone not always answered by Design.
- Information often gets held up by senior management.

Other departments

During the placement the communication auditor had many informal discussions with staff from other departments – those not identified for the survey questionnaire – whose contact with Design was less frequent such as Retail, Samples, Systems, etc. The approach in such cases was to ask what were the positive/negative elements of communication with Design. Again, much of what was provided veered towards the anecdotal one-off examples, but there was a general feeling that the Design Department was somewhat aloof, and only made contact when absolutely necessary. Many acknowledged that the physical location of the Design Studio, detached and on the top level of the Skopos complex, reinforced this perception. Individually, the Design staff were seen as friendly and were usually able to provide the necessary information when asked.

Summary

The majority of views given in this section were, with a few exceptions, the same as those provided by the survey questionnaire. It is interesting to note that many of the communication 'problems' cited by the Design Department such as incomplete information or ignorance of department working methods, mirror those of other departments. There is also a consensus of opinion that Design is too distant and that information passed through a senior member can often reach its destination incomplete. The use of IT was a remedy frequently given but the primary remedy is an expressed desire for departments to 'talk' to each other *en masse* at regular meetings. Some individuals even stated they would attend inter-departmental meetings in their own time, such as lunch breaks, if management would arrange them. Finally, it is worth stressing that it was expressed to the auditor by many staff that inter-departmental communication was not in a state of crisis. Communication was regarded as being 'acceptable', but cases of ineffective communication frequently occur which need not.

Technology assessment

Throughout this report reference has been made to the use of IT as means of improving communication. This section focuses separately on technology. The assessment was divided into two parts: (1) assessing the current technology; and (2) considering needs.

Current technology

Other Skopos departments have access to computers installed with task-specific programs such as stock control, credit control, accounts programs and so on. In the Design Department there are currently five computers. Two are installed with Microsoft Office – one is for sole use by the Design Director and is used mainly for word processing, the other is mainly used by the Design secretary although it is accessible to all staff. This is primarily used for compiling lists or writing letters. Another computer also accessible to all staff but mainly used by the Design secretary, is installed with IBM JBA System 400. This is used by the company only to catalogue and order fabric from the Stores Department. Finally, an Apple Mac computer is used mainly for its QuarkXpress package by the graphic designer to create company literature and promotional material.

Interview with Systems Manager

To obtain a greater insight into the current status of IT at the company the Systems Manager was consulted and asked to comment on what he would like to see taking place in the company on the technology front. The Systems Manager advised that it was paradoxical for a design-led company which Skopos claims to be, to be short-sighted in recognizing the opportunities new technology could bring. An example given was that it was only very recently that CAD had been acquired and is only available on one monitor. Asked to comment on using existing technology such as the AS400 system, it was stated that this was not really practical. A messaging facility did exist on the system but this was rarely used and would only be practical if all staff had their own computer. To compound matters, only a few people actually knew how to use the system, moreover, there is little reason to use it as it is mainly used for stock control. Asked to provide an insight into the level of computer literacy within the company, the Systems Manager stated that this was to be found wanting in that most staff have only been trained to operate specific programs which relate to their job. It was put to the Systems Manager that the apparent lethargy in investing in new technology might be dictated by the naïvety of senior management. This was confirmed, and it was stated that to his knowledge only one member of senior management was computer-literate. Asked to focus on communication and take a 'magic wand' approach, the Systems Manager commented that email would be the ideal solution should money be available. His own preference would be to invest in Lotus Notes GroupWare documents. The Systems Manager was further asked whether the company had ever considered project management software. Apparently Microsoft Project 4 is held but has never been installed.

Needs and attitudes

A technology assessment interview was simultaneously held with members of the Design Department at the Interview 2 stage. The purpose of the interview was to assess attitudes towards using new technology and the extent to which they think it could assist them in communication. The interviewees were asked to state:

- if they had access to a computer;
- would they wish to use new technology;
- what type would be installed.

It was found that all members of the department did have access to computers but these were only used on a regular basis by the Design Director, the Design secretary and the graphic designer. Varying responses were given when asked whether they would like to use new technology:

- probably not;
- only if relevant to job – if Design required it;
- yes, if trained;
- would use more often for communicating – email, fax.

Interviewees were asked to state the type of new technology they would like to see installed and how might this help them to communicate more effectively:

- computer for each designer;
- CAD/CAM system needed eventually;
- networking would show visually what was meant rather than relying on written instructions;
- email, fax would save movement around the complex;
- laptops for outside visits.

The overall impression given was that the Design Department would cautiously welcome new technology but with a few reservations. Concern was expressed about the need for training. Several interviewees openly stated that they were ignorant of computers and would need guidance just to learn the basics. Another understandable concern was how new technology might affect their jobs – would this include job changes – loss or enhancement? In spite of these concerns, the fact that new technology could be used as an effective communicating tool was unanimously welcomed and any time that could be freed for creative work would be beneficial. Likewise, the Design Director agreed that in the long term new technology would be useful and that it had been discussed at board level in the past.

Recommendations of the audit

This report provides a number of recommendations to help remedy the status quo and is summed up in terms of:

- What needs to be done now.
- What needs to be done soon.
- What needs to be addressed when time and money permit.

What needs to be done now

Recommendation 1: Design Department meetings

Communication first of all needs to be improved within the Design Department itself, especially between the Design Director and Design staff. Meetings for department members should be organized on a regular basis and adhered to. As most of the communication within the department is conducted on a one-to-one basis, a forum is required to enable staff to exchange views with each other. Regular meetings will allow staff to problem-solve, exchange ideas on current projects, and discuss positive/negative aspects of communication. Recommendations are:

- Meetings should be conducted on a regular basis – e.g. quarterly initially.
- They should be on a set day of each month/period.
- They should take place during identified 'quiet' periods of the working day.
- Matters arising should be minuted and used for inter-departmental meetings.

Regular meetings between the Design Director and Design staff will help alleviate the problem of bottlenecking and create a greater sense of department unity – poor internal communication was cited by the majority of Design staff. It is important to note that staff like to be informed of current developments even if it does not relate directly to them.

The Design Director, being the gatekeeper for much of the information arriving into the department should make a concerted effort to share information received from external sources, particularly information relating to new projects. Suggested strategies are:

- Design Director to continuously compile a list of points for each meeting.
- Inform staff that all views/suggestions put forward at meetings are valued.
- Inform staff that efforts will be made to action useful suggestions.
- Points arising from this communication audit report should be made known to department staff.

Recommendation 2: inter-departmental meetings

It is recommended that regular meetings be organized between the Design Department and those departments with whom most communication problems arise, namely, Sales, Stores and Production departments. The report highlights that departments had certain naïve notions of the working methods and procedures of other departments. By bringing departments together, staff can be fully informed of the information required by other departments, not only in what they require but why they require it. By entering face-to-face communication with colleagues from other departments staff will be able to obtain immediate feedback and exchange views in addressing common problems. Face-to-face meetings will also help dispel the perception that the Design Department is a clique isolated from the body of the company. In implementing this recommendation it is suggested that:

- Department heads take responsibility in organizing inter-departmental meetings on a rota basis.
- Meetings should be arranged for a set day/month at mutually convenient times.
- Agendas should be agreed in advance and meetings minuted.
- Staff be informed that all contributions are welcomed.
- Initial meeting should inform staff of points arising from this report.

Recommendation 3: a list of job duties and responsibilities

To ease information overload on Department Heads, and to ensure communication is made to the correct person, it is recommended that a list be compiled by all departments with whom Design has regular communication. The list should show names of department staff alongside which should be shown the job duties and responsibilities. The list should also briefly state whether the individual has specific knowledge on a subject in addition to that outlined in their job description. Where possible, the list should nominate individuals other than the Department Head who can be contacted about specific problems, clarify details, or who can approve work in the absence of the Department Head. Telephone extensions should also be shown. It is suggested that:

- The Department Head consults with staff regarding the information to be included and agree upon responsibilities.
- Each department list should be 'bound' together into one document.
- Each member should be given a copy for their own use.
- A member of staff should be nominated to keep this document updated.

Recommendation 4: completing forms

It is recommended that there should be standard procedures in completing forms. In particular, departments using trial request forms and special design/colour request forms should be advised to always complete boxes for:

- job number;
- date received/required/requested by and date;
- name of client;
- value and size;
- expected order date;
- preferred freight method, ref. no.;
- delivery address and invoice address;
- the special instructions.

Other departments should also be made aware of the lead times or the special/colour request form. Attention should be drawn to the section stating that ten working days should be allowed if screens are available. In all cases, full and clear information must be given on all forms sent to the Design Department. Failure to do so will result in Design staff having to re-contact the sender.

Recommendation 5: fabric ordering system

Problems are found to arise in the fabric ordering system. Inter-departmental meetings should aim to ensure that this is addressed. It is recommended that further training be given to those Design staff ordering fabric on the AS400 system. This training should be given in consultation with the Stores Department to assess needs. It is further recommended that discussions are undertaken with the Systems Manager to assess the possibility of incorporating more options into the ordering system on the order entry screen.

What needs to be done soon

Recommendation 1: company bulletin

It is recommended that the QuarkXpress package on the Apple Mac be utilized to resurrect the company 'bulletin' which has been dormant for several years. Within this bulletin, space should be made available to provide 'Design News', such as current developments in the department and news of new collections, etc. The bulletin should be viewed as another channel through which Design can communicate, albeit in a more informal way. This will again help resolve the perception of the department being distant and isolated.

Recommendation 2: project management software

With interest being shown in project management, it is recommended that the Design Director consults with the Systems Manager to assess the usefulness of installing project management software for his own use. Microsoft Project 4 has been available in the company for some time but has never been installed. In assessing whether project management would be worthwhile, consideration should be given to: whether project management would 'free' more creative time for the Design Director. Or if other packages should be considered.

Recommendation 3: technology – continuous review

It is recommended that the department makes regular enquiries to IT suppliers to assess the type of IT currently available, to continually assess which systems would be relevant to their needs, and to make comparisons on prices and services offered by suppliers. This recommendation is made in the knowledge that further IT investment is on the company agenda in the long term and is not restricted only to the Design Department. Investigating new technology at an early stage will signal to staff that new or upgraded systems will eventually become part of their working environment. By doing this now, and by regularly consulting staff, employees will be prepared for change and feel confident in the benefits new technology will bring.

What needs to be done when time and money permit

Recommendation 1: new technology

As a design-led company it is essential that Skopos embrace new technology, not only for its use as a designing tool but also as a communication tool. It is recommended that fax machines be obtained for both the Design Department and other departments with which there is frequent communication. It is further recommended that the company consider email and the eventual possibility of networking. As previously recommended, there should be an ongoing investigation into what type of new technology will suit the company's needs. An eventual aim of supplying employees with their own computer will allow for email facility as well as allowing visuals to be sent from department to department partly replacing paper forms and memos. As part of this ongoing review it is further recommended that:

- CAD/CAM be a long-term aim of the company.
- A team be set up to undertake the task of continually assessing new technology best suited to the company's needs and assessing suppliers who can provide the appropriate equipment and services.
- That Design/Sales staff are eventually equipped with laptops – useful when visiting clients.

Recommendation 2: design policy

No written design policy has ever existed at Skopos as it is stated that Design Department members would intuitively know what the department does and what its aims are. This report recommends that a design policy be formulated for the benefit of those who do not have this intuitive know-ledge. By formulating a design policy, all those with whom Design communicates or those involved in the design process will know both how and why design decisions are made. In effect, the design policy should be considered another channel of communication expressing why the Design Department does what it does. In consideration that Skopos is a design-led company owing its success to design, then it should follow that the aims and objectives of the Design Department reflect those of the company as a whole. Furthermore:

- A design policy will help modify the perception that Design is isolated.
- Copies of the policy can be sent to educational enquiries, saving time in writing personalized letters.
- Extracts from policy could be used in publicity material.

Company feedback

At the end of the company placement an interim presentation of the main findings was given to the Design Director and the Studio Manager. The purpose of the presentation was to inform the company that research had confirmed that communication 'problems' did exist between departments and that a number of recommendations would be formulated to hopefully remedy the situation.

Following this, abridged copies of the report were handed to the company for their consideration. The company stated that some of the recommendations had already been implemented, such as arranging Design Department meetings, compiling a list of job duties and responsibilities and the revision of colour separation and special design request forms. Other recommendations supplied would be receiving attention later.

Overall, the company advised that the audit had been useful and recommendations were welcomed.

Conclusion

General findings

This report finds that Skopos can be regarded as a 'traditional' company in that all the major decision-making is led from the top through a hierarchical chain of line managers. Although Skopos employees have the autonomy to exchange information with other departments through a number of channels, it is the Department Head who acts as the filter for much of the information coming into the department. The brief given for this audit was to research the communication that takes place between Design and other departments and provide recommendations for improving communication. This audit finds that the majority of those responding to questionnaires and interviews perceive themselves to be good communicators who are usually able to send and receive information in an appropriate style, and through an appropriate channel, enabling the job in hand to be successfully completed. This perception extends further in that poor communication is usually seen as a problem not usually attributable to themselves but to individuals in other departments. Various reasons are given by all departments in support of this, for example, information is often received too late, is incomplete or goes to the wrong person. Similarly, all departments identified for this audit believe that the procedures and working methods of their own department are not fully understood by others and because of this confusion arises.

In comparison, the Design Department was less satisfied than other Skopos departments about how they communicated with each other. It was felt that many of the communication exchanges between themselves and other departments involved clarifying information sent to them or chasing work sent to other departments. The audit found that the main criticism of the Design Department by other departments was that it was too distant and Design staff were often perceived as a clique. The report speculates that this perception is perhaps reinforced by the physical location of the Design Studio at the top of the Skopos complex.

The audit found that only 15 per cent of the Design staff thought that communication in their own department was generally good, compared to 73 per cent in other departments. An explanation for this was that staff felt they were not receiving the full information required to complete the job in hand without having to make further enquiries. It was also found that Design staff were more likely to receive information individually through a superior and are less likely to have department meetings. Although Design staff agreed more than other departments that their Department Head was more likely to listen and take action upon suggestions, it was noted that the Department Head was probably overloaded and because of this there was likely to be a bottleneck in the communication process.

The period during which the audit was conducted is usually regarded as a quiet period in the company year. During this period it was found that a member of the Design Department can still expect to spend 50 minutes each day on average in exchanging work-related information and the Design Director up to $3\frac{1}{2}$ hours.

Although these figures can only be regarded as 'typical' for the period during which the audit was conducted, it is evident that communication forms a relatively large part of the designer's day and is likely to be even greater during busier periods.

Individuals are aware that new technology will become increasingly important in their working lives and, although many are cautious of its implications, the majority welcomed the benefits new technology could bring in improving communication. The type of new technology, and the investment needed to acquire it, will be dependent upon senior management, long-term company objectives, and is a recommended area for further study.

For many years the methods by which Design and other Skopos departments have communicated with each other have remained static. Staff have become resigned to the fact that the current communication processes are likely to continue unless action is taken with the full support of senior management. In conclusion, this audit finds that internal communication is in need of overhaul and those concerned should prepare for, and enter into, a dialogue to bring about change.

Review questions

1 The auditor used the Task, Relationship, Organization (TRO) mechanism to gain a quick understanding of the company culture. What other ways would you suggest that could equally have been valid?

2 Discuss the importance of effective and efficient inter-departmental communication in a customer-centred organization, in particular, the relationship between Production and Sales.

3 Referring to the text, discuss other benefits that new technologies could provide, in particular to the communication process.

4 What problems could you see arising as a result of incomplete information between departments from within the company? How would you resolve this issue?

5 Would you recommend the company implement a recognized Quality Management System or TQM? Discuss the benefits to both the organization and their customers.

6 It was widely considered that the Design Department was a separate entity within the company. Discuss how you would overcome this commonly held view in practical terms.

7 Regarding the development of new fabrics and printed ranges, why is it important that there is direct and effective means of communication between the Design and Sales Departments?
8 Why is it important that there is a strong sense of direction and leadership from management at Skopos? Provide possible ways in which they could disseminate information from the top down throughout the company.
9 Referring to the text, it was noted that the Design Director is often overloaded with information from different departments, leading to a breakdown in the communication process. How would you seek to reduce this cause of conflict?
10 At a more fundamental level, would you recommend that the company adopt a different management style when managing design projects, if so, what would you suggest and why?

Project questions

1 Consider the audit methodology employed at Skopos describing the relative benefits of the audit procedures against what may have been achieved with a detailed large-scale questionnaire to all employees.
2 Devise a questionnaire (based on this audit) in such a way that it may be transferred to a similar manufacturing company. If possible, in the future, use it.
3 Select three questions in the audit and develop a relationship between them, which will result in key management change. These policy changes should then be described.
4 What are the important links between communication within the company and future aspects of managing design in operational terms?
5 Consider the recommendations to the company and, given an appropriately generous budget, specify an IT purchasing plan for the Design Officer. This should be accompanied by a management plan linked to the expected changes.

References

Hamilton, S.C. (1987) *A Communication Audit Handbook*, London: Pitman Publishing.
Wiio, O.A. (1978) *Contingencies of Organisational Communication*, Helsinki: Helsinki School of Economics.

Further reading

Battye, S. (1993) *Skopos Promotional Literature*, Dewsbury: Skopos.
Barham, K. (1989) *Shaping the Corporate Future*, London: Unwin.
Cateora, P. (1990) *International Marketing*, Boston: Irwin.

Daniels, T.D. (1994) *Perspective on Organisational Communication*, Madison, WI: Brown and Benchmark.

Dibb, S. (ed.) (1994) *Marketing Concepts and Strategies*, London: Houghton Mifflin.

Dicken, P. (1992) *Global Shift*, London: Paul Chapman.

Dourado, P. (1993) 'Little global difficulties', *Independent on Sunday*, 5 September, p. 69.

Falcione, R. (1980) *Organisational Communication*, London: Sage.

Goldhaber, G.M. (1988) *A Handbook of Organisational Communication*, New Jersey: Ablex Publishers.

Griffiths, J. (1995) 'Ford gets the whip out', *Financial Times*, 9 March, p. 13.

Henzler, H. and Rall, W. (1986) 'Facing up to the globalisation challenge', *McKinsey Quarterly*, Winter, pp. 52–68.

Hoeklin, L. (1995) *Managing Cultural Differences*, London: Addison-Wesley.

Hill, C.W.L. (1994) *Competing in the Global Marketplace*, Boston: Richard Irwin.

Keegan, W.J. (1989) *Global Marketing Management*, New Jersey: Prentice-Hall.

Levitt, T. 'The globalisation of markets', *Harvard Business Review*, May–June, 1983, pp. 10–27.

Lorenz, A. (1994) 'Ford takes a global plunge', *Sunday Times*, 24 April, p. 13.

Lorenz, C. (1992) *The Design Dimension*, London: Blackwell.

Lydiate, L. (ed.) (1992) *Professional Practice in Design Consultancy*, London: Design Council.

Ohmae, K. (1994) *The Borderless World*, London: HarperCollins.

Perlmutter, H.V. (1995) 'Becoming globally civilised', *Financial Times*, Mastering Management: Part 6, 1 December, pp. 5–6.

Porter, M. (1992) *The Strategic Role of International Marketing*, Global Marketing Management: Harvard Business School.

Specht, M. (1989) 'Heineken thinks pan-Europe', *Advertising Age*, 30 January, p. 44.

Tibbetts, J. (1992) 'The international market', in L. Lydiate (ed.) *Professional Practice in Design Consultancy*, London: Design Council.

Index

234   *Index*